SAT®
GRAMMAR

ADVANCED
PRACTICE
SERIES

- For the Redesigned SAT
- Full Practice Tests
- Essential Tips and Tactics

ies
TEST
PREP

Authors
Arianna Astuni, President IES
Khalid Khashoggi, CEO IES

Editorial
Patrick Kennedy, Executive Editor
Christopher Carbonell, Editorial Director
Cassidy Yong, Editorial Assistant

Contributors
Arianna Astuni
Christopher Carbonell
Chris Holliday
Caitlin Hoynes-O'Connor
Patrick Kennedy
Daniel Lee
Rajvi Patel

Published by IES Publications
www.IESpublications.com

ON BEHALF OF
Integrated Educational Services, Inc.
355 Main Street
Metuchen, NJ 08840
www.iestestprep.com

We would like to thank the IES Publications team as well as the teachers and students at IES2400 who have contributed to the creation of this book. We would also like to thank our Chief Marketing Officer, Sonia Choi, for her invaluable input.

ISBN: 978-0-9964064-1-3

QUESTIONS OR COMMENTS? Visit us at iestestprep.com

TABLE OF CONTENTS

GRAMMAR LESSONS

CHAPTER 1
Subject-Verb Agreement 11-18
CHAPTER 2
Parallelism 19-24
CHAPTER 3
Comparison 25-32
CHAPTER 4
Subject-Pronoun Agreement 33-40
CHAPTER 5
Pronoun Case 41-48
CHAPTER 6
Dangling Modifier 49-54
CHAPTER 7
Adjective Vs. Adverb 55-60
CHAPTER 8
Irregular Verbs 61-66
CHAPTER 9
Verb Tense 67-72
CHAPTER 10
Idiom 73-78
CHAPTER 11
Diction 79-84
CHAPTER 12
Sentence Structure 85-94
CHAPTER 13
Subjunctive Mood-Hypothetical 95-100
CHAPTER 14
Concision, Style, and Word Usage 101-106
CHAPTER 15
Cohesion and Organization 107-118
CHAPTER 16
Punctuation 119-126
CHAPTER 17
Graphs 127-136
CHAPTER 18
Grammar Technique and Review 137-145

PRACTICE TESTS

Test 1 146-163

Test 2 164-181

Test 3 182-199

Test 4 200-215

Test 5 216-233

Test 6 234-249

Test 7 250-267

Test 8 268-285

Test 9 286-301

Test 10 302-319

INTRODUCTION

Welcome to the NEW *SAT* Grammar Practice Book* of the *IES Advanced Practice Series.* This specialized workbook is one volume in an SAT preparation series that has been developed by elite SAT teachers at Integrated Educational Services, Inc. (IES). Renowned for its easy, accurate, and efficient SAT techniques, IES is a leader in the world of SAT preparation. Founded 15 years ago, our company is proud to have contributed to the academic and professional growth of countless students. With its innovative methods, IES is confident that this workbook will be integral to dramatically increasing writing scores.

IES prides itself on delivering comprehensive grammar knowledge that can be understood and applied regardless of a student's personal understanding of the English language. In this IES workbook, the SAT Grammar has been distilled into seventeen major types based on analysis of the most recent College Board material. Over the course of seventeen efficient lessons, every SAT Grammar problem will be taught with a clear example followed by an explanation. Our experience has proven that SAT Grammar is best approached by using simplified, clear, and straightforward terms. It is not necessary to be a grammarian or a linguist to ace the SAT Grammar section. However, it is important to be thoroughly practiced and knowledgeable about the IES grammar lessons and techniques.

Follow our rules, tips, strategies, and methods to a perfect score!

** SAT is a registered trademark of the College Board, which was not involved in the production of, and does not endorse, this product.*

Dear student,

As I was preparing this book for print, I was reminded of something that I often saw while teaching the old SAT—and that I have continued to see in my New SAT and New PSAT classes. Often, students finish SAT Writing sections and immediately declare, "that was so easy!" only to find that they have actually committed numerous mistakes. Many of these students do not know how to break from colloquial speech habits. Some of them have excellent reading and writing skills, but more than first impressions and quick instincts are needed for success on the New SAT Grammar test. To excel here, you need rules.

There is nothing obscure about the rules for clear, effective writing that the New SAT tests. Many of them rely on basic visual clues; all of them can be mastered through consistent practice with SAT Writing and Language passages. In this book, we at Integrated Educational Services give you a comprehensive breakdown of the test, covering fundamental grammar topics and accompanying these with abundant practice exercises. Once you have completed these, you can practice on ten tests that replicate the rigors and nuances of the latest College Board material. And perhaps most importantly, you will build the confidence you will need when test day arrives.

Although the SAT has changed, the test itself can still be made supremely manageable and predictable. IES has spent the past fifteen years teaching students to take control of grammar, writing, and composition. Now it's your turn. Once you have finished this book, you will be able to look over the New SAT and say, with certainty, "that was so easy!"

Wishing you all the best in your test-taking endeavors.

Sincerely,

Arianna Astuni
President, IES

HOW TO USE THIS PRACTICE BOOK

Our lessons are structured around the three **E's**: **E**xample, **E**xplanation, and **E**xercise. Following these "E drills" will prepare you for every grammar problem on the SAT. You will learn visual clues that indicate the specific grammar type being tested in a particular question. You will no longer need to plug in each answer choice until you find the right one. Instead, you will learn to eliminate wrong answer choices quickly and accurately by using the knowledge that this workbook contains.

To master the SAT Grammar, you must know *what* you are being tested on and *how* to notice it. You must break old grammar habits that come from the use of colloquial speech and everyday slang. You cannot rely on how a sentence "sounds." On the SAT, you must apply the rules of grammar that we have collected and clarified in the seventeen lessons that follow. With this workbook, you will learn the difference between a "style" change (changing the answer to a random word you "like" better) and a grammatical change (using the laws of grammar).

Most of all, you can use these seventeen lessons to effectively identify your weak areas. Then, practice, practice, practice until you reach your target score.

Included

- 17 Essential Grammar Rules Made Easy
- Over 200 Study Skills Questions
- 440 Practice Test Questions
- 10 Full Grammar Practice Tests

Key

Pay attention to anything near this graphic. Information accompanied by this pencil is crucial to understanding this book's techniques.

These tips are provided to give you additional knowledge of essential SAT Grammar.

These are special notes that provide more information about a particular lesson.

GRAMMAR LESSONS

Chapter 1

SUBJECT-VERB AGREEMENT

1 SUBJECT–VERB AGREEMENT LESSON 1

SUBJECT: The noun or pronoun that indicates what the sentence is about

VERB: The action of the noun or pronoun

REMEMBER: Subject/verb agreement is commonly tested by using: is/are, was/were, and has/have. If these words are underlined, check for subject/verb agreement.

AGREEMENT: All **subjects** and verbs must agree in number.

WHEN YOU SEE a verb underlined, you must ask yourself:

"Who (or what) is doing the verb, and do both subject and verb agree in number?"

SINGULAR	PLURAL
The **girl** jumps.	The **girls** jump.
He is happy.	**They** are happy.

LESSON 1.1

PREPOSITION: Any word (in, at, of, for, to, over, among, between, under…) that indicates a relationship between a noun and another part of the sentence

PREPOSITIONAL PHRASE: Any phrase (in the house, at the mall, to the store, for a jog, under the table…) that begins with a preposition and ends before the verb

Eliminate all PREPOSITIONAL PHRASES. The subject will never be in a prepositional phrase. Prepositional phrases contain extra details that often mislead the reader. CROSSING THEM OUT makes it easier to identify the subject.

EXAMPLE

The cars *in the lot* are clean.

The cars ~~in the lot~~ are clean. → Cross out "in the lot"

The ***cars are*** clean. ✓

One *of the girls* is visiting.

One ~~of the girls~~ is visiting. → Cross out "of the girls"

One is visiting. ✓

LESSON 1.2

INTERRUPTER: Any detail positioned between two commas

Eliminate all INTERRUPTERS. The subject will never be in an interrupter. Interrupters contain extra details that often mislead the reader. CROSSING THEM OUT makes it easier to identify the subject.

EXAMPLE

Patrick, *in addition to Tom and Mark,* is coming to the reception.
Patrick, ~~in addition to Tom and Mark~~, is coming to the reception. → Cross out "in addition to Tom and Mark,"

Patrick is coming to the reception. ✓

LESSON 1.3 **TRICKY SINGULAR:** A singular word that sounds plural or is commonly misused as a plural

Look out for TRICKY SINGULARS (neither, either, everyone, everybody, someone, somebody, anybody, anything, each, anyone, no one, everything, little, and much).

EXAMPLE

Neither of the twins *is* sick.

Neither ~~of the twins~~ *is* sick. → Cross out "of the twins"

Neither is sick. ✓

Either of the rooms at the hotel *is* available.

Either ~~of the rooms at the hotel~~ *is* available. → Cross out "of the rooms at the hotel"

Either is available. ✓

LESSON 1.4 **TRICKY PLURAL:** A plural word that sounds singular or is commonly misused as a singular

Look out for TRICKY PLURALS (Plural/Singular: data/datum, phenomena/phenomenon, media/medium, and criteria/criterion).

EXAMPLE

The *data* from the computer *are* on my disc.

The *data* ~~from the computer~~ *are* on my disc. → Cross out "from the computer"

The ***data are*** on my disc. ✓

The *criteria* for the assigned essay *are* very complex.

The *criteria* ~~for the assigned essay~~ *are* very complex. → Cross out "for the assigned essay"

The ***criteria are*** very complex. ✓

LESSON 1.5 **NEITHER/NOR AND EITHER/OR:** Two subjects separated by a standard phrase

Look out for NEITHER/NOR and EITHER/OR phrases. Although NEITHER and EITHER are singular, when grouped with NOR/OR, the word that ends the phrase determines the verb.

FORMULA:

Either A or B → B determines the verb

Neither A nor B → B determines the verb

EXAMPLE

Either John or ***Mary is*** right. ✓

Neither John nor ***the Parkers are*** wrong. ✓

TIPS

Sometimes the "B Phrase" includes a prepositional phrase. Apply the technique:

Either the Smiths or *one* of the Johnsons *was* expected to bring the salad.

Either the Smiths or *one* ~~of the Johnsons~~ *was* expected to bring the salad. → Cross out "of the Johnsons"

Either the Smiths or ***one was*** expected to bring the salad. ✓

LESSON 1.6 **INVERTED SENTENCE:** The verb comes before the subject in a sentence

Look out for anything INVERTED (VERB/SUBJECT). Sentences that start with the word "there" and compound sentences that have more than one subject/verb combination tend to be inverted.

HOW TO CHECK THE VERB:

Simply un-invert (flip) the subject and verb.

EXAMPLE

There <u>is</u> a **cat** in the house.

FLIPPED: ***cat is*** ✓

During the day, there <u>is</u> **ten cats** in the garage.

FLIPPED: *ten cats is* ✗

ten cats are ✓

TIPS

When subject nouns are LINKED with an "AND," the subject is PLURAL.

✓ <u>The house **and** the car</u> *were* ruined by the storm.

✓ <u>John **and** Mary</u> *eat* chocolate all day.

✓ <u>The dog **and** the cat</u> *are* in trouble for eating the cake on the counter.

1

Use this page for additional notes. The following pages have exercises regarding Subject/Verb Agreement.

1

EXERCISE ONE

DIRECTIONS: Using the strategies you learned on pages 12 - 14, fix the verb(s) where necessary.

EXAMPLE:

Neither of the twins ~~are~~ *is* happy about the convention being canceled.

1. By Anita's estimate, there is at least a hundred birds in the tropical rain forest exhibit.

2. There has always been too many conflicting clauses and stipulations in the company's hiring policy.

3. There is a public park, a swimming pool, and a miniature golf course just down the road from the house where I grew up.

4. The principles of morality, government, and perception was all investigated by British philosopher John Locke.

5. Neither Mr. Carruthers nor his son were invited to this year's golf outing.

6. Neither of the contestants were willing to use dishonest methods and thus risk her reputation.

7. The overwhelming support of both emerging and established authors have undeniably enriched the world literature scene.

8. The proceeds from the auction of Ms. Dutton's estate was distributed among her children.

9. Neither the cheerleaders nor the football players themselves believes that the coach has had a positive influence on the team.

10. Either a German novel or a French novel are going to be assigned to the class for summer reading.

11. There is only five more miles to go until we reach our destination.

12. Weather phenomena, from deadly tornadoes to gentle spring rain, is analyzed in great detail on an informative new television show.

13. The building inspectors were astonished to discover that there was three hidden rooms in the basement of the old mansion.

14. Every tenured faculty member of the department of literature and languages were present at Dr. McNulty's retirement party.

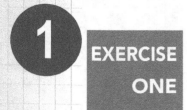

EXERCISE TWO

These are examples of questions that you will see on the SAT concerning Subject–Verb Agreement. Follow the directions below.

1

Questions 1-7 are based on the following passage.

Subject / Verb Agreement

For large numbers of both film critics and casual movie-goers, the greatest Japanese filmmaker isn't a man who created blockbusters or sci-fi epics, as George Lucas and Steven Spielberg have done. Instead, [1] there is many who would grant the title "greatest Japanese filmmaker" to Yasujiro Ozu, whose films feature highly realistic stories. What [2] are the typical Ozu movie like? Very often, the film starts with a family or other small group of people dealing with everyday problems. By the end, the overall situation has changed, possibly because of a marriage, travel plans, or an unexpected new friendship. [3] There are the usual extent of Ozu's plot, and the camera shots [4] seems very simple and direct, completely free of confusion.

So why is Ozu astonishing? There [5] is a few intriguing answers to this question. The first is that Ozu's films are about fascinating moments in history. From 1920 to 1960—the period when Ozu was very active—the Japanese wanted to modernize their economy while preserving their cultural traditions. This tension between old and new [6] make Ozu's work fascinating. Another reason for Ozu's prowess is that Ozu is a great storyteller. In his film *Tokyo Story*, for instance, two aging parents visit their children. From the old father and mother to their grandchildren, each of the characters in *Tokyo Story* [7] is depicted with a combination of gentle humor and compassion.

1

A) NO CHANGE
B) there are
C) there was
D) they're

2

A) NO CHANGE
B) were
C) will
D) is

3

A) NO CHANGE
B) This is
C) There is
D) These are

4

A) NO CHANGE
B) seemed
C) seem
D) seeming

5

A) NO CHANGE
B) was
C) were
D) are

6

A) NO CHANGE
B) makes
C) are making
D) made

7

A) NO CHANGE
B) was
C) have been
D) are

(ANSWERS ON NEXT PAGE)

1 ANSWER KEY

SUBJECT–VERB AGREEMENT
LESSON 1

EXERCISE 1:

1. By Anita's estimate, there ***are*** at least a hundred ***birds*** in the tropical rain forest exhibit. **(inverted)**

2. There ***have*** always been too many conflicting ***clauses and stipulations*** in the company's hiring policy. **(inverted)**

3. There ***are*** a ***public park, a swimming pool, and a miniature golf course*** just down the road from the house where I grew up. **(inverted)**

4. The ***principles*** of morality, government, and perception ***were*** all investigated by British philosopher John Locke. **(prepositional phrase)**

5. Neither Mr. Carruthers nor his ***son was*** invited to this year's golf outing. **(neither/nor)**

6. ***Neither*** of the contestants ***was*** willing to use dishonest methods and thus risk her reputation. **(tricky singular/ prepositional phrase)**

7. The overwhelming ***support*** of both emerging and established authors ***has*** undeniably enriched the world literature scene. (**prepositional phrase)**

8. The ***proceeds*** from the auction of Ms. Dutton's estate ***were*** distributed among her children. **(prepositional phrase)**

9. Neither the cheerleaders nor the ***football players*** themselves ***believe*** that the coach has had a positive influence on the team. **(neither/nor)**

10. Either a German novel or a French ***novel is*** going to be assigned to the class for summer reading. **(either/or)**

11. There ***are*** only five more ***miles*** to go until we reach our destination. **(inverted)**

12. Weather ***phenomena,*** from deadly tornadoes to gentle spring rain, ***are*** analyzed in great detail on an informative new television show. **(interrupter/tricky plural)**

13. The building inspectors were astonished to discover that there ***were*** three hidden ***rooms*** in the basement of the old mansion. **(inverted)**

14. Every tenured faculty ***member*** of the department of literature and languages ***was*** present at Dr. McNulty's retirement party. **(prepositional phrase)**

EXERCISE 2:

1. B
2. D
3. B
4. C
5. D
6. B
7. A

Chapter 2
PARALLELISM

2

PARALLELISM LESSON 2

Making a sentence parallel simply involves making the sentence balanced. Grammar is based on parallel structure.

THE LAWS OF PARALLELISM demand that words or phrases be in the same form of speech (adjectives, verbs, nouns) and use the same structure. Often, balancing a phrase requires the removal of extraneous words.

WHEN YOU SEE lists, comparisons, standard phrases, pronouns, and conjunctions, CHECK for parallelism.

comparisons:	more than, as much as, is, like
standard phrases:	not only/but also, so/that, either/or, neither/nor, prefer/to
pronouns:	one, you
conjunctions:	and, but

LESSON 2.1 **BALANCING LISTS**

EXAMPLE

She went swimming, running, and danced all night. ✗

She went swimming, running, and ***dancing*** all night. ✓

This is a call for all professors, editors, and people who collaborate. ✗

This is a call for all professors, editors, and ***collaborators***. ✓

LESSON 2.2 **BALANCING COMPARISONS**

EXAMPLE

Jefferson actually liked to participate in the science league more than he liked playing basketball. ✗

Jefferson actually liked ***participating*** in the science league more than he liked ***playing*** basketball. ✓

Jefferson actually liked ***to participate*** in the science league more than he liked ***to play*** basketball. ✓

LESSON 2.3 **BALANCING TWO SIDES OF A STANDARD PHRASE**

EXAMPLE

Judging by the look on his face, Paul is either nervous or filled with excitement. ✗

Judging by the look on his face, Paul is either nervous or ***excited***. ✓

I prefer eating salty foods to sweet foods. ✗

I prefer eating salty foods to ***eating*** sweet foods. ✓

LESSON 2.4 BALANCING PRONOUNS

EXAMPLE

One should always do what you want. ✗

One should always do what ***one*** wants. ✓

You should always do what ***you*** want. ✓

LESSON 2.5 BALANCING TWO SIDES OF A CONJUNCTION

EXAMPLE

To prepare for the party, we should set the table and making the pasta. ✗

To prepare for the party, we should set the table and ***make*** the pasta. ✓

John's book is informative but full of entertainment. ✗

John's book is informative but ***entertaining***. ✓

TIPS

As mentioned before, sometimes balancing a sentence merely requires the OMISSION of extraneous words.

✗ The students were happy to learn the lesson, finish the homework, and *they could* enjoy the weekend.

✓ The students were happy to learn the lesson, finish the homework, and enjoy the weekend.

Use this space for additional notes. The following pages have exercises regarding Parallelism.

2

EXERCISE ONE

DIRECTIONS: Using the strategies you learned on pages 20 - 21, balance the sentence if necessary.

EXAMPLE:

Loving

~~To love~~ is essential, but so is working on your career.

1. In preparation for the train heist, the outlaws obtained ropes and ladders, disguised themselves in black clothing, and they also devised a foolproof escape plan.

2. If you are interested in learning about Italian cinema, one should watch the film *La Strada.*

3. The ballerina was neither committed to a single performance style nor was she willing to ally herself with only one dance troupe.

4. Many students would agree that actually traveling the world is more exciting than when you simply read about faraway places.

5. In recent times, some investment bankers have been more interested in amassing wealth than in how scrupulous the business practices they follow are.

6. To say that Meredith works out "now and then" is underestimating her devotion to health and fitness.

7. Norman yearned not only to write innovative poetry, but also he yearned to create experimental sculptures and architectural designs.

8. Walking through the old haunted house was like a return to all my childhood fears.

9. The Caribbean heritage festival attracted traditional dancers, community service organizers, and documentaries by directors from around the world.

10. Richard is worried not only about how his teachers perceive him, but also about his peers reacting to his personality.

11. Delilah prefers the music of the Rolling Stones to the music which was made by the Beatles.

12. Visitors discovered that the performance art exhibit was not only innovative, but also it educated.

13. My uncle purchased steaks and sausage links, set up his new deck furniture, and he also sent out invitations for his Friday cookout.

14. Compared to its competitors, the new bistro is more spacious and it is more efficiently managed.

15. Linda is neither comfortable speaking in front of others nor is she capable of making her points succinctly.

EXERCISE TWO

These are examples of questions that you will see on the SAT concerning Parallelism. Follow the directions below.

2

Questions 1-5 are based on the following passage.

Parallelism

[1] To write was always easier for her than talking. Jane Wu, author of *The Ties That Bind Us*, seems to have been born the quintessential author. She has other hobbies, of course. [2] She enjoys playing golf, tennis, and to play chess. She sometimes collects stray cats and delivers them to a shelter where the kind people [3] care for these unwanted creatures and are finding homes for them. But she does all of this in a perfunctory way. It is in her novels that she is both [4] at home and peacefully. The novels are the place where her passion comes alive. Her [5] characters fly and are dancing through their emotionally vigorous lives—creating sharp contrasts with Wu's own persona of calmness and introspection.

1

A) NO CHANGE
B) To write was always easier for her than having talked.
C) Writing was always easier for her than to talk.
D) Writing was always easier for her than talking.

2

A) NO CHANGE
B) to play golf, to play tennis, and to play chess.
C) playing golf, tennis, and chess.
D) playing golf, playing tennis, and chess.

3

A) NO CHANGE
B) care for these unwanted creatures and try to find homes for them.
C) cares for these unwanted creatures, also trying to find homes for them.
D) caring for these unwanted creatures and try to find homes for them

4

A) NO CHANGE
B) at home and at peace.
C) at home and peace.
D) homeful and peaceful.

5

A) NO CHANGE
B) are flying and are dancing
C) fly and dance
D) flying and dancing

(ANSWERS ON NEXT PAGE)

2

ANSWER KEY

PARALLELISM
LESSON 2

EXERCISE 1: *THERE ARE MANY WAYS TO CORRECT THE SENTENCES, BUT THE FOLLOWING CORRECTIONS REFLECT SAT STANDARDS.*

1. In preparation for the train heist, the outlaws obtained ropes and ladders, disguised themselves in black clothing, ***and devised*** a foolproof escape plan.

2. If you are interested in learning about Italian cinema, ***you*** should watch the film *La Strada*.

3. The ballerina was neither committed to a single performance style ***nor willing*** to ally herself with only one dance troupe.

4. Many students would agree that actually traveling the world is more exciting than ***simply reading*** about faraway places.

5. In recent times, some investment bankers have been more interested in amassing wealth than in ***following scrupulous business practices.***

6. To say that Meredith works out "now and then" is ***to underestimate*** her devotion to health and fitness.

7. Norman yearned not only to write innovative poetry, ***but also to create*** experimental sculptures and architectural designs.

8. Walking through the old haunted house was like ***returning*** to all my childhood fears.

9. The Caribbean heritage festival attracted traditional dancers, community service organizers, and ***documentary directors*** from around the world.

10. Richard is worried not only about how his teachers perceive him, but also ***about how his peers react*** to his personality.

11. Delilah prefers the music of the Rolling Stones to ***the music of*** the Beatles.

12. Visitors discovered that the performance art exhibit was not only innovative, ***but also educational.***

13. My uncle purchased steaks and sausage links, set up his new deck furniture, ***and sent out*** invitations for his Friday cookout.

14. Compared to its competitors, the new bistro is more spacious and ***more efficiently managed.***

15. Linda is neither comfortable speaking in front of others ***nor capable*** of making her points succinctly.

EXERCISE 2:

1. D
2. C
3. B
4. B
5. C

Chapter 3
COMPARISON

3

COMPARISON LESSON 3

Comparison problems are often tricky to catch because the reader infers the correct comparison. Checking for comparison requires the use of visual parallelism. Be aware of what is being compared in the sentence. These comparisons must be LOGICAL.

WHEN YOU SEE these words in a sentence, check for the problems described in the following lessons.

COMPARISONS	**as, than, like, to, between, among**
"A" PHRASE	**a student, a player, a musician**
WORDS THAT DESCRIBE QUANTITY	**fewer/ less, number/ amount, many/ much**

LESSON 3.1 ILLOGICAL COMPARISONS

EXAMPLE
In my opinion, there is no story more intriguing than Othello. ✕

EXPLANATION
The word *than* signals that there is a comparison in this sentence. This is not a logical comparison because we must compare a "story" to a "story."

In my opinion, there is no ***story*** more intriguing than ***the story of*** Othello. ✓

EXAMPLE
Her inclination to eat a cupcake is much stronger than to go for a jog. ✕

EXPLANATION
This sentence is wrong because her "inclination [to eat a cupcake]" is being compared to "to go for a jog." You must compare *inclination* and *inclination,* not *inclination* and *to go for a jog.*

Her ***inclination*** to eat a cupcake is much stronger than her ***inclination*** to go for a jog. ✓

EXAMPLE
Napoleon Bonaparte is more famous than any leader in French history. ✕

EXPLANATION
This sentence is wrong because Napoleon Bonaparte was a leader himself, and he could not have been more famous than himself. We must compare him to *other* leaders.

Napoleon Bonaparte is more famous than any ***other*** leader in French history. ✓

When checking for ILLOGICAL COMPARISON, think of parallelism: *Pineapples to apples,* NOT *pineapples to eating apples!*

LESSON 3.2 NUMBER AGREEMENT/"A" PHRASE

Things that you compare have to agree in *number*. Both are either *singular* or *plural*.

EXAMPLE Though their parents wished otherwise, they were both struggling to be a musician. ✗

EXPLANATION Because the word "musician" is referring to "they," we must use *musicians*.

Though their parents wished otherwise, ***they*** were both struggling to be ***musicians***. ✓

EXAMPLE Both Kristi and Kim are an administrator in the office. ✗

EXPLANATION Because "administrator" is referring to "Kristi and Kim," we must use *administrators*.

Both ***Kristi and Kim*** are ***administrators*** in the office. ✓

LESSON 3.3 COUNTABLE/NOT COUNTABLE

DESCRIBES THINGS THAT ARE **COUNTABLE** (hot dogs, dollars, kisses)	DESCRIBES THINGS THAT ARE **NOT COUNTABLE** (food, money, love)
fewer / number / many	**less / amount / much**

EXAMPLE There are much more architectural decorations on this skyscraper than I had expected. ✗

EXPLANATION This sentence is wrong because *decorations* can be counted. We must use *many*.

There are ***many*** more architectural ***decorations*** on this skyscraper than I had expected. ✓

EXAMPLE No one could guess the number of candy in the jar. ✗

EXPLANATION This sentence is wrong because *candy* cannot be counted. We must use *amount*.

No one could guess the ***amount*** of ***candy*** in the jar. ✓

LESSON 3.4 COMPARING EXACTLY TWO VS. THREE OR MORE

COMPARING ONLY TWO THINGS	COMPARING THREE OR MORE THINGS
between	**among**
more	**most**
-er ending words: better, faster, stronger	**-est ending words:** best, fastest, strongest

EXAMPLE Of the dozens of kids in the club, Sarah was the more popular. ✗

EXPLANATION Because there are dozens of kids (3 or more), we must use *most*.

Of the dozens of kids in the club, Sarah was the ***most*** popular. ✓

EXAMPLE There was no animosity between Joe, Chris, and Patrick. ✗

EXPLANATION Because there are three people, we must use *among*.

There was no animosity ***among*** Joe, Chris, and Patrick. ✓

TIPS

When you see BETWEEN or AMONG, remember:

BETWEEN

Compares exactly two things
Always use "and"
Always use "me", not "I"

EXAMPLE

The decision is between John or *I*. ✗

The decision is between John ***and me***. ✓

AMONG

Compares three things or more
Always use "and"
Always use "me", not "I"

EXAMPLE

Among Mary, Rhonda or *I*, Mary is the prettiest. ✗

Among Mary, Rhonda ***and me***, Mary is the prettiest. ✓

3

Use this page for additional notes. The following pages have exercises regarding Comparison.

3

DIRECTIONS: Using the strategies you learned on pages 26 - 28, fix the comparison error if necessary.

EXAMPLE:

in traveling across

More people are interested in traveling across the United States than ~~in~~ Europe.

1. The ship could not maneuver effectively because too ~~much~~ *Many* barrels of provisions and cases of ammunition had been stored on board.

2. In nineteenth-century America, activists such as Elizabeth Cady Stanton and Susan B. Anthony urged women to become ~~a participant~~ *participants* in the democratic process.

3. The word problem asked students to determine the ~~amount~~ *number* of marbles that could fill a cylindrical jar.

4. He believes that wearing sandals in summer is better for his health ~~than~~ sneakers. *wearing — in the summer*

5. Senator Joseph McCarthy rose to notoriety by determining which citizens of the United States had a ~~communist belief~~. *communist beliefs*

6. Terry is firmly convinced that the best comic novels are P.D. Wodehouse. ✓

7. After much deliberation, the judges decided that Grover was ~~the better~~ *the best* of the seven performers who had appeared in the talent show.

8. It is hard to deny that flying in a private jet is a much more glamorous way to travel ~~than a~~ commercial plane. *then traveling in a*

9. Only a few of the air force cadets were interested in becoming ~~an astronaut~~. *astronauts*

10. Like so many ~~other~~ academic essays on literature, Sharon bombards readers with awkward sentences and unclear definitions. *writers of*

11. The gardening and yard maintenance duties were equally divided ~~between~~ *among* Jacques, Frederic, and me.

12. Independence and determination are ~~a quality~~ *qualities* that will lead you to success in your college studies.

EXERCISE TWO

These are examples of questions that you will see on the SAT concerning Comparisons. Follow the directions below.

Questions 1-8 are based on the following passage.

Comparison

Sharks, real sharks, have been making quite a splash in this summer's news cycle. Forget the yearly "Shark Week" television events; shark sightings and shark attacks have been reported on almost every beach on the East Coast. The hysteria is almost surreal and can be likened [1] to *Jaws*, the movie. Every fisherman wants to nab the "big one" and be [2] heroes. Every swimmer wants to brave the waters—only to boast later that he or she "survived." [3] Between the aspiring fishermen, the frenzied media, and the foolhardy beach-goers, there is a morbid fascination in these events. Of all the species in the ocean, sharks were always the [4] scarier. There is no story more intriguing than [5] the story of a shark attack survivor, yet welcoming an attack for the sake of a good story is lunacy.

Sensationalism aside, some commentators have made conscientious efforts to get to the heart of the situation. Their efforts, though, have not yielded decisive answers. It is unclear whether there are [6] much more sharks than usual in the oceans today, and unclear when and why a population increase might have taken place. Have we polluted the water [7] like the earth, and thus forced the sharks to hunt innocent swimmers for food? Is this phenomenon due to global warming? At least for the present, scientists don't have [8] many information to share.

1

A) NO CHANGE
B) to the hysteria depicted in the movie *Jaws*.
C) to *Jaws*, the movie's depicted hysteria.
D) to *Jaws*, the movie's, shark attacks.

2

A) NO CHANGE
B) heroines.
C) a hero.
D) hero.

3

A) NO CHANGE
B) Among
C) In between
D) Even

4

A) NO CHANGE
B) most scariest.
C) more scarier.
D) scariest.

5

A) NO CHANGE
B) the attack of
C) those of
D) DELETE the underlined portion.

6

A) NO CHANGE
B) more
C) less
D) many

7

A) NO CHANGE
B) like the earth is polluted
C) like we polluted the earth
D) as the earth

8

A) NO CHANGE
B) any
C) much
D) many more

(ANSWERS ON NEXT PAGE)

3

ANSWER KEY

COMPARISON
LESSON 3

EXERCISE 1: *THERE ARE MANY WAYS TO CORRECT THE SENTENCES, BUT THE FOLLOWING CORRECTIONS REFLECT SAT STANDARDS.*

1. The ship could not maneuver effectively because too ***many*** barrels of provisions and cases of ammunition had been stored on board.

2. In nineteenth-century America, activists such as Elizabeth Cady Stanton and Susan B. Anthony urged women to become ***participants*** in the democratic process.

3. The word problem asked students to determine the ***number*** of marbles that could fill a cylindrical jar.

4. He believes that wearing sandals in summer is better for his health than ***wearing sneakers***.

5. Senator Joseph McCarthy rose to notoriety by determining which citizens of the United States had ***communist beliefs***.

6. Terry is firmly convinced that the best comic novels are ***those of P.D. Wodehouse***.

7. After much deliberation, the judges decided that Grover was the ***best*** of the seven performers who had appeared in the talent show.

8. It is hard to deny that flying in a private jet is a much more glamorous way to travel than ***flying in a commercial plane***.

9. Only a few of the air force cadets were interested in becoming ***astronauts***.

10. Like so many other academic essays on literature, ***Sharon's essays bombard*** readers with awkward sentences and unclear definitions.

11. The gardening and yard maintenance duties were equally divided ***among*** Jacques, Frederic, and me.

12. Independence and determination are ***qualities*** that will lead you to success in your college studies.

EXERCISE 2:

1. B
2. C
3. B
4. D
5. A
6. B
7. C
8. C

Chapter 4

SUBJECT-PRONOUN AGREEMENT

4

SUBJECT–PRONOUN AGREEMENT LESSON 4

PRONOUN: The word that takes the place of the noun

EXAMPLES: I, you, we, us, our, me, he, she, him, her, they, their, it, its

FORMULA: *Janet* is tired because *she* studied for the SAT all day.

WHEN YOU SEE a PRONOUN underlined, you must ask yourself:

"Who (or what) is this pronoun referring to and do both (subject and pronoun) agree in number?"

SINGULAR	PLURAL
He/ She, It	They
Her/ Him, It	Them
His/ Her, Its	Their

LESSON 4.1 DON'T MISTAKE SINGULAR SUBJECTS FOR PLURAL SUBJECTS.

EXAMPLE

SUBJECT	PRONOUN
The University of Massachusetts (one place) = the radio station =	IT
people (more than one person) = the doctors = students =	THEY
each of the girls (Tricky Singular) =	SHE
everybody (Tricky Singular) =	HE OR SHE

LESSON 4.2 JUST LIKE SUBJECT/VERB AGREEMENT, BE AWARE OF TRICKY SINGULARS.

TRICKY SINGULARS
EITHER, NEITHER, EVERYONE, EVERYBODY, SOMEONE, SOMEBODY, ANYBODY, ANYTHING, EACH, ANYONE, NO ONE, EVERYTHING, LITTLE, MUCH

EXAMPLE *Everyone* should brush *their* teeth three times a day. ✗

EXPLANATION *Everyone* is a tricky singular.

Everyone should brush ***his*** or ***her*** teeth three times a day. ✓

TIPS

Do NOT cross out prepositional phrases. The pronoun's subject may be in the prepositional phrase.

The quality of the *multivitamins* depends entirely on *its* ingredients. ✗

What has the ingredients? The quality or the multivitamins?

The quality of the ***multivitamins*** depends entirely on ***their*** ingredients. ✓

LESSON 4.3 BE AWARE OF TRICKY PRONOUNS.

***What, where, when, why, who,* and *how* are all interrogative pronouns that can begin a question or refer to an unknown. BUT, sometimes they refer directly to the subject.**

USE **WHAT** ONLY TO REFER TO A THING.

EXAMPLE The quality of the product is ***what's*** important. ✓

EXPLANATION ***What*** refers to quality. Quality is important.

USE **WHERE** ONLY TO REFER TO A PLACE.

EXAMPLE Seattle is ***where*** I got engaged. ✓

EXPLANATION ***Where*** refers to Seattle. I got engaged in Seattle.

USE **IN WHICH** IF THE "WHERE" IS NOT LITERAL.

EXAMPLE This is a story where the hero dies. ✗

This is a story ***in which*** the hero dies. ✓

EXAMPLE I like movies where the guy gets the girl. ✗

I like movies ***in which*** the guy gets the girl. ✓

USE **WHEN** ONLY TO REFER TO A TIME.

EXAMPLE 2014 is ***when*** the incident happened. ✓

EXPLANATION ***When*** refers to 2014. The incident happened in 2014.

USE **WHY** ONLY TO REFER TO A REASON.

EXAMPLE Please tell me ***why*** you refuse to wear a helmet. ✓

EXPLANATION ***Why*** refers to the reason you refuse to wear a helmet. (Please tell me the ***reason*** you refuse to wear a helmet.)

USE **WHO** TO REFER TO A PERSON. (Do not use THAT when referring to a person.)

EXAMPLE The students that ate got sick. ✗

The students ***who*** ate got sick. ✓

USE **HOW** ONLY TO REFER TO AN EXPLANATION.

EXAMPLE Studying hard is ***how*** I aced my SAT. ✓

EXPLANATION ***How*** refers to studying hard. (I aced my SAT by studying hard.)

LESSON 4.4 LOOK OUT FOR AMBIGUOUS PRONOUNS.

If the pronoun in the sentence can refer to more than one thing, it is ambiguous. The connection between the subject and the pronoun should be clear.

EXAMPLE Austin told Joe that ***he*** had some spinach in his teeth. ✕

EXPLANATION Who "had spinach in his teeth?" Austin or Joe?

EXAMPLE Deep-sea exploration has occurred, but ***they*** still haven't found any new species. ✕

EXPLANATION Who "haven't found any new species?"

Use this page for additional notes. The following pages have exercises regarding Subject/Pronoun Agreement.

4

EXERCISE ONE

DIRECTIONS: Using the strategies you learned on pages 34 - 36, fix the pronoun(s) if necessary.

EXAMPLE:

Each year, the local churches collect money to support ~~its~~ *their* charity programs.

1. Everyone that wants a part in the play should report to the auditorium with their script.

2. I still vividly remember that it was Jacksonville, not Orlando, when I got engaged.

3. Someone forgot their credit card in the lobby of the hotel.

4. The insects, though each distinct in their own way, were all equally despised by Hannah.

5. After a long and contentious deliberation, the soccer association decided that they would punish the offending player by suspending them for two months.

6. Even though the Center for Disease Control has been charged with the task of researching methods to prevent harmful diseases, they often publish findings that are largely ignored by the public.

7. Sometimes, high school students bite off more than they can chew with sports, clubs, and academics.

8. No parent wants to hear that their child is the one that has a bad reputation at school.

9. The Bronx Zoo in New York City is very much concerned with providing their animals with a good quality of life by housing them in habitats that reflect its indigenous environments.

10. Both Lady Gaga and Madonna are known for their stage performances, but she has the more powerful voice.

4

(ANSWERS ON NEXT PAGE)

4

ANSWER KEY

PRONOUN ERRORS
LESSON 4

EXERCISE 1:

1. ***Everyone who*** wants a part in the play should report to the auditorium with ***his or her*** script.

2. I still vividly remember that it was ***Jacksonville***, not Orlando, ***where*** I got engaged.

3. ***Someone*** forgot ***his or her*** credit card in the lobby of the hotel.

4. The insects, though ***each*** distinct in ***its*** own way, were all equally despised by Hannah.

5. After a long and contentious deliberation, ***the soccer association*** decided that ***it*** would punish ***the offending player*** by suspending ***him or her*** for two months.

6. Even though the ***Center for Disease Control*** has been charged with the task of researching methods to prevent harmful diseases, ***it*** often publishes findings that are largely ignored by the public.

7. Sometimes, ***high school students*** bite off more than ***they*** can chew with sports, clubs, and academics. ***(no error)***

8. No ***parent*** wants to hear that ***his or her child*** is the one ***who*** has a bad reputation at school.

9. ***The Bronx Zoo*** in New York City is very much concerned with providing ***its animals*** with a good quality of life by housing them in habitats that reflect ***their*** indigenous environments.

10. Both ***Lady Gaga*** and ***Madonna*** are known for their stage performances, but ***she (ambiguous pronoun, must name woman)*** has the more powerful voice.

Chapter 5

PRONOUN CASE

5

PRONOUN CASE LESSON 5

WHEN YOU SEE a PRONOUN you must ask yourself:

"Is this pronoun in the proper form?"

Similar to SUBJECT/PRONOUN, **PRONOUN CASE** focuses on the correct use of a pronoun in relation to the rest of the sentence. Below are general instances in which the SAT will test PRONOUN CASE.

LESSON 5.1 PEOPLE OR GROUPS

You will see a pronoun combined with ANOTHER PRONOUN, PERSON, or GROUP by a conjunction.

EXAMPLE

The sports team and he...	Sally and they...

Read the following sentence:

Every Sunday at the playground, <u>the other children and her</u> pretended to be valiant knights.

Did you see the problem? If not, here is what you should do when you see a pronoun used in combination with another person or group:

STOP and PLACE YOUR FINGER over the other person or group and REREAD the sentence.

Every Sunday at the playground, ~~the other children and~~ her pretended to be valiant knights.

her pretended ✗	*she* pretended ✓

Every Sunday at the playground, the other children and ***she*** pretended to be valiant knights. ✓

EXAMPLE

The school presented the award to Andre and he.

The school presented the award to ~~Andre and~~ he.

presented the award to he ✗

presented the award to *him* ✓

The school presented the award to Andre and ***him***. ✓

EXAMPLE

Us and the other parents went to the beach.

Us ~~and the other parents~~ went to the beach.

Us went ✗

We went ✓

We and the other parents went to the beach. ✓

LESSON 5.2 THAN OR AS

Pronoun Case may also appear in comparisons usually indicated by the words THAN or AS:

No one did better than her.	No one has scored as many touchdowns as him.

In both sentences, there is an implied verb after the pronoun. Here is what you should do: INSERT the implied verb to REVEAL the correct pronoun.

No one did better than her (did).	No one has scored as many touchdowns as him (scored).
her did ✗	him scored ✗
she did ✓	*he* scored ✓
No one did better than ***she***. ✓	No one has scored as many touchdowns as ***he***. ✓

EXAMPLE

Betty is faster than me. Betty is faster than me (am).	Chris is as noisy as her. Chris is as noisy as her (is).
me am ✗	her is ✗
I am ✓	*she* is ✓
Betty is faster than *I*. ✓	Chris is as noisy as *she*. ✓

LESSON 5.3 REFLEXIVE PRONOUNS

Another way that you will see PRONOUN CASE is in REFLEXIVE PRONOUNS such as *himself, herself, themselves, ourselves,* and *myself.* Note: *myself* is the most commonly used on the SAT. If you see *me* or *myself* underlined, check to make sure that the pronoun is being used properly.

To celebrate my graduation, I scheduled a party for me and the other graduates.

I scheduled a party for me ✗

I scheduled a party for *myself* ✓

To celebrate my graduation, I scheduled a party for ***myself*** and the other graduates. ✓

5

LESSON 5.4	BETWEEN / AMONG

Do you recall the tip from comparison about "BETWEEN" and "AMONG"? Always use "me" not "I". The same rule applies in these cases. When you see the words *between* and *among* use the OBJECTIVE form of the pronoun. See table below.

SUBJECTIVE	OBJECTIVE
I	**Me**
He	**Him**
She	**Her**
We	**Us**

EXAMPLE

Between Mary and I ✗	Between Mary and *me* ✓

Among Stacy, Richard, and she ✗	Among Stacy, Richard, and her ✓

5

EXERCISE ONE

DIRECTIONS: Using the strategies you learned on pages 42 - 44, circle the correct pronoun.

EXAMPLE: I am better at tennis than (her / she (is)) and thus I win every game.

1. Despite our differences, Yolanda and (I / me) must work together on this science project.

2. No one is sorrier than (I / me) that you lost your dog.

3. Gertrude was trying to provoke me the whole night, but I had to remind (me / myself) not to dignify her antics with a response.

4. After the shopping spree, we all agreed that no one had spent more than (she / her).

5. Did Dad bring any exotic souvenirs home for Keshav and (I / me)?

6. (We / Us) and the rest of our posse decided that, in order to assert our territory on the beach, we would need to bring a blanket and multiple chairs.

7. The man making the broccoli and cheddar soup accidentally spilled it all over my Yorkshire Terrier and (I / me).

8. (He and I / Him and me) work well together.

9. Even though I wore my best dress and my most dramatic hairdo, none of the boys at the event would dance with (I / me).

10. Over the course of 28 years, Kelly, Linda, and (he / him) cultivated a bountiful pumpkin patch.

11. The other Civil War reenactors and (she / her) got into a dispute with the municipal parks department about the use of real cannons.

12. Since we were provided with a pamphlet about the mating habits of apes, it was easy for (she and I / her and me) to spot indications of romance at the gorilla exhibit.

5

EXERCISE TWO

These are examples of questions that you will see on the SAT concerning Subject–Pronoun and Pronoun Case. Follow the directions below.

Questions 1-7 are based on the following passage.

Pronoun Errors

By working together, a hardy group of pet enthusiasts has created a community organization with the potential to do an enormous amount of good. In 2007, People Pick-Me-Up began when two recent college graduates began bringing [1] our pets—rabbits, parakeets, and a cheerful golden retriever—to a local nursing home. The idea of using "visiting pets" to comfort others quickly caught on. Now, People Pick-Me-Up has over twenty members and is recognized in a large number of local newspapers. The group's activities include [2] their regular visits to nursing homes and veterans' hospitals as well as occasional sessions at camps for children from troubled families.

The successes of People Pick-Me-Up can be explained by [3] their dedication to the immediate community—in this case, a few counties in suburban Connecticut. "We have had plenty of opportunities to expand, but [4] one would rather build stronger connections to the people we know," says Ron MacKinner, one of the two People Pick-Me-Up founding members. However, MacKinner doesn't see staying local as turning [5] its back on people in need. He is confident that other organizations will see the good work that People Pick-Me-Up has done, and he has the business savvy to effectively

1

A) NO CHANGE
B) their
C) it's
D) the

2

A) NO CHANGE
B) they're regular visits
C) its regular visits
D) it's regular visits

3

A) NO CHANGE
B) there
C) its
D) our

4

A) NO CHANGE
B) we
C) he
D) they

5

A) NO CHANGE
B) it's
C) their
D) his

EXERCISE TWO

These are examples of questions that you will see on the SAT concerning Subject–Pronoun and Pronoun Case. Follow the directions below.

publicize even a single-area charity. As it turns out, MacKinner's background is in communications and marketing, both of which **6** <u>him</u> studied at the university level.

Indeed, MacKinner's "stay close, inspire far" strategy has begun to show positive results, as other pet therapy groups have begun to follow the approach set by MacKinner. One newly-established organization in rural Pennsylvania even cites the good work done by People Pick-Me-Up as **7** <u>their</u> specific inspiration.

6

A) NO CHANGE
B) they
C) he
D) we

7

A) NO CHANGE
B) its
C) it's
D) there

(ANSWERS ON NEXT PAGE)

5 ANSWER KEY PRONOUN CASE

LESSON 5

EXERCISE 1:

1. Despite our differences, Yolanda and ***I*** must work together on this science project.

2. No one is sorrier than ***I*** that you lost your dog.

3. Gertrude was trying to provoke me the whole night, but I had to remind ***myself*** not to dignify her antics with a response.

4. After the shopping spree, we all agreed that no one had spent more than ***she***.

5. Did Dad bring any exotic souvenirs home for Keshav and ***me***?

6. ***We*** and the rest of our posse decided that in order to assert our territory on the beach, we would need to bring a blanket and multiple chairs.

7. The man making the broccoli and cheddar soup accidentally spilled it all over my Yorkshire Terrier and ***me***.

8. ***He and I*** work well together.

9. Even though I wore my best dress and my most dramatic hairdo, none of the boys at the event would dance with ***me***.

10. Over the course of 28 years, Kelly, Linda, and ***he*** cultivated a bountiful pumpkin patch.

11. The other Civil War reenactors and ***she*** got into a dispute with the municipal parks department about the use of real cannons.

12. Since we were provided with a pamphlet about the mating habits of apes, it was easy for ***her and me*** to spot indications of romance at the gorilla exhibit.

EXERCISE 2:

1. B
2. C
3. C
4. B
5. D
6. C
7. B

Chapter 6

DANGLING MODIFIER

6

DANGLING MODIFIER LESSON 6

A DANGLING MODIFIER IS A DESCRIPTIVE PHRASE FOLLOWED BY THE WRONG SUBJECT.

MODIFIER: Descriptive phrase

Regularly lifting heavy packages, John hurt his back. ✓

SUBJECT: The person or other noun that the modifier describes

WHEN YOU SEE a sentence beginning with a modifier...

Ask yourself, **WHO** or **WHAT** does this descriptive phrase apply to?

LESSON 6.1	PLACING THE SUBJECT AFTER THE MODIFIER (THUS AFTER THE COMMA)
EXAMPLE	Known to be poisonous, the unsuspecting tourist was bitten by the rattlesnake. ✗
EXPLANATION	*Who* is known to be poisonous—the tourist, or the rattlesnake?
	Known to be poisonous, the rattlesnake bit the unsuspecting tourist. ✓
EXAMPLE	Walking down the street, Jane saw a shooting star. ✓
EXPLANATION	If JANE is walking down the street, then JANE must come right after the comma.

LESSON 6.2	THE APOSTROPHE TRAP

BE CAREFUL not to pick a subject that is a possessive noun, or a subject with an apostrophe (Picasso's paintings; Carol's legs). The apostrophe means ownership, so the word following it cannot be separated from the person. They must remain together unless the apostrophe is removed.

EXAMPLE	Walking down the street, Jane's head was almost cut off by a shooting star. ✗
EXPLANATION	*Jane's head* was not walking down the street.
EXCEPTION	Pounding like a hammer, Jane's headache would not stop. ✓
EXPLANATION	*Jane's headache* was pounding like a hammer, so there is no dangling modifier.

LESSON 6.3 DANGLING MODIFIERS AT THE END OF THE SENTENCE

EXAMPLE Raj swallowed his last bite of watermelon parking the truck. ✗

EXPLANATION *His last bite of watermelon* was not parking the truck.

Parking the truck, Raj swallowed his last bite of watermelon. ✓

Use this page for additional notes. The following pages have exercises regarding Dangling Modifier.

6

EXERCISE ONE

DIRECTIONS: Using the strategies you learned on pages 50 - 51, fix the Dangling Modifier if necessary.

EXAMPLE:

While attending college, her family was happy to see Cindy every weekend.

1. Without any formal training, the landscape paintings by Rhonda were beautiful.

2. Famous for having popularized colorful socks, Harry's shoes also have a stylish flair.

3. Before taking off into the sunset, the kiss the cowboy shared with his lover was passionate.

4. The teacher was proud that by lightening the homework load, her students' performance and participation in class increased.

5. Kandi invented a new toilet that cleans itself when pulling a lever.

6. Hoping that her performance had been good enough to earn her a spot on the cheerleading squad, Caroline waited in the hallway.

7. Worn out after years of use, Jacob needed to replace his favorite pair of jeans.

8. Perhaps his finest work, Picasso created a mural-sized painting in black and white called *Guernica.*

9. Easily the most sought-after countertop material, most people want granite for its durability and attractiveness.

10. Having climbed for days, the torrential downpour forced the disheartened travelers to abandon their goal of reaching the summit.

EXERCISE TWO

These are examples of questions that you will see on the SAT concerning Dangling Modifier. Follow the directions below.

6

Questions 1-6 are based on the following passage.

Dangling Modifier

When watching movies and television shows, [1] it is often common for viewers to be bombarded with tense depictions of stern parents and their rebellious teenagers. Knowing full well the entertainment value of such vivid [2] stereotypes, television producers capitalize on one segment of the parent-teenager relationship. Yet popular entertainment may be wrong about today's "generation gap." Since the advent of the Internet and its possibilities of increased connectivity, [3] psychiatrist's theories have found that the much-sensationalized divide that flourished in the days of James Dean, the Brat Pack, and *My So-Called Life* doesn't fit the reality of [4] today, listening to the same music and wearing the same styles.

The case of recent *American Idol* contestant Amy McKeithan is firm evidence of such tendencies. Hoping that her performance had gone well, [5] Amy's anxiety pushed her directly to her mother, who was waiting in the wings. "I do not trust any of my friends to guide me or critique me," says Amy definitively. "My mom knows this industry and its style trends better than any teenager does." Family ties, somewhat unexpectedly, can endure thanks to of-the-moment entertainment. And because they view the world in more or less the same way, [6] computers will only continue to become closer and closer.

1

A) NO CHANGE
B) viewers are often bombarded
C) they are common for viewers bombarded
D) viewer's bombardment is common

2

A) NO CHANGE
B) stereotypes, parents
C) stereotypes, teenagers
D) stereotypes, we

3

A) NO CHANGE
B) psychiatrists have
C) TV stations have
D) technology has

4

A) NO CHANGE
B) today's parents and teens, listening to the same music and wearing the same styles.
C) music and styles.
D) today's parents and teens, who listen to the same music and wear the same styles.

5

A) NO CHANGE
B) it pushed Amy directly
C) Amy pushed her way directly
D) the generation gap pushed her directly

6

A) NO CHANGE
B) parents and teens
C) trends
D) family happiness

(ANSWERS ON NEXT PAGE)

6

ANSWER KEY

DANGLING MODIFIER

LESSON 6

EXERCISE 1: *THERE ARE MANY WAYS TO CORRECT THE SENTENCES, BUT THE FOLLOWING CORRECTIONS REFLECT SAT STANDARDS.*

1. Without any formal training, Rhonda made beautiful landscape paintings.

2. Famous for having popularized colorful socks, Harry also wears shoes with a stylish flair.

3. Before taking off into the sunset, the cowboy shared a passionate kiss with his lover.

4. The teacher was proud that by lightening the homework load, she increased her students' performance and participation in class.

5. Kandi invented a new toilet that cleans itself when its lever is pulled.

6. Hoping that her performance had been good enough to earn her a spot on the cheerleading squad, Caroline waited in the hallway. ***(no error)***

7. Worn out after years of use, Jacob's favorite pair of jeans need to be replaced.

8. Perhaps his finest work, Picasso's *Guernica* is a mural-sized painting in black and white.

9. Easily the most sought-after countertop material, granite is wanted for its durability and attractiveness.

10. Having climbed for days, the travelers were disheartened that the torrential downpour forced them to abandon their goal of reaching the summit.

EXERCISE 2:

1. B
2. A
3. B
4. D
5. C
6. B

Chapter 7

ADJECTIVE VS. ADVERB

7

ADJECTIVE VS. ADVERB LESSON 7

WHEN YOU SEE a descriptive word UNDERLINED – stop and ask yourself:

"What is it describing? Is it describing a noun, verb, or adjective?"

Lilly is **AMAZING** at baseball.
Madison **SLOWLY** jogged on Sunday.
The movie was **DISTURBINGLY** horrific.

LESSON 7.1 **ADJECTIVE:** The word that describes a noun

EXAMPLE

1. Jane is *beautiful.* Beautiful describes *Jane.*
2. The beat is *constant.* Constant describes *the beat.*
3. She is a *safe* driver. Safe describes *her as a driver.*

LESSON 7.2 **ADVERB:** The word that describes a verb or an adjective

EXAMPLE **Adverbs describing verbs**

1. Jane runs *beautifully.* Beautifully describes how Jane *runs.*
2. The beat is *constantly* playing. Constantly describes how the beat is *playing.*
3. Drive *safely.* Safely describes how to *drive.*

EXAMPLE **Adverbs describing adjectives**

1. She is *amazingly* quick. Amazingly describes how *quick* she is.
2. She is *breathtakingly* pretty. Breathtakingly describes how *pretty* she is.
3. The casserole came out of the oven with a *horrifically* burnt top layer. Horrifically describes how *burnt* the top layer was.

TIPS

ADJECTIVE VS. ADVERB seems like an easy type to detect. However, the College Board test makers are very adept at picking adjectives and adverbs that do not sound wrong even when used incorrectly.

Use this page for additional notes. As you complete practice tests, write down the adjectives and adverbs that you find. This list can be used for further study. The following pages have exercises regarding Adjective vs. Adverb.

7

EXERCISE ONE

DIRECTIONS: Using the strategies you learned on page 56, correct the adjective or adverb if needed.

EXAMPLE:

swiftly

The calm river became wild due to the ~~swift~~ changing storm.

1. Although my dentist does a thoroughly job cleaning my teeth, he lacks charisma.

2. Jennifer and Austin were awarded the highest honors in the class for their ingenious science projects.

3. No matter how hard you try, you will never steal the recipe for my moist and sweetly brownies.

4. Whenever he mows the lawn, Akshay sings enthusiastic because nobody can hear him above the roar of the lawnmower.

5. Even though I understand that my comments were offensive, you should cut me a break because I only meant them joking.

6. In today's society, finding affordable and sustainable energy sources is more important than owning irresponsible immense homes.

7. Sravani is our new intern at the office; her acumen and diligence make her a likely candidate for an officially position.

8. Despite the fact that the black bear at my local nature reserve is general harmless, inconsiderate tourists sometimes move this animal to wrath.

9. Maya Angelou, a gifted poet, literary legend, and fervently dancer, died on May 28, 2014, at the ripe old age of 86.

10. Just because you are more skilled at the steel drums than I, you do not have the right to regard me condescendingly.

EXERCISE TWO

These are examples of questions that you will see on the SAT concerning Adjective Vs. Adverb. Follow the directions below.

Questions 1-7 are based on the following passage.

Adjective Vs. Adverb

Twenty-first century elementary education arbitrarily groups students together—no matter their abilities, intellects, or special needs. Among the first-graders at Guthrie Ridge Grammar School, Sandra is clearly [1] more smarter than Caroline. Harold is the [2] most tallest in the class and even looks a full year or two older than any of his peers. The walls are covered with [3] creatively drawings—some of them barely stick figures, others [4] amazingly adept. Some students [5] walk slow, still nervous and unsure of their surroundings; others seem to [6] dance frantic through the halls of the school. Are more advanced children merely held back by this hodgepodge approach to learning, or are the slower ones pushed to learn [7] more quickly?

1

A) NO CHANGE
B) smarter
C) more smart
D) smartest

2

A) NO CHANGE
B) taller
C) tallest
D) more taller

3

A) NO CHANGE
B) creatively drawn
C) more creative drawings
D) creative drawings

4

A) NO CHANGE
B) amazing adept.
C) adept amazingly.
D) adeptly amazingly.

5

A) NO CHANGE
B) walk slowly
C) walk slower
D) walk slowest

6

A) NO CHANGE
B) frantic dance
C) dance frantically
D) frantically dancing

7

A) NO CHANGE
B) more quick
C) more quicker
D) quickest

(ANSWERS ON NEXT PAGE)

7

ANSWER KEY

ADJECTIVE VS. ADVERB

LESSON 7

EXERCISE 1:

1. Although my dentist does a ***thorough*** job cleaning my teeth, he lacks charisma.

2. Jennifer and Austin were awarded the highest honors in the class for their ingenious science projects. ***(no error)***

3. No matter how hard you try, you will never steal the recipe for my moist and ***sweet*** brownies.

4. Whenever he mows the lawn, Akshay sings ***enthusiastically*** because nobody can hear him above the roar of the lawnmower.

5. Even though I understand that my comments were offensive, you should cut me a break because I only meant them ***jokingly***.

6. In today's society, finding affordable and sustainable energy sources is more important than owning ***irresponsibly*** immense homes.

7. Sravani is our new intern at the office; her acumen and diligence make her a likely candidate for an ***official*** position.

8. Despite the fact that the black bear at my local nature reserve is ***generally*** harmless, inconsiderate tourists sometimes move this animal to wrath.

9. Maya Angelou, a gifted poet, literary legend, and ***fervent*** dancer, died on May 28, 2014, at the ripe old age of 86.

10. Just because you are more skilled at the steel drums than I, you do not have the right to regard me condescendingly. ***(no error)***

EXERCISE 2:

1. B
2. C
3. D
4. A
5. B
6. C
7. A

Chapter 8

IRREGULAR VERBS

8

IRREGULAR VERBS LESSON 8

IRREGULAR VERBS: Verbs that are not conjugated by simply adding an "s" or "ed". Irregular verbs change spelling when tense changes.

WHEN YOU SEE a verb underlined, you must ask yourself:

Is there a "had/have" before it?
Does this verb change spelling when the tense changes?

NORMAL VERB	
slap → slapped	step → stepped
→ had slapped	→ had stepped

IRREGULAR VERB	
break → broke	drink → drank
→ had broken	→ had drunk

LESSON 8.1 IRREGULAR VERBS

Changing "IRREGULAR VERBS" to past tense or to the "had/have" tenses is not straightforward. An easy way to spot irregular verbs on the SAT is to look for an irregular verb alone or an irregular verb paired with a *had* or *have*.

EXAMPLE

drive → drove	know → knew	creep → crept
→ had/have driven	→ had/have known	→ had/have crept

TIPS

Anytime there is a ***had*** or ***have*** in front of an irregular verb, it changes its spelling to incorporate a ***u, m***, or ***n***. In simplest terms, if you see an irregular verb with a ***u, m***, or ***n*** in it, it must have ***had*** or ***have***. See below.

EXAMPLE By the time Jeffery *had drove* to California, the rocky road ice cream stored in the trunk of his car was completely melted and inedible.

EXPLANATION The verb *drive* is conjugated to *drove* to indicate past tense. However, because there is a *had* next to it, we must change *drove* to *driven.*

By the time Jeffery ***had driven*** to California, the rocky road ice cream stored in the trunk of his car was completely melted and inedible. ✓

NOTE: There are some exceptions to the *u, m, n* rule, but they are not tested on the SAT.

TIPS

WHENEVER YOU SEE "had" or "have" right before a verb, check that the verb is in the correct form. Refer to the list on the next page for an illustration of this principle. This list is not comprehensive, but it will give you a good foundation for checking this type of error in the future.

COMMON IRREGULAR VERBS ON THE SAT

INFINITIVE	PAST TENSE	"HAD" OR "HAS"/"HAVE"
To arise	Arose	Arisen
To awake	Awoke	Awoken
To beat	Beat	Beaten
To begin	Began	Begun
To bite	Bit	Bitten
To blow	Blew	Blown
To break	Broke	Broken
To choose	Chose	Chosen
To do	Did	Done
To draw	Drew	Drawn
To drink	Drank	Drunk
To drive	Drove	Driven
To eat	Ate	Eaten
To freeze	Froze	Frozen
To fly	Flew	Flown
To forsake	Forsook	Forsaken
To forget	Forgot	Forgotten
To go	Went	Gone
To know	Knew	Known
To ride	Rode	Ridden
To run	Ran	Run
To sing	Sang	Sung
To sink	Sank	Sunk
To speak	Spoke	Spoken
To spring	Sprang	Sprung
To swim	Swam	Swum
To take	Took	Taken
To tear	Tore	Torn
To write	Wrote	Written

TIPS

NOTE the common change in the third column. The verbs now have a *u*, *m*, or *n*. When the helping verb is added, the main verb takes on a new form.

8

EXERCISE ONE

DIRECTIONS: Using the strategies you learned on pages 62 - 63, fix the irregular verb if necessary.

EXAMPLE: *forgotten*
Have we ~~forgot~~ the necessity of human kindness?

1. I should have knew that Henry was going to betray me: his shifty eyes were a dead giveaway.

2. Mickey told me that you had beat the principal in the student-faculty tennis tournament.

3. Even though the sandcastles that we built last summer have sunk into the ground, my memories of that idyllic vacation will never fade away.

4. I would have wrote the letter if the stationery I wanted to use had been available.

5. Since Ananya is such a kind girl, I did not expect you to have spoke to her in such a nasty tone.

6. Until thirty-five years ago, Sachin had always rode his bicycle to school.

7. If you had froze the steak, it would not have gone bad so soon.

8. The students should have taken the extension that the professor offered them; instead, they insisted on finishing on time with just a mediocre presentation.

9. Janet decided that she needed to go to the bathroom only after the concert had began.

10. In his youth, Kenji, like his friends, had forsook his former lifestyle to pursue the freedom of living as a vagabond in California.

EXERCISE TWO

These are examples of questions that you will see on the SAT concerning Irregular Verbs. Follow the directions below.

8

Questions 1-8 are based on the following passage.

Irregular Verb

A few years ago, news magazines carried the story of a woman named Janet Bascomb, who had [1] forsook her everyday life in a suburb of Denver. A few months into a protracted trip abroad, she [2] writes a letter that explained her unfulfilled desires, her longing to experience the violent jolt of a life of adventure. Indeed, Janet's journey seems to [3] have took her to a remote part of the world. There, without a phone or a post office, she [4] swum with the dolphins and laid in the sun.

Janet drank coconut juice when possible—at times, in energetic embrace of her new existence, even [5] spring into action to catch a fish for dinner. If she [6] had knew that her days would end like this, she would most likely [7] have spoke once more with her family, perhaps to offer a slow and proper "good-bye." As it was, she had [8] flew half way around the world thinking that she'd see all her closest relatives again.

1

A) NO CHANGE
B) forsaked
C) forsaken
D) forsakes

2

A) NO CHANGE
B) wrote
C) had wrote
D) has written

3

A) NO CHANGE
B) has taken
C) take
D) have taken

4

A) NO CHANGE
B) swam
C) swims
D) had swum

5

A) NO CHANGE
B) had sprung
C) springing
D) will spring

6

A) NO CHANGE
B) had known
C) knew
D) knows

7

A) NO CHANGE
B) speak
C) have spoken
D) had spoken

8

A) NO CHANGE
B) flown
C) flies
D) flied

(ANSWERS ON NEXT PAGE)

8 ANSWER KEY

IRREGULAR VERBS
LESSON 8

EXERCISE 1:

1. I should have ***known*** that Henry was going to betray me: his shifty eyes were a dead giveaway.

2. Mickey told me that you ***had beaten*** the principal in the student-faculty tennis tournament.

3. Even though the sandcastles that we built last summer have sunk into the ground, my memories of that idyllic vacation will never fade away. ***(no error)***

4. I would have ***written*** the letter if the stationery I wanted to use had been available.

5. Since Ananya is such a kind girl, I did not expect you to have ***spoken*** to her in such a nasty tone.

6. Until thirty-five years ago, Sachin had always ***ridden*** his bicycle to school.

7. If you had ***frozen*** the steak, it would not have gone bad so soon.

8. The students should have taken the extension that the professor offered them; instead, they insisted on finishing on time with just a mediocre presentation. ***(no error)***

9. Janet decided that she needed to go to the bathroom only after the concert had ***begun***.

10. In his youth, Kenji, like his friends, had ***forsaken*** his former lifestyle to pursue the freedom of living as a vagabond in California.

EXERCISE 2:

1. C
2. B
3. D
4. B
5. C
6. B
7. C
8. B

Chapter 9

VERB TENSE

9

VERB TENSE LESSON 9

There are a multitude of tenses in the English language. It is not necessary for the purpose of the SAT to learn and/or memorize every single tense.

The best way to master verb tense questions is to recognize when you are being tested on tense:

WHEN YOU SEE the following references to time in a sentence, use your basic knowledge of tense to check for an error.

YEARS	1969, nineteenth century
DATES	On October 6th, 1999
TIME	2PM, 15 hours
TENSE WORDS	year, later, after, since, yesterday, tomorrow, ago, past, future

Though the SAT does not test your in-depth knowledge of tenses, it will expect you to know the basic guidelines in this chapter:

LESSON 9.1 HAS/HAVE

When you see HAS or HAVE before the verb, it should refer to an action or condition that began in the past, has continued to the present, and perhaps may continue into the future.

EXAMPLE

I went to see the fireworks since I was four years old. ✗

I ***have been going*** to see fireworks since I was four years old. ✓

LESSON 9.2 HAD

When you see HAD before the verb, it should refer to an event or condition that occurred prior to another event in the past.

EXAMPLE

By the time George organized his closet, his mother berated him about his filthy room. ✗

By the time George organized his closet, his mother ***had berated*** him about his filthy room. ✓

LESSON 9.3 PAST TENSE (PART 1)

When the sentence establishes PAST TENSE, verbs describing action should not end in *ing*.

EXAMPLE

Fifty years ago, Isabella marrying a rich banker just for his money. ✗

Fifty years ago, Isabella ***married*** a rich banker just for his money. ✓

LESSON 9.4 PAST TENSE (PART 2)

If you see an underlined verb and you are unsure if you should change the tense, USE THE CONTEXT of the rest of the sentence to clarify the tense of the verb in question.

EXAMPLE

Megha *arrives* at the train station just when the ticket booth closed. ✗

Megha ***arrived*** at the train station just when the ticket booth closed. ✓

TIPS

The word "being" is often wrong.

Jonathan *being remembered* because of his valiant efforts during the hurricane rescue and his legacy will endure. ✗

Jonathan ***will be remembered*** because of his valiant efforts during the hurricane rescue and his legacy will endure. ✓

Use this space for additional notes. The following pages have exercises regarding Verb Tense.

9 EXERCISE ONE

DIRECTIONS: Using the strategies you learned on pages 68 - 69, fix the Verb Tense if necessary.

EXAMPLE: *has continued*

Ramona was hired as a director at a small company and ~~was continuing~~ in this capacity ever since.

1. In 1979, the Islamic Republic of Iran being established.

2. Sandy regretted his decision to ignore his parents' curfew: when he gets home late, they were waiting at the door with a list of punishments.

3. After Olga had thrown me out of her apartment, I thought that perhaps I should not have tried to bathe my pet goat in her shower.

4. Fiona was writing her novel for nine hours straight, and she is still going strong.

5. In 1969, the famous Woodstock concert attracting hordes of people.

6. Phil only returned my call after I have fallen asleep.

7. We are happy to have you in our home, but tomorrow, while we are preparing dinner, we hope you did the laundry.

8. I refuse to leave the casino so soon after arriving; it was only twenty minutes.

9. Matilda plans to arrive at four o'clock, when the dancers performed their ballet routine.

10. If you were so concerned about Lauren's decision to get a tattoo of a jack-o-lantern on her neck, then maybe you should have said something before she did so.

EXERCISE TWO

These are examples of questions that you will see on the SAT concerning Verb Tense. Follow the directions below.

Questions 1-6 are based on the following passage.

Verb Tense

Society is making efforts to turn its back on technology. The very devices that were created to **1** <u>have made</u> our lives easier and more efficient have ultimately brought upon us a pandemic of addiction. The cell phone is one clear example. Every moment of life has shifted from experiences worth "seeing" to those that must be "recorded." Some argue that such recording **2** <u>could have been</u> detrimental to real education and real emotional health. What **3** <u>occur</u>, for the users of such technology, is that they merely record and then forget to internalize the *actual* experiences. For instance, a picture of Mount Fuji becomes just that—a picture to be uploaded for others to see. Our active roles **4** <u>is</u> no longer to witness, to feel, and to learn but instead "to click" and "to post." Our feelings come not from what we see independently but instead are defined by people's reactions to the images we have distributed. In the future, what **5** <u>was</u> in front of us at firsthand will not matter as much as what will be on some acquaintance's screen. The question remains: if we **6** <u>knew</u> in the past that our perceptions of the world could be so altered and so cheapened, would we have created this technology?

1
A) NO CHANGE
B) make
C) be making
D) had made

2
A) NO CHANGE
B) was
C) can be
D) had been

3
A) NO CHANGE
B) occurring
C) are occurring
D) occurs

4
A) NO CHANGE
B) are
C) was
D) being

5
A) NO CHANGE
B) has been
C) will be
D) have been

6
A) NO CHANGE
B) know
C) will know
D) had known

(ANSWERS ON NEXT PAGE)

9

ANSWER KEY

VERB TENSE
LESSON 9

EXERCISE 1:

1. In 1979, the Islamic Republic of Iran ***was*** established.

2. Sandy regretted his decision to ignore his parents' curfew: when he ***got*** home late, they were waiting at the door with a list of punishments.

3. After Olga had thrown me out of her apartment, I thought that perhaps I should not have tried to bathe my pet goat in her shower. ***(no error)***

4. Fiona ***has been*** writing her novel for nine hours straight, and she is still going strong.

5. In 1969, the famous Woodstock concert ***attracted*** hordes of people.

6. Phil only returned my call after I ***had*** fallen asleep.

7. We are happy to have you in our home, but tomorrow, while we are preparing dinner, we hope you ***will do*** the laundry.

8. I refuse to leave the casino so soon after arriving; it ***has only been*** twenty minutes.

9. Matilda plans to arrive at four o'clock, when the dancers ***will perform*** their ballet routine.

10. If you were so concerned about Lauren's decision to get a tattoo of a jack-o-lantern on her neck, then maybe you should have said something before she did so. ***(no error)***

EXERCISE 2:

1. B
2. C
3. D
4. B
5. C
6. D

Chapter 10
IDIOM

10

IDIOM LESSON 10

An **Idiom** is simply the customary way of saying a particular phrase. The idioms on the SAT should not to be confused with colloquial expressions such as "all ears" or "across the board." **Instead, an idiomatic error occurs when the preposition is used incorrectly.**

WHEN YOU SEE a preposition or a prepositional phrase underlined, STOP and CHECK:

Is this the correct preposition?

FORMULA: preposition + phrase OR preposition alone

EXAMPLES: *listen to, at the mall, from, of*

LESSON 10.1 IDIOMATIC ERRORS

The best way to master IDIOMATIC ERRORS on the SAT is to keep a list of the idioms, prepositions, and prepositional phrases that you come across in any SAT practice test that you might do.

EXAMPLE

She was arguing *against* her mother. ✕

She was arguing ***with*** her mother. ✓

TIPS

When you come across an idiom that is not on your list, use the written idiom in three short and simple sentences in your head and see which preposition you use most often. If it is a different preposition than the one written, you may be looking at an idiom error. Still, remember to follow the format of the sentence. See below.

LESSON 10.2 INCORRECT PREPOSITION

EXAMPLE For my birthday, my parents insisted *about* taking me to dinner. ✕

EXPLANATION To check if the preposition *about* is used correctly, quickly create three sentences in your head using the word (or phrase) before the preposition. Here, that word is *insisted.*

SENTENCE 1: They insisted *on* driving their own car.

SENTENCE 2: She insisted *on* paying me back.

SENTENCE 3: He insisted *on* opening the door for me.

For my birthday, my parents insisted ***on*** taking me to dinner. ✓

LESSON 10.3 COLLOQUIAL SPEECH ERRORS

The SAT will occasionally use COLLOQUIAL SPEECH, or slang, to hide an error.

EXAMPLE She should of gone to the market herself if she was that hungry. ✗

EXPLANATION Did you catch the error? The SAT selectively hides the error based on colloquial speech. In this case, *should of* sounds similar to *should've*, which is the contraction for the phrase *should have*.

She should of gone to the market herself if she was that hungry. ✗

She should'*ve* gone to the market herself is she was that hungry. ✓

She should *have* gone to the market herself if she was that hungry. ✓

TIPS Following the principle explained above, **WHEN YOU SEE** *should of*, *could of*, or *would of*, **these phrases are wrong**.

Use this space for additional notes. The following pages have exercises regarding Idiom.

10

EXERCISE ONE

DIRECTIONS: Using the strategies you learned on pages 74 - 75, complete the idiomatic phrase.

EXAMPLE:

Johnathan was familiar ________ social media and digital marketing strategies.

1. The defendant was accompanied ________________ two police officers.

2. I refuse to be held responsible ________________ something I didn't do.

3. She has a tendency ________________ cower when someone yells at her.

4. After watching the movie, he was convinced ________________ the existence of aliens.

5. The scientist's findings were inconsistent ________________ other researchers' results.

6. The actor was celebrated ________________ his philanthropic work in developing countries.

7. Eric was criticized ________________ being indecisive in making life choices.

8. I prefer iced tea ________________ sweetened soda.

9. The record player I bought Bruce looks similar ________________ older record players.

10. The students constantly complained ________________ the amount of homework they received.

EXERCISE TWO

These are examples of questions that you will see on the SAT concerning Idiom. Follow the directions below.

Questions 1-7 are based on the following passage.

Idiom

I have always enjoyed traditional ballet, and I even participated [1] at a few dance recitals as I was growing up. Yet I first experienced the world of non-classical dance [2] with seeing my first modern, experimental dance performance this past summer. For my birthday, I was given a ticket to a production by the Alvin Ailey Dance Company. This celebrated troupe was performing just a brief train ride away [3] to my hometown, presenting a repertoire of works based [4] by both African-American traditions and modern theories of dynamism.

It took me a little while to understand exactly how an Alvin Ailey piece is meant to be interpreted; [5] in contrast to a traditional long ballet such as *Swan Lake*, there is neither a storyline nor a definable main character. However, it soon became clear to me that everything in an Ailey routine has a purpose. Each set of dances refers [6] at historical or cultural forces, or to ideas from society and religion.

Perhaps the most cogent expression of this artistic vision is the dance composition *Revelations*, which is regarded as an Alvin Ailey masterpiece. A performance [7] by different movements, *Revelations* includes references to the sacrament of Baptism, to evil and sin, and to the pleasures of worship and community. The finale reconciles these themes in moment of true joy and redemption.

1

A) NO CHANGE
B) in
C) on
D) with

2

A) NO CHANGE
B) to see
C) by seeing
D) as seeing

3

A) NO CHANGE
B) at
C) from
D) near

4

A) NO CHANGE
B) for
C) to
D) on

5

A) NO CHANGE
B) contrasting to
C) in contrast with
D) contrary with

6

A) NO CHANGE
B) into
C) to
D) by

7

A) NO CHANGE
B) with
C) in
D) from

(ANSWERS ON NEXT PAGE)

10 ANSWER KEY
IDIOM
LESSON 10

EXERCISE 1:

1. The defendant was accompanied ___*by*___ two police officers.

2. I refuse to be held responsible ___*for*___ something I didn't do.

3. She has a tendency ___*to*___ cower when someone yells at her.

4. After watching the movie, he was convinced ___*of*___ the existence of aliens.

5. The scientist's findings were inconsistent ___*with*___ other researchers' results.

6. The actor was celebrated ___*for*___ his philanthropic work in developing countries.

7. Eric was criticized ___*for*___ being indecisive in making life choices.

8. I prefer iced tea ___*to*___ sweetened soda.

9. The record player I bought Bruce looks similar ___*to*___ older record players.

10. The students constantly complained ___*about*___ the amount of homework they received.

EXERCISE 2:

1. B
2. C
3. C
4. D
5. A
6. C
7. B

Chapter 11
DICTION

11

DICTION LESSON 11

Diction simply means "word choice."

WHEN YOU SEE a word that sounds similar to another word, STOP and CHECK:

"Is this the correct word?"

The SAT may use a word that appears to be the intended word, but does not make sense in context. Sometimes, a word will sound almost right, but not quite. It is usually a word that is commonly confused with another due to spelling or sound.

TIPS

The best way to combat diction errors is to **KNOW YOUR VOCABULARY.** Generally, only 1 to 2 Diction errors appear on any given test. On the next page is a chart of the most common diction errors on the SAT.

LESSON 11.1 DICTION

A common DICTION error is mixing *proceed(s)* and *precede(s).*
***Proceed(s)* can function as a verb or noun depending on the context of the sentence:**
***Proceed(s)* as a VERB means "to advance." / *Proceeds* as a NOUN refers to money.**
***Precede(s)* as a VERB will ALWAYS mean "to come before."**
Below are examples of diction errors involving the words *proceed(s)* and *precede(s).*

EXAMPLE

We decided to precede with the business venture even though the market is volatile. ✗

EXPLANATION

Precede means to come before. We didn't decide *to come before* the business venture. We decided to *advance*, or *continue* with the business venture, or *proceed* with it.

We decided to ***proceed*** with the business venture even though the market is volatile. ✓

EXAMPLE

The precedes from the fundraiser helped to build wells in a dozen impoverished villages. ✗

EXPLANATION

Here, based on the context of the sentence, we know that we are looking for a word that means *the funds received for charitable purposes.* Therefore, *precedes* is incorrect. The correct word would be *proceeds.*

The ***proceeds*** from the fundraiser helped to build wells in a dozen impoverished villages. ✓

COMMON DICTION ERRORS ON THE SAT

ACCEPT To agree or consent to	**EXCEPT** To exclude; to leave out
ADOPT To take in	**ADAPT** To adjust
AFFECT To influence	**EFFECT** (n) result; (v) to bring about
ALLUDE To refer to	**ELUDE** To escape from
ALLUSION An indirect reference (often to literature)	**ILLUSION** An unreal image; a false impression
AMBIVALENT Uncertain, having mixed feelings	**AMBIGUOUS** Unclear
ANECDOTE A short account based on real life experience	**ANTIDOTE** A remedy
ASSURE To comfort in order to dispel doubts	**ENSURE** To confirm; to make certain
COLLABORATE To work together	**CORROBORATE** To confirm
COMPLEMENT An addition that enhances or improves	**COMPLIMENT** Praise
COUNSEL To advise, to offer guidance	**COUNCIL** An advisory body that meets regularly
DEFER To put off; to comply	**REFER** To bring up; to consult
DELUDE Deceive	**DILUTE** To reduce strength
DISCRETE Separate, distinct	**DISCREET** Reserved in speech and action, circumspect
DISINTERESTED Neutral, impartial	**UNINTERESTED** Not interested
ELEGANT Well-designed	**ELOQUENT** Articulate or well-spoken
ELICIT To draw out or bring forth	**ILLICIT** Not legally allowed
FLAUNT To show off	**FLOUT** To exhibit scorn or contempt
IMMINENT Likely to occur at any moment	**EMINENT** High in rank or repute
INAPT Unsuitable	**INEPT** Unskilled
INEQUITY Inequality	**INIQUITY** Immorality
INHABIT To occupy	**INHIBIT** To constrain
PERSPECTIVE Viewpoint	**PROSPECTIVE** Potential, possible
RELUCTANT Unwilling	**RETICENT** Silent, reserved

11

EXERCISE ONE

DIRECTIONS: Identify the diction error using the information from pages 80 - 81.

EXAMPLE:

complemented

Using the same color for the furniture ~~complimented~~ the interior decorator's overall aesthetic.

1. The president was finally impeached for flaunting governmental procedures.

2. We decided that it was time to precede to the lodge before it got any darker in the woods.

3. When he eluded to "Big Brother" in his novel, we all knew that he was really talking about communism.

4. We were thrilled to get such an imminent professor on our teaching staff.

5. As an expert, John was used to people referring to his decisions.

6. If the hospital refuses to stock anecdotes for rare spider bites, more people will inevitably die.

7. A euphemism involves deluding harsh criticism in order to sound nicer.

8. The hieroglyphics are essentially ambivalent; scientists must rely on the "Rosetta Stone" to decipher them.

9. We were amazed at the eloquence of her dress since she usually wears jeans and hiking boots.

10. The corroboration was so successful because every department head played a role in the creative process.

EXERCISE TWO

These are examples of questions that you will see on the SAT concerning Diction. Follow the directions below.

Questions 1-6 are based on the following passage.

Diction

For many years, the prospect of electric and partially electric cars was seen by the market as an [1] eminent reality. Now, hybrid cars are everywhere on American roads, as evidenced by the runaway popularity of the efficient and affordable Toyota Prius. This vehicle's success [2] collaborates earlier marketing research on the economic viability of "green" cars, even though many buyers of hybrid and electric cars are not solely concerned with saving money. Consumers are now purchasing [3] eloquent and expensive models such as the BMW i8 and the Tesla Model S. While some of these buyers merely want to [4] flout their wealth or indulge a selfish [5] allusion of greatness, others want to associate themselves with a popular and worthwhile [6] prospective on life: environmental activism.

1

A) NO CHANGE
B) imminent
C) monetary
D) minute

2

A) NO CHANGE
B) corrodes
C) corroborates
D) colludes

3

A) NO CHANGE
B) eloquently
C) locution
D) elegant

4

A) NO CHANGE
B) flaunt
C) flourish
D) flame

5

A) NO CHANGE
B) elusion
C) illusion
D) alternation

6

A) NO CHANGE
B) perspective
C) perception
D) prospect

(ANSWERS ON NEXT PAGE)

11 ANSWER KEY

DICTION
LESSON 11

EXERCISE 1:

1. The president was finally impeached for ~~**flaunting**~~ ***flouting*** the governmental procedures.

2. We decided that it was time to ~~**precede**~~ ***proceed*** to the lodge before it got any darker in the woods.

3. When he ~~**eluded**~~ ***alluded*** to Big Brother in his novel, we all knew that he was really talking about communism.

4. We were thrilled to get such an ~~**imminent**~~ ***eminent*** professor on our teaching staff.

5. As an expert, John was used to people ~~**referring**~~ ***deferring*** to his decisions.

6. If the hospital refuses to stock ~~**anecdotes**~~ ***antidotes*** for rare spider bites, more people will inevitably die.

7. A euphemism involves ~~**deludes**~~ ***diluting*** harsh criticism in order to sound nicer.

8. The hieroglyphics are essentially ~~**ambivalent**~~ ***ambiguous;*** scientists must rely on the "Rosetta Stone" to decipher them.

9. We were amazed at the ~~**eloquence**~~ ***elegance*** of her dress since she usually wears jeans and hiking boots.

10. The ~~**corroboration**~~ ***collaboration*** was so successful because every department head played a role in the creative process.

EXERCISE 2:

1. B
2. C
3. D
4. B
5. C
6. B

Chapter 12

SENTENCE STRUCTURE

12

SENTENCE STRUCTURE LESSON 12

SENTENCE STRUCTURE refers to the arrangement of ideas in a sentence. The arrangement should be logical and should adhere to the laws of grammar. If a sentence is illogical, it is necessary to consider the common problems below. Each problem will have a specific visual clue that will act as a guide to identifying the errors in the sentence.

LESSON 12.1 COMMA SPLICES AND RUN-ON SENTENCES

A COMMA SPLICE occurs when two full sentences (commonly called independent clauses) are combined using only a comma. To fix a comma splice problem on the SAT, you have to use a colon (:), a semi-colon (;), or a transition word (but, and, yet, or, so, for, nor).

EXAMPLE

John went to Vermont to ski, he had a really good time. ✗

John went to Vermont to ski, ***and*** he had a really good time. ✓

I have taken several yoga classes over the years, my favorite is Vinyasa Yoga. ✗

I have taken several yoga classes over the years, **but** my favorite is Vinyasa Yoga. ✓

TIPS

BE CAREFUL when fixing comma splices. Inserting a transition word after the comma fixes the problem, but never insert a transition word *followed by* a comma. This often creates a clause that can stand alone as a sentence. This does not fix the comma splice. See below.

EXAMPLE

Cars are notoriously bad for the environment, *but*, the development of alternative fuel has mitigated the automobile's impact on emissions. ✗

Cars are notoriously bad for the environment, ***but*** the development of alternative fuel has mitigated the automobile's impact of emissions. ✓

LESSON 12.2 THE COLON AND SEMI-COLON

Use a SEMI-COLON (;) when joining two closely related independent clauses in a single sentence. When using a semi-colon, make sure that the two adjoining clauses can stand alone as sentences. Avoid using a semi-colon WITH a conjunction.

EXAMPLE

The film's plot was confusing; and the audience members didn't understand it. ✗

The film's plot was confusing; the audience members didn't understand it. ✓

A COLON (:) is used in basically the same way a semi-colon is used, except that a colon implies that an explanation will follow.

EXAMPLE The house needs a serious renovation and the basement is not structurally sound. **(Clarify more)**

EXPLANATION The sentence is grammatically correct. However, if you replace *and* with a colon, this replacement clarifies *why* the house needs a serious renovation.

The house needs a serious renovation: the basement is not structurally sound. **(Clear)** ✓

LESSON 12.3 TRANSITION WORDS

A TRANSITION WORD error occurs when the transition word given does not follow the logic of the sentence.

EXAMPLE She seemed very upset at work today, and she looked happier when she left. ✗

EXPLANATION The content of the sentence signals a CONTRAST in tone (upset to happier), but the transition word *and* implies agreement. Therefore, we must replace *and* with a word that will follow the logic of the sentence *(but, yet)*.

She seemed very upset at work, ***but*** she looked happier when she left. ✓

TIPS

Sometimes there will be two similar conjunctions given in the same sentence. Be aware of these errors as they are often disguised. See below.

EXAMPLE Although it rained at the family picnic, but everyone still had a good time. ✗

EXPLANATION *Although* and *but* signify the same relationship shift (rained to good time), so including both transition words causes a redundancy error. Omit one.

Although it rained at the family picnic, everyone still had a good time. ✓
It rained at the family picnic, but everyone still had a good time. ✓

TIPS

WHEN YOU SEE one of the following in the grammar section, check to make sure that this word is preceded by a semi-colon (;) **if it begins an independent clause.**

However • Therefore • Moreover
Consequently • Nevertheless

EXAMPLE	Many people know that eating breakfast is essential, nevertheless, most people skip this meal. ✗
EXPLANATION	In this sentence, *nevertheless* begins the independent clause *most people skip this meal.* Use a semi-colon before *nevertheless* to connect the independent clauses.
	Many people know that eating breakfast is essential; nevertheless, most people skip this meal. ✓

LESSON 12.4 STANDARD PHRASES

WHEN YOU SEE the first or second half of a standard phrase underlined, check that the other half is placed appropriately.

The SAT will test you on the correct completion of standard phrases. There are many standard phrases in the English language, but here are some common examples found on the SAT.

STANDARD PHRASE EXAMPLES		
NEITHER...NOR	I was neither happy about the service or satisfied by the food at that restaurant. ✗	I was neither happy about the service ***nor*** satisfied by the food at that restaurant. ✓
EITHER...OR	Either we take the car into the city and hope we find parking and on the other hand we take the train in. ✗	Either we take the car into the city and hope we find parking ***or*** we take the train in. ✓
NOT ONLY...BUT ALSO	The dogs at the shelter were not only cramped in their cages but in addition to that they were not fed at regular intervals. ✗	The dogs at the shelter were not only cramped in their cages ***but also*** not fed at regular intervals. ✓
AS...AS	Janet is just as deserving of the teacher of the year award than Jeff. ✗	Janet is just as deserving of the teacher of the year award ***as*** Jeff. ✓
BOTH...AND	Carol is both jealous of her brother's soccer skill in addition to being mad at him for stealing her ball. ✗	Carol is both jealous of her brother's soccer skill ***and*** mad at him for stealing her ball. ✓

LESSON 12.5 REDUNDANCY

REDUNDANCY occurs when words or phrases with the same meaning are repeated.

EXAMPLE

In the year 1912, ✗

EXPLANATION

Year is not needed when a specific year is given.

In 1912, ✓

EXAMPLE

Every year the college's alumni gather for the annual jamboree. ✗

EXPLANATION

Every year and *annual* mean the same thing.

Every year the college's alumni gather for the jamboree. ✓
The college's alumni gather for the annual jamboree. ✓

REASON/BECAUSE/SINCE/WHY
The words REASON, BECAUSE, SINCE, and WHY cannot be in the same sentence. These words all indicate explanation; therefore, it would be redundant to use them in conjunction with one another. If you see these words used in the same sentence, try replacing one of the words with *THAT*.

EXAMPLE

The *reason* I arrived late was *because* I didn't hear my alarm clock. ✗

EXPLANATION

The *explanation* for my lateness *was that I didn't hear my alarm clock.* Use the word *that* in place of *because.*

The reason I arrived late was ***that*** I didn't hear my alarm clock. ✓

Use this space for additional notes. The following pages have exercises regarding Sentence Structure.

EXERCISE ONE

DIRECTIONS: Using what you learned on pages 86 - 89, identify the Sentence Structure error: comma splice, semi-colon, colon, redundancy, standard phrase, transition word, or none.

EXAMPLE:

Many argue that the criticism of art is primarily subjective, this often leads to varying opinions on the definition of art. (Comma splice)

1. Even though one studied much more than the other studied, both students similarly got the same grade on the test. *redundant*

2. Math is Marc's favorite subject, he is naturally very skilled in it. *Comma splice*

3. Although it has taken me three decades, I have realized that not everything in life is either black nor white. *or either, neither nor, or, and*

4. I don't think that teaching, for most, is simply a job, teachers often genuinely care about their students. *correct sentence*

5. Because I deactivated my social networking account, but I now feel disconnected from all my friends who live far away.

6. I know it was an irresponsible decision to stay out past curfew, furthermore I had so much fun with my friends that I think it was worth getting grounded.

7. My favorite book is a thousand pages long: but it still feels too short every time I read it.

8. Joan not only is fully qualified for this job, as well as very highly recommended by her peers.

9. I drink coffee in the morning every single day; but today I decided to eat fruit instead.

10. The reason we scaled the side of the mountain was because we wanted to get to the peak faster.

EXERCISE TWO

These are examples of questions that you will see on the SAT concerning Sentence Structure. Follow the directions below.

Questions 1-8 are based on the following passage.

Sentence Structure

redundancy

Did you know that there is an author who is equally loved by children and adults all over the world **1** the same? Perhaps you have heard of this great writer, Roald Dahl. His books have been adapted into popular **2** movies; including some with wild special effects. If you think it's incredible that Dahl's books possess such large appeal, you might find a look at his lifestyle enlightening. He lived through adventures as interesting **3** than anything you will find in his celebrated novels *Charlie and the Chocolate Factory* and *James and the Giant Peach*.

During World War II, Dahl was a fighter pilot, constantly putting his life in danger **4** or protect his home country. When he turned to fiction, Dahl took a different kind of risk. His books criticize the world of adults and prize characters such as dreamers, freethinkers, and rebels—characters who oppose everything that makes life uninteresting. Some people believe that Dahl's writings enthusiastically represent the 1960s counterculture and other **5** movements. Only using fantasy scenarios instead of real-life political statements.

1
A) NO CHANGE
B) similarly?
C) the same.
D) DELETE the underlined portion and end with a question mark.

redundancy

2
A) NO CHANGE
B) movies, including
C) movies, they include
D) movies. Include

incorrect use of semicolon

3
A) NO CHANGE
B) to
C) as
D) with

as to as parralism standard phrase

4
A) NO CHANGE
B) and
C) to
D) but

incorrect use of transition word

5
A) NO CHANGE
B) movements, only
C) movements only
D) movements; only

12

EXERCISE TWO

These are examples of questions that you will see on the SAT concerning Sentence Structure. Follow the directions below.

One well-known example of Dahl's spirit of adventure is *James and the Giant Peach*. In this novel, a young boy named James loses his parents **6** and even makes new **7** friends: huge insects who take James on a perilous yet bracing journey. **8** Because both adults and children can relate to this desire to live unpredictably, a factor that explains the popularity of Dahl's many prose creations.

6

A) NO CHANGE
B) so he
C) but also
D) but

7

A) NO CHANGE
B) friends; huge
C) friends. Huge
D) friends huge

8

A) NO CHANGE
B) Both
C) Because
D) Since both

(ANSWERS ON NEXT PAGE)

12

ANSWER KEY

SENTENCE STRUCTURE

LESSON 12

EXERCISE 1:

1. redundancy
2. comma splice
3. standard phrase
4. no error
5. transition word
6. transition word
7. colon
8. standard phrase
9. semi-colon
10. redundancy

EXERCISE 2:

1. D
2. B
3. C
4. C
5. B
6. D
7. A
8. B

Chapter 13

SUBJUNCTIVE MOOD-HYPOTHETICAL

13

SUBJUNCTIVE MOOD-HYPOTHETICAL LESSON 13

WHEN YOU SEE "IF" **or** suggestions/ proposals indicated by the word "THAT" this will indicate the SUBJUNCTIVE MOOD or simply, the HYPOTHETICAL.

he proposes that / he insists that
he asks that / he suggests that

The word *if* or *that* indicates a situation that either **HAS NOT HAPPENED YET** or **DID NOT HAPPEN AT ALL.**

LESSON 13.1 WISH/CONDITIONAL

FORMAT: If I were... I would... OR If I were to.... I would

EXAMPLE

If I **was** stronger, I would be able to lift that heavy box. ✕

EXPLANATION

Based on the context of the sentence, a wish or desire is indicated. Therefore, *was* must be changed to *were*.

If I ***were*** stronger, I would be able to lift that heavy box. ✓

EXAMPLE

If she **was to** own a farm, she would be self-sustaining. ✕

EXPLANATION

Based on the context of the sentence, she will be self-sustaining on the condition that she owns a farm. Therefore, *was to* must be changed to *were to*.

If she ***were to*** own a farm, she would be self-sustaining. ✓

LESSON 13.2 PAST SUBJUNCTIVE

FORMAT: If I had.... I would have

EXAMPLE

If he **would have** remembered earlier, he would not have missed his appointment. ✕

EXPLANATION

Notice that this sentence is in PAST TENSE, implying that this DID NOT HAPPEN AT ALL. Therefore, *would have* must be changed to *had*.

If he ***had*** remembered earlier, he would not have missed his appointment. ✓

LESSON 13.3 SUGGESTIONS/PROPOSALS

If you see the word *that*, stop and check for the following common problems:

EXAMPLE

The child desperately begs that his mother gives him candy. ✗

EXPLANATION

Notice that his mother *has not yet* given him candy.
TO SOLVE, there are TWO steps:

(1) Find the verb that is being suggested or proposed.

The child desperately begs that his mother ***gives*** him candy. ✗

He's begging for her ***to give***.

(2) Insert the infinitive of the verb (to + verb) WITHOUT the preposition *to*.

The child desperately begs that his mother (~~to~~ give) him candy.

The child desperately begs that his mother ***give*** him candy. ✓

TIPS

Remember that ***is*** and ***are*** is conjugated from the infinitive verb ***to be***. See below.

EXAMPLE

He proposed that his birthday is celebrated at the community pool. ✗

EXPLANATION

Follow the TWO steps as indicated above:

(1) Find the verb that is being suggested or proposed.

He proposed that his birthday ***is*** celebrated at the community pool.

He is proposing for his birthday ***to be***.

(2) Insert the infinitive of the verb (to + verb) WITHOUT the preposition to.

He proposed that his birthday (~~to~~ be) celebrated at the community pool.

He proposed that his birthday ***be*** celebrated at the community pool. ✓

TIPS

Would indicates a situation that is still possible. ***Would have*** indicates a situation that is a missed opportunity. ***Will*** indicates a definite future.

EXAMPLE

If you were to keep these tips in mind, you ***would*** be well-prepared.

If you had kept these tips in mind, you ***would have*** been better prepared.

If you keep these tips in mind, you ***will*** be well-prepared.

13

EXERCISE ONE

DIRECTIONS: Correct the sentences using the strategies from pages 96 - 97 if needed.

EXAMPLE:

If it ~~was~~ *were* more docile, Dorothy's horse would be perfect for equestrian training.

1. If Jackson had wrapped his elbow before he played, he would not have suffered from severe muscle strain.

2. If he was alive, he would be proud of his son.

3. I wish I was still living in my hometown, Cincinnati.

4. The manager insists that the parking lot is locked at night.

5. The board of directors recommends that he joins the special committee.

6. I wish the vacation was longer.

7. If I would have known Petunia's real intentions, I would have insisted on a prenuptial agreement.

8. If I was an Academy Award winner, I would be more confident in producing my own work.

9. If he were to invite the neighbors to his mother's home for Easter, his sister would be upset.

10. If I was Lee, I would play the guitar every day.

11. I suggest that the last applicant plays the piano for the audition.

12. I propose that John is asked to sing.

(ANSWERS ON NEXT PAGE)

13

ANSWER KEY

SUBJUNCTIVE MOOD-HYPOTHETICAL

LESSON 13

EXERCISE 1:

1. If Jackson had wrapped his elbow before he played, he would not have suffered from severe muscle strain. ***(no error)***
2. If he ***were*** alive, he would be proud of his son.
3. I wish I ***were*** still living in my hometown, Cincinnati.
4. The manager insists that the parking lot ***be*** locked at night.
5. The board of directors recommends that he ***join*** the special committee.
6. I wish the vacation ***were*** longer.
7. If I ***had*** known Petunia's real intentions, I would have insisted on a prenuptial agreement.
8. If I ***were*** an Academy Award winner, I would be more confident in producing my own work.
9. If he were to invite the neighbors to his mother's home for Easter, his sister would be upset. ***(no error)***
10. If I ***were*** Lee, I would play the guitar every day.
11. I suggest that the last applicant ***play*** the piano for the audition.
12. I propose that John ***be*** asked to sing.

Chapter 14

CONCISION, STYLE, & WORD USAGE

14

CONCISION, STYLE, AND WORD USAGE LESSON 14

A concision, style, or word usage error occurs when the underlined portion of a sentence does not match how the passage is written. To correct, use the sentences above and below.

WHEN YOU SEE an underlined portion that does not contain an explicit grammatical error:

Ask yourself:

◊ Am I using language that is consistent with the style of the passage?

◊ Am I avoiding wordiness and ambiguity?

LESSON 14.1 CONCISION

CONCISION: using as few words as possible to convey the correct meaning.

WORDINESS: expressing an idea with more words than are necessary.

Choose the shortest possible option while still conveying the original meaning of the sentence.

REDUNDANCY: repeating the same information.

Be wary of two words or phrases that seem different but mean the same thing. Here are some redundancies that the SAT will test:

"may possibly"

"initially begin"

"repeat again"

"soon quickly"

LESSON 14.2 STYLE

STYLE: the tone of the passage.

AMBIGUITY: unclear reference to ideas in the rest of the sentence, paragraph, or passage (often the word "things")

Avoid ambiguity and choose a tone that is consistent with that of the passage. Typically, the passage will be written in a "formal yet accessible" tone; the writing is scholarly but does not use unnecessarily complex vocabulary or sentence structure.

General range that the SAT will test:

CONVERSATIONAL	FORMAL YET ACCESSIBLE	ESOTERIC
"bare-bones"	"simple"	"facile"
"how-tos"	"directions"	"protocols"
"law troubles"	"legal issues"	"litigious concerns"
"hodge-podge"	"mixed"	"multifarious"
"hemmed in"	"limited"	"proscribed"
"double-dealing"	"dishonesty"	"chicanery"

EXAMPLE [**GIVEN**: the rest of the passage has a formal yet accessible tone]

The problems with genetically modified crops <u>should not be ignored.</u>

A) NO CHANGE ✓
B) oblige us to exercise meticulousness. (too esoteric)
C) are things to which we must pay attention. (too wordy; "things" is vague)
D) should not be put on the back burner. (too conversational)

TIPS

REMEMBER:

These edits are CONTEXTUAL, so your job is to MATCH the prevailing tone of the passage. When the passage seems conversational, choose a conversational revision. However, highly esoteric vocabulary will rarely ever be correct.

LESSON 14.3 WORD USAGE

Sometimes, the answer options will present four different vocabulary words. They will typically be similar in meaning and might even be similar in tone, but these words are NOT used interchangeably.

In order to achieve correct word usage, you must be able to identify not only the meaning and tone of the word, but also the correct CONTEXT in which it is used.

Use the words in the surrounding sentence to establish the CONTEXT for your word.

PRACTICE Match the following words with their correct contexts. (answers are on page 106.)

1. ___Profound	A. describes necessary job skills
2. ___Important	B. describes the tone of an opinionated politician
3. ___Emphatic	C. describes a famous scholar
4. ___Eminent	D. describes a deeply significant experience
5. ___Firm	E. describes fresh fruit
6. ___Taut	F. describes an inflexible system of rules
7. ___Rigid	G. describes the tension of a tightrope
8. ___Tight	H. describes the seal on an unopened jar
9. ___Fulfilled	I. describes the feeling after eating a large meal
10. ___Satiated	J. describes a spiritually satisfied person
11. ___Complacent	K. describes a quantity that is enough
12. ___Sufficient	L. describes a smug person
13. ___Austere	M. describes a clear contrast
14. ___Stark	N. describes a typo that cannot be overlooked
15. ___Egregious	O. describes an unremitting heat wave
16. ___Unmitigated	P. describes a strict and severe headmaster

14

EXERCISE ONE

DIRECTIONS: Using the strategies you learned on pages 102 - 103, circle the best option within the parentheses. Note: (--) means do not add any phrase.

EXAMPLE:
The new intern followed the very explicit (how-tos | directions | protocols) that were provided in the training manual.

1. If government officials and corporate leaders work together, they will (wallow in a happy commune | luxuriate in mutual prosperity | enjoy shared benefits | make good times).

2. Dance is an artistic form of self-expression, but (to speak of it in a more practical way | more practically | speaking in a way more practical | in a more practical consideration) it is a good way to stay in shape.

3. By 2009, sixteen practice books were available (for distribution | to be distributed widely | for their distribution | for them to be distributed).

4. The mayor judges his city's potential by the annual influx of new residents, growth in jobs, and number of (inventions created | inventions | big ideas that were patented | creations being made).

5. The economist warned that merely (having a higher population than other cities | the people moving in | having more people | increasing the population) will not increase revenue.

6. The phenomenon has spread to New York, New Jersey, Pennsylvania, and other states (-- | on top of that | likewise | in addition).

7. By changing their electrical supply to a more environment-friendly source, the tenants of the building were able to enjoy annual electricity cost reductions of $20,000 (-- | every year | per year | each year).

8. The conditions of the public restroom were so unsanitary that the facility was closed down for being (corrupting | unclean | icky | bedraggled).

9. (The reception of Jen's ideas was underwhelming, even unexciting | The way that they received Jen's ideas was even unexciting and underwhelming | The reception of Jen's ideas was underwhelming | There was a reception of Jen's ideas that was both underwhelming and unexciting), so she lost enthusiasm for her project.

10. Although time-consuming and mentally taxing, (the choice to write | writing | you should choose to write because it | choosing to write) is a rewarding endeavor.

EXERCISE TWO

14

These questions match the format of the Concision, Style, and Word Usage errors that you will see on the SAT. Follow the directions below.

Questions 1-6 are based on the following passage.

Concision, Style, and Word Usage

Chicago was in disarray after the Haymarket [1] Riots of the year 1886; the police decidedly [2] ignored their own laws that they made and barged into demonstrators' homes, making more arrests than most courthouses could handle. Anarchist labor unions, believing that the government should have less control over workers' lives, agitated for equality in the workforce and an eight-hour workday. This came at a time when demonstrations [3] were not peaceful then: corporations hired ruffians to harass demonstrators. The police only feigned a moral and ethical code, taking every chance they could to viciously attack the protesters. [4] In response, the unions reacted with predominantly peaceful protests, only becoming violent when [5] provoked. The press, however, [6] worked against the labor unions—slandering their leaders and condemning anarchy, forever sullying this philosophy in the national mind of America.

1

A) NO CHANGE
B) Riots in the year 1886
C) Riots that happened in 1886
D) Riots of 1886

2

A) NO CHANGE
B) ignored their own laws
C) ignored the laws of their own making
D) did not pay heed to their own laws

3

A) NO CHANGE
B) were not peaceful at that time
C) were not peaceful
D) were anything but peaceful

4

A) NO CHANGE
B) The unions responded with mainly protests that were predominantly peaceful,
C) In response, the unions mainly had predominantly peaceful protests,
D) The unions responded with predominantly peaceful protests,

5

A) NO CHANGE
B) egged on.
C) irritated.
D) set off.

6

A) NO CHANGE
B) toiled in opposition against
C) got on the bad side of
D) were antagonizing to

(ANSWERS ON NEXT PAGE)

14

ANSWER KEY — CONCISION, STYLE, AND WORD USAGE

LESSON 14

EXERCISE 1:

1. If government officials and corporate leaders work together, they will (wallow in a happy commune | luxuriate in mutual prosperity | enjoy shared benefits | make good times).

2. Dance is an artistic form of self-expression, but (to speak of it in a more practical way | more practically | speaking in a way more practical | in a more practical consideration) it is a good way to stay in shape.

3. By 2009, sixteen practice books were available (for distribution | to be distributed widely | for their distribution | for them to be distributed).

4. The mayor judges his city's potential by the annual influx of new residents, growth in jobs, and number of (inventions created | inventions | big ideas that were patented | creations being made).

5. The economist warned that merely (having a higher population than other cities | the people moving in | having more people | increasing the population) will not increase revenue.

6. The phenomenon has spread to New York, New Jersey, Pennsylvania, and other states (-- | on top of that | likewise | in addition).

7. By changing their electrical supply to a more environment-friendly source, the tenants of the building were able to enjoy annual electricity cost reductions of $20,000 (-- | every year | per year | each year).

8. The conditions of the public restroom were so unsanitary that the facility was closed down for being (corrupting | unclean | icky | bedraggled).

9. (The reception of Jen's ideas was underwhelming, even unexciting | The way that they received Jen's ideas was even unexciting and underwhelming | The reception of Jen's ideas was underwhelming | There was a reception of Jen's ideas that was both underwhelming and unexciting), so she lost enthusiasm for her project.

10. Although time-consuming and mentally taxing, (the choice to write | writing | you should choose to write because it | choosing to write) is a rewarding endeavor.

EXERCISE 2:

1. D
2. B
3. C
4. D
5. A
6. A

PRACTICE:

1. D
2. A
3. B
4. C
5. E
6. G
7. F
8. H
9. J
10. I
11. L
12. K
13. P
14. M
15. N
16. O

Chapter 15

COHESION AND ORGANIZATION

15

COHESION AND ORGANIZATION LESSON 15

Cohesion and Organization errors disrupt the logical sequence of ideas for a paragraph or for an entire passage. Corrections for these errors can include reorganizing the order of sentences or paragraphs, deleting sentences, or adding sentences.

WHEN YOU SEE questions that ask about conclusions or introductions, questions that ask where a sentence or paragraph should be placed, questions that ask whether a sentence should be added or deleted, and questions that ask which choice most effectively accomplishes a goal:

Ask yourself:

◊ Am I following the exact wording of the question?

◊ Do the sentences or paragraphs form a logical transition with those before and after?

LESSON 15.1 COHESION AND ORGANIZATION

COHESION: the continuity from sentence to sentence, with regards to style and content.

ORGANIZATION: the logical presentation of ideas in the passage, especially with regards to sentence order.

BREAKDOWN LOGICAL SEQUENCE OF IDEAS

Sentences should be positioned so that they flow seamlessly from a given sentence to the following sentence. As a general rule, ideas in a paragraph should go from general to specific and back to general:

FIRST SENTENCE OF THE PARAGRAPH: States the general topic and central point of the paragraph.

MIDDLE SENTENCES OF THE PARAGRAPH: Provide specific details and analyses that are relevant to the topic and that support the central point of the paragraph.

LAST SENTENCE OF THE PARAGRAPH: Restates the general topic and central point of the paragraph.

NOTE: Sometimes the question asks where an existing sentence should be placed, and sometimes the question states that the writer plans to add a sentence and asks you where it should be placed. In both cases, the standards by which you make your choice are the same:

1

To make this paragraph most logical, sentence 4 should be placed

A) where it is now.
B) after sentence 1.
C) after sentence 2.
D) after sentence 5.

2

The writer wants to add the following sentence to the paragraph.

> The courtiers were too busy constructing a nonsense image of Camelot.

The best placement for the sentence is immediately

A) before sentence 1.
B) after sentence 1.
C) after sentence 2.
D) after sentence 3.

Place the sentence so that it does not abruptly change the topic of the paragraph, and so that it enhances and clarifies the meaning of the previous and the following sentences

EXAMPLE

[1] Jocelyn was a generally well-behaved girl. [2] She did her homework promptly, played nicely with her friends, and was respectful to her parents. [3] However, sometimes she acted out of character, breaking the rules. [4] On these nights, she simply could not resist the temptation that the sweet night air and beckoning tree posed.

The writer plans to add the following sentence.

> For instance, sometimes Jocelyn would sneak out after dark, without her parents' permission, to climb the tree that she so dearly loved.

To make this paragraph most logical, the sentence should be placed

A) after sentence 1.
B) after sentence 2.
C) after sentence 3. ✓
D) after sentence 4.

EXPLANATION

A) (the new sentence is NOT an instance of Jocelyn being "well-behaved.")
B) (the new sentence is NOT an instance of Jocelyn being "respectful to her parents.")
C) (the new sentence IS an instance of "her breaking the rules.")
D) (sentence 4 would be unclear without the appropriate introduction to "these nights" and the "tree.")

NOTE: Sometimes the question will ask where to place a certain paragraph in the context of the passage as a whole. In these cases, the same standards apply as those involving sentence placement:

EXAMPLE When you read a paragraph, keep in mind what each paragraph does (see below). This will help you answer the questions about paragraph placement more aptly.

[GIVEN THAT...]

[Paragraph 1 introduces a museum.]

[Paragraph 2 describes the details of a specific exhibit.]

[Paragraph 3 introduces a specific exhibit within that museum.]

[Paragraph 4 expands on the details of that specific exhibit.]

[Paragraph 5 mentions how museum visitors respond to that specific exhibit.]

To make the passage most logical, paragraph 2 should be placed

A) where it is now.
B) after paragraph 3. ✓
C) after paragraph 4.
D) after paragraph 5.

EXPLANATION

A) (details may confuse the reader without an introduction to the exhibit)
B) (describing details of the exhibit should be placed BEFORE *expanding* on those details)
C) (expanding on details should come after the details)
D) (describing details at the end would interrupt the flow between the paragraphs about the details of the exhibit.)

LESSON 15.2 USING YOUR UNDERSTANDING OF THE PASSAGE

Over the course of the passage, you must:

- ◊ Identify the main focus of the passage.
- ◊ Identify the more specific topics of the paragraphs.
- ◊ Understand the writer's stance on the topic he or she has written about.

Ensure that content that is RETAINED IN or ADDED TO the passage clarifies or supports the writer's point. Make sure to DELETE content that is irrelevant to the topic of the paragraph or passage, DELETE content that is redundant, and DELETE content that directly contradicts the writer's point.

NOTE: Some questions ask whether an underlined portion should be deleted, and some ask whether a given sentence should be added to the passage. In order to answer these questions, you must apply your understanding of the passage as a whole:

EXAMPLE

Green energy sources represent a valuable opportunity to improve the environment and maintain our current standard of living in a sustainable way. Wind power, solar power, and even wave power—an emerging field that harnesses the kinetic energy of waves in the ocean—are growing sectors of the energy economy and should not be ignored....

[GIVEN THAT THE FOLLOWING PARAGRAPH IS ABOUT WAVE POWER.]

The writer is considering deleting the underlined portion. Should the writer make this deletion?

A) Yes, because the underlined portion detracts from the paragraph's focus on green energy.
B) Yes, because the information in the underlined portion is provided in the previous sentence.
C) No, because the underlined portion defines a term that is important to the passage. ✓
D) No, because the underlined portion gives an example of a particular ocean that can efficiently provide wave power.

TIPS

In the answer choices for these types of questions:

The BECAUSE is just as important as the YES or NO. Carefully read all answer options before selecting one. If you use your knowledge of the entire passage, it is possible to PREDICT the answer to be YES or NO prior to process of elimination.

LESSON 15.3 FOLLOWING INSTRUCTIONS IN THE QUESTION

Often, questions will be worded as follows:

- ◊ The writer wants to do X. Which choice best accomplishes this goal?
- ◊ Which choice does X?

Choose the option that fulfills the instructions given as X. Some options will satisfy one part of X but not all. These are incorrect.

EXAMPLE

Reading every day has many benefits.

The writer wants to *provide a specific example of a positive effect of reading every day*. Which choice best accomplishes this goal?

A) NO CHANGE
B) Those who read often find that their eyesight is significantly improved.
C) Reading every day can mean that you have less time for other activities.
D) Reading daily has improved my IQ score by 10 percentage points. ✓

EXPLANATION

A) (does not give "a specific example")
B) (does not specify "reading every day")
C) (does not give a "positive effect")
D) (provides a "specific positive effect")

NOTE: Sometimes, more than one answer option will make sense. If this is the case, pick the one that is most concise:

EXAMPLE

Typically, the forest begins to show evidence of browsing in early autumn. This follows several weeks of deer population growth.

Which choice most effectively combines the two sentences at the underlined portion?

A) autumn, following ✓
B) autumn, and this browsing follows
C) autumn, and such browsing follows
D) autumn, and this evidence follows

Use this space to write additional notes about Cohesion and Organization errors.

15 EXERCISE ONE

These questions match the format of the Cohesion and Organization errors that you will see on the SAT. Follow the directions below.

Questions 1-8 are based on the following passage.

—1—

One of the advantages of living in a part of France that borders the English Channel is that I can get not only the TV channels of France but also those of the UK. I would like to say that I switch between the two, enjoying two different views of the world. Sadly, the truth is that I have neither the ability nor the patience to follow French programs.

—2—

[1] This is not to say that I spend my evenings watching the news. [2] It is ironic that even with such a plethora of choices, there are some evenings when I look through the TV schedules and declare that there is nothing worth watching. [3] There is a channel that only shows endless repeats of shows from the past. [4] There I find my favorite program when the news is not on. [5] It is neither British nor French. [6] Rather, this program is an American TV series that ran for over ten years. **1**

—3—

French television is placid, urbane, patronizing, and boring. It is also a poor venue for women. Of course, women do appear, but rarely as central performers in a program. On early evening chat shows, they are always supporters of the central male "star of the **2** <u>show." He is a</u> charismatic guy who flashes frequent smiles: he clearly thinks that he is irresistible. The participants laugh a great deal and the "star"

1

The writer plans to add the following sentence to this paragraph.

> On nights like that, there is only one thing to do: give way to one of my television guilty pleasures.

To make this paragraph most logical, the sentence should be placed

A) before sentence 1.
B) after sentence 1.
C) after sentence 2.
D) after sentence 3.

2

Which choice most effectively combines the two sentences at the underlined portion?

A) show," a
B) show," he is a
C) show;" a
D) show" a

talks, interminably. French news bulletins are invariably presented by men and present a view of the world that is centered completely on Paris, as if the rest of France did not exist. Politicians are treated with deference and are never questioned aggressively. The major evening program is inevitably a movie, regularly French but sometimes an American or English film that has been poorly dubbed. **3** There is no variation throughout the week, except on Saturday nights when the film is replaced with an endless cabaret featuring very old French singers.

— 4 —

British news programs, unlike those of France, are aggressive, investigative, critical of politics, and wide-ranging in their attempts to provoke, infuriate, and entertain their viewers. No matter which news channel is in question, British reporters from war zones or other dangerous areas are as likely to be female as male. **4** <u>They will also be of different ethnic origins.</u> What the viewer sees on television reflects the full spectrum of UK society. The accents of those who present the news range from Northern Irish to West Indian to Asian. As a result, television is a much more important element in the society of the UK: in France, it is, by and large, ignored.

3

At this point, the writer is considering adding the following sentence.

> But my absolute favorite French program is one about traditional food in agrarian communities.

Should the writer make this addition here?

A) Yes, because it reinforces the passage's main point about the superior quality of French television.
B) Yes, because it acknowledges the writer's preference for areas of France outside of Paris.
C) No, because it discusses a mode of entertainment that is irrelevant to the passage.
D) No, because it undermines the passage's emphasis on the inferior quality of French television.

4

Which choice gives an additional supporting example that emphasizes how British news programs feature a more diverse staff than do French news programs?

A) NO CHANGE
B) They also are all highly educated.
C) They invariably are more blunt than French reporters.
D) They also do a better job of speaking clearly.

15 EXERCISE ONE

These questions match the format of the Cohesion and Organization errors that you will see on the SAT. Follow the directions below.

—5—

[1] *Murder, She Wrote* features an amateur detective, loosely based on Agatha Christie's Miss Marple but transformed into an American writer of detective novels. [2] But **5** even though she tends to solve crimes, her appearance in that town means that very shortly at least one murder will occur. [3] Sadly, the police are quite incapable of solving the crime and are determined to imprison the innocent. [4] Her name is Jessica Fletcher and she lives in Cabot Cove in New England. [5] Happily, in between finishing the latest novel in time for its publication deadline, giving lectures at various academic institutions and stopping by the homes of her rich and famous friends, Jessica is able to sort things out to the admiration of the professionals and the gratitude of the falsely accused—and all in forty-five minutes! [6] The show is total nonsense **6** : absurd plots, mechanical acting, and appalling scripts. [7] However, from the moment the opening bars of the show's opening theme are sounded, I am hooked. **7**

Question 8 asks about the previous passage as a whole.

5

The writer wants to include a phrase that conveys the broad applicability of the claim in the sentence. Which choice best accomplishes this goal?

A) NO CHANGE
B) no matter where she is
C) disregarding any hope of plausibility
D) since she brings bad luck with her

6

The writer is considering deleting the underlined portion (ending the sentence with a period). Should the writer make this deletion?

A) Yes, because the information in the underlined portion blurs the paragraph's focus by introducing new ideas that are not explained.
B) Yes, because the underlined portion repeats information that has been provided in an earlier paragraph.
C) No, because the information in the underlined portion clarifies the writer's assertion about the show.
D) No, because the information in the underlined portion reinforces the thesis of the passage.

7

To make this paragraph most logical, sentence 4 should be placed

A) where it is now
B) after sentence 1.
C) after sentence 2.
D) after sentence 5.

Think about the previous passage as a whole as you answer question 8.

8

To make this passage most logical, paragraph 2 should be placed

A) where it is now.
B) after paragraph 3.
C) after paragraph 4.
D) after paragraph 5.

EXERCISE TWO

These questions match the format of the Cohesion and Organization errors that you will see on the SAT. Follow the directions below.

Questions 9-16 are based on the following passage.

The way I write an essay is like this: I think of a topic that I want to have a go at. Then I write a long first **9** paragraph. I try to make it striking and invitingly phrased. Then I let the second paragraph develop. Then, I look at what I have composed and ask the question that I should really have thought about before I started: where do I think this piece is going? Then I start to reread and cut all the unnecessary and showy stuff I have put in the first paragraph. **10**

For example, when asked about what I actually like about Baltimore (where I live) and why I remain here (apart from the inability to escape because I cannot drive), I determine the tone from my view of the subject, from writing as honestly as I can. I know that whenever I write anything which is quite good, I do so by behaving like a camera and **11** using technology to aid my creative process. The energy that comes from doing what you love is inspiring. I felt a similar sensation when I was directing plays. The energy spurs on ideas and the honest eye stops me from being too clever for words. And all of it is just fun, too.

9

Which choice most effectively combines the two sentences at the underlined portion?

A) paragraph, and trying
B) paragraph; trying
C) paragraph, trying
D) paragraph to try

10

At this point, the writer is considering adding the following sentence.

> Writing is different for everyone, so it is probable that other people have different strategies.

Should the writer make this addition here?

A) Yes, because it adds a relevant fact to the writer's discussion of writing.
B) Yes, because it clarifies the writer's claim about his personal writing process.
C) No, because it merely reformulates the thought expressed in the preceding sentence.
D) No, because it detracts from the paragraph's focus on the writer's individual writing process.

11

Which choice most effectively reinforces the writer's main point about "behaving like a camera"?

A) NO CHANGE
B) expressing myself artistically.
C) recording what I see in my mind's eye.
D) creating memories that I can look back on.

15 EXERCISE TWO

These questions match the format of the Cohesion and Organization errors that you will see on the SAT. Follow the directions below.

[1] **12** Nevertheless, teaching writing was similar. [2] I liked nearly all the classes I used to teach—well, for sure, there were some difficult times, but on the whole I looked forward to each day. [3] **13** I treated my classes as though they were theater performances. [4] After all, in the theater you have to work the audience, to engage it, to surprise it, to make it want to come back the next time to see what is going to happen. [5] I think (and I don't want to sound arrogant here) that students used to look forward to the next class to find out what was going to happen, and because I had enthusiasm for what I was presenting, they began to look at each of our sessions not as a chore but as something rather fun. [6] You give a student a good grade because what the student has produced is good. [7] You give a student a top grade only when there is nothing further to be said on what the student has produced. [8] When anyone in my class got the top mark possible, the news went round the **14** school. [9] That student felt deservedly proud. [10] A teacher does not tell a student what to think. [11] A teacher helps a student to *want* to think. **15**

12

Which choice most smoothly and effectively introduces the writer's discussion of teaching in this paragraph?

A) NO CHANGE
B) I felt the same way about teaching writing.
C) Teaching writing, it evoked the same feelings in me.
D) I also felt a certain way when I was doing paid work, like teaching writing.

13

The writer is considering deleting the underlined sentence. Should the sentence be kept or deleted?

A) Kept, because it introduces a comparison that continues in the paragraph.
B) Kept, because it substantiates the writer's claim that teaching is not for everyone.
C) Deleted, because it merely reformulates the thought expressed in the preceding sentence.
D) Deleted, because it interrupts the discussion of teaching writing.

14

Which choice most effectively combines the two sentences at the underlined portion?

A) school, and the
B) school, the
C) school; and the
D) school, which the

15

The writer plans to add the following sentence to this paragraph.

> This enjoyment is not just a matter of "playing to the gallery" and giving in to the student—too many teachers do that—but of maintaining a certain strictness of quality.

To make this paragraph most logical, the sentence should be placed

A) after sentence 2.
B) after sentence 4.
C) after sentence 5.
D) after sentence 10.

EXERCISE TWO

These questions match the format of the Cohesion and Organization errors that you will see on the SAT. Follow the directions below.

[1] All I know is that my ex-students still write about what they discovered in my lessons, and I feel proud of that. [2] Personally, I was a useless student at school—awkward, completely lost, and miserable in a boarding house. [3] I wanted to escape and didn't know how to break free. [4] When I did become a teacher, one of the main things I wanted to do was to make sure that nobody felt as lost and muddled and awful as I did when I was a teenager (or in my twenties, for that matter). [5] But I have digressed, once again, carried away by my memories of life, swept off in a sea of emotion. [6] At least, the tone is clear, no? 16

16

To make this paragraph most logical, sentence 3 should be placed

A) where it is now.
B) after sentence 1.
C) after sentence 4.
D) after sentence 5.

ANSWER KEY

COHESION AND ORGANIZATION
LESSON 15

EXERCISE 1:

1. C

2. A

3. D

4. A

5. B

6. C

7. B

8. C

EXERCISE 2:

9. C

10. D

11. C

12. B

13. A

14. A

15. C

16. A

Chapter 16
PUNCTUATION

16

PUNCTUATION LESSON 16

Punctuation errors occur when a punctuation is misused according to the standards of conventional English. Much like the rules of Sentence Structure, the rules of punctuation logically arrange and present the ideas in a sentence.

WHEN YOU SEE answer options that have semicolons, colons, em dashes, apostrophes, or quotations:

;	**semicolon**
:	**colon**
—	**em dash**
’	**apostrophe**
“”	**quotation**

Ask yourself:

◊ Am I following the semicolon rule?

◊ Am I avoiding creating or retaining a comma splice?

◊ Am I avoiding unnecessary punctuation?

◊ Am I using possessive nouns appropriately?

◊ Am I avoiding redundancy?

◊ Am I setting off modifiers from the rest of the sentence?

LESSON 16.1 SEMICOLONS, COMMA SPLICES, AND REDUNDANCY

The semicolon rule and comma splice rules should be familiar to you from lesson 11 (sentence structure):

SEMICOLON RULE: a semicolon must separate two independent clauses that CAN STAND ALONE AS 2 SEPARATE SENTENCES.

Make sure that on both sides of the semicolon you have two distinct, independent clauses.

COMMA SPLICE: in layman's terms, a comma splice is a type of error in which TWO FULL SENTENCES are combined using only a comma.

Make sure that you do not choose an option that creates or retains a comma splice.

REDUNDANCY: in punctuation questions, generally a "subject, subject verb"

Redundancy in punctuation questions will look something like this:

. . . Shirley, she is . . . ✗	. . . Shirley is . . . ✓	OR . . . she is . . . ✓
. . . my car, it is . . . ✗	. . . my car is . . . ✓	OR . . . it is . . . ✓
. . . happiness, this feeling is . . . ✗	. . . happiness is . . . ✓	OR . . . this feeing is . . . ✓

EXAMPLE

I tend to bite my nails when I am nervous; this feeling is usually because I have a presentation to make in school.

A) NO CHANGE (creates redundancy)
B) nervous, ✓
C) nervous, this is (creates a comma splice; redundant)
D) nervous; (violates semicolon rule)

My school has just ratified a new set of rules, some of them are exceedingly strict.

A) NO CHANGE (retains a comma splice)
B) rules (retains comma splice)
C) of which ✓
D) DELETE the underlined portion (retains comma splice)

LESSON 16.2 COMMONLY CONFUSED POSSESSIVES AND CONTRACTIONS

POSSESSIVES: words that indicate ownership.

CONTRACTIONS: words that combine two words.

EXAMPLES Its versus It's versus Its'

Its is the possessive version of a singular noun.

The car's air conditioning is broken. = Its air conditioning is broken.

It's is a contraction, the combined form of "it is" or "it has"

The car has been painted green. = It's been painted green.

The car is green. = It's green.

TIPS **Its' is NEVER CORRECT, and actually does not exist in English.**

EXAMPLES There versus Their versus They're

There describes a place that is not here. *There* is neither a contraction nor a possessive.

I am parking the car in the garage. = I am parking the car in there.

Their is the possessive version of a plural noun.

The kids' toys are blue. = Their toys are blue.

They're is a contraction, the combined form of "they are"

They are well-behaved. = They're well-behaved.

EXAMPLES Noun's versus Nouns' versus Nouns's versus Nouns

Using "Insect" as the noun:

Insect's is the possessive form of a singular noun.

The wings of that insect are green = The insect's wings are green.

Insects' is the possessive form of a plural noun.

The wings of those insects are green = The insects' wings are green.

Insects is plural, not possessive.

More than one insect = Insects

Insects's is NEVER CORRECT.

TIPS

For words ending with *y*, use these examples when indicating ownership:

The laws of the country = The country's laws, NOT the countries' laws

The skin of the body = The body's skin, NOT the bodies' skin.

LESSON 16.3 PUNCTUATION FOR MODIFIERS

MODIFIERS: descriptive phrases that provide extra information AND are not central to the structure of the sentence.

EXPLANATION

The lawnmower is old and broken. NOT A MODIFIER.

The lawnmower, old and broken, is going to be replaced soon. A MODIFIER.

To set off modifiers from the rest of the sentence, make sure that you use the SAME punctuation on either side of the modifier.

EXAMPLE

The lawnmower, old and broken, is going to be replaced soon.

A) NO CHANGE ✓
B) broken is
C) broken; is
D) broken—is

My sister—or, at least, the closest thing to a sister that I have just got married.

A) NO CHANGE
B) have, just
C) have—just ✓
D) have: just

LESSON 16.4 UNNECESSARY PUNCTUATION

Dogs, love to please their owners.

A) NO CHANGE
B) Dogs: love
C) Dogs; love
D) Dogs love ✓

I couldn't stop poking fun at my professor, Mr. Green's, bright orange bifocals.

A) NO CHANGE
B) professor, Mr. Green's
C) professor Mr. Green's,
D) professor Mr. Green's ✓

EXPLANATION

There is no punctuation needed between the subject (Dogs) and their verb (love).

Commas inappropriately separate parts of the noun phrase ("my professor Mr. Green's bright orange bifocals").

LESSON 16.5 ITEMS IN A LIST

Use commas or the word *and* to separate items in a list, and use a colon to introduce a list.

EXAMPLES

Alexander's pets, plants; and peaches are all downstairs.

A) NO CHANGE (violates semicolon rule; fails to recognize that items are part of a list)
B) plants, and ✓
C) plants: and (fails to recognize that items are part of a list)
D) plants, and, (adds unnecessary comma)

Alexander has moved his belongings: his pets, plants, and peaches.

A) NO CHANGE (appropriately uses a colon to introduce a list) ✓
B) belongings; (violates semicolon rule)
C) belongings, (incorrectly positions "belongings" as a member of the list)
D) belongings (needs a colon to introduce the list)

Use this space to write additional notes about Punctuation errors.

16

EXERCISE ONE

DIRECTIONS: Using the strategies you learned on pages 120 - 123, fix punctuation errors if necessary.

EXAMPLE:

contrary—that

Jonathan believed—despite all evidence to the <u>contrary, that</u> Mrs. Devereaux was innocent.

1. Akshay learned many gardening skills this summer, such as, weeding, planting, and harvesting.

2. Its perfectly clear that Davina simply has a better work ethic than you do.

3. I enjoy spending my Friday nights watching *Battlestar Galactica*, it is a science fiction thriller about space exploration.

4. Harry's biggest role model, his coach, Miss Floyd, taught him the value of determination.

5. A recent article by two journalists at Hunter College, Dr. Jones and Dr. Black, claims, that sleeping for exactly seven hours a night can improve cognition in adults over forty.

6.The transportation commission has found that trucks weighing over four tons can do significant damage to roadway's.

7. Although he always wanted to go to Maine, he never managed to move they're.

8. Dairy farmers, environmentalists; and government officials are collaborating on a project that would reduce methane emissions by as much as thirty percent.

9. Anna Hanes, my old teacher from when I was in second grade just got back in touch with me.

10. I can think of a very good reason for your poor grades in school: your lack of interest.

11. I just read a compelling criticism of painter, Pablo Picasso's, *Geurnica.*

12. After working all day, Ashley found that her legs were sore, her arms were tired.

EXERCISE TWO

16

These questions match the format of the Punctuation errors that you will see on the redesigned SAT. Follow the directions below.

Questions 1-8 are based on the following passage.

Punctuation

[1] Marmoset's exhibit a rather shallow range of fearful responses when confronted with stressful [2] situations, these reactions include distress calls, bouts of crippling [3] anxiety, and, major increases in cortisol levels. These small, squirrel-like [4] primates, use a technique dubbed "mobbing" to deal with tense scenarios, relying on [5] it's numbers and collective voices for support. The high-pitched and [6] excited calls they produce when mobbing, called [7] tsiks: are thought by researchers to directly serve to decrease cortisol levels, perhaps acting to calm marmosets and give them a sense of security. Growing to only a diminutive eight [8] inches, these monkeys must rely on their collective voice to feign great numbers or, at the very least, to produce confusion concerning their specific locations.

1

A) NO CHANGE
B) Marmosets
C) Marmosets'
D) Marmosets's

2

A) NO CHANGE
B) situations, however, these
C) situations: these
D) situations, some of these

3

A) NO CHANGE
B) anxiety, and:
C) anxiety; and
D) anxiety, and

4

A) NO CHANGE
B) primates use
C) primates, use,
D) primates; use

5

A) NO CHANGE
B) its
C) they're
D) their

6

A) NO CHANGE
B) excited, calls
C) excited calls,
D) excited: calls

7

A) NO CHANGE
B) tsiks,
C) tsiks
D) tsiks:

8

A) NO CHANGE
B) inches; these
C) inches. These
D) inches—these

(ANSWERS ON NEXT PAGE)

16 **ANSWER KEY**

PUNCTUATION
LESSON 16

EXERCISE 1: *THERE ARE MANY WAYS TO CORRECT THE SENTENCES, BUT THE FOLLOWING CORRECTIONS REFLECT SAT STANDARDS.*

1. Akshay learned many gardening skills this summer, ***such as weeding, planting, and harvesting.***

2. ***It's*** perfectly clear that Davina simply has a better work ethic than you do.

3. I enjoy spending my Friday nights watching *Battlestar Galactica*, ***a science fiction thriller about space exploration.***

4. Harry's biggest role model, ***his coach Miss Floyd***, taught him the value of determination.

5. A recent article by two journalists at Hunter College, Dr. Jones and Dr. Black, ***claims that*** sleeping for exactly seven hours a night can improve cognition in adults over forty.

6. The transportation commission has found that trucks weighing over four tons can do significant damage to ***roadways.***

7. Although he always wanted to go to Maine, he never managed to move ***there***.

8. ***Dairy farmers, environmentalists, and government*** officials are collaborating on a project that would reduce methane emissions by as much as thirty percent.

9. Anna Hanes, my old teacher from when I was in second ***grade, just*** got back in touch with me.

10. I can think of a very good reason for your poor grades in school: your lack of interest. (***no error***)

11. I just read a compelling criticism of ***painter Pablo Picasso's*** **Guernica**.

12. After working all day, Ashley found that her legs were ***sore and*** her arms were tired.

EXERCISE 2:

1. B

2. C

3. D

4. B

5. D

6. A

7. B

8. A

Chapter 17

GRAPHS

GRAPHS LESSON 17

On the SAT, passages will occassionally have a graphic or visual representation of a concept or idea that the writer is discussing. You will be asked to ensure that the underlined portion of the sentence accurately represents the data and information presented by the graphic or visual representation.

WHEN YOU SEE questions that ask you to make a revision to the passage based on the information provided in a graph, table, chart, map, or other visual that supplements the passage...

Ask yourself:

◊ Do I know how the information in the graphic relates to the information in the passage?

◊ Do I know how to accurately interpret the information in the graphic?

LESSON 17.1 ACCURATE INTERPRETATION

ACCURATE: directly supported by the information presented in the graphic

INTERPRETATION: translating the visual information from the graphic into words.

EXAMPLE UNDERSTANDING KEY COMPONENTS

Before reading the answer options, circle or underline any key components of the graphic—the title, the legend, the units, and any other labels or captions. Make sure you understand how these components interact.

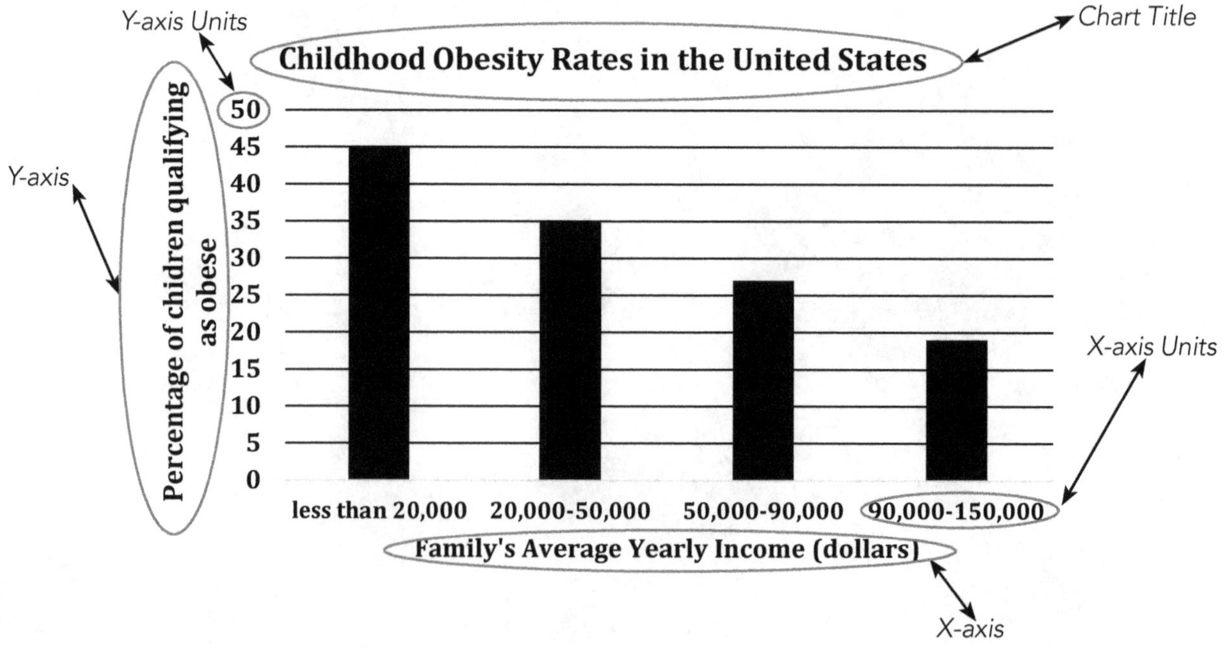

EXAMPLE **APPLYING KEY COMPONENTS**

To briefly test your understanding of the graphic, randomly choose one point on the graphic and put it into words. To maintain accuracy, keep the words you use close to the words used in the graphic.

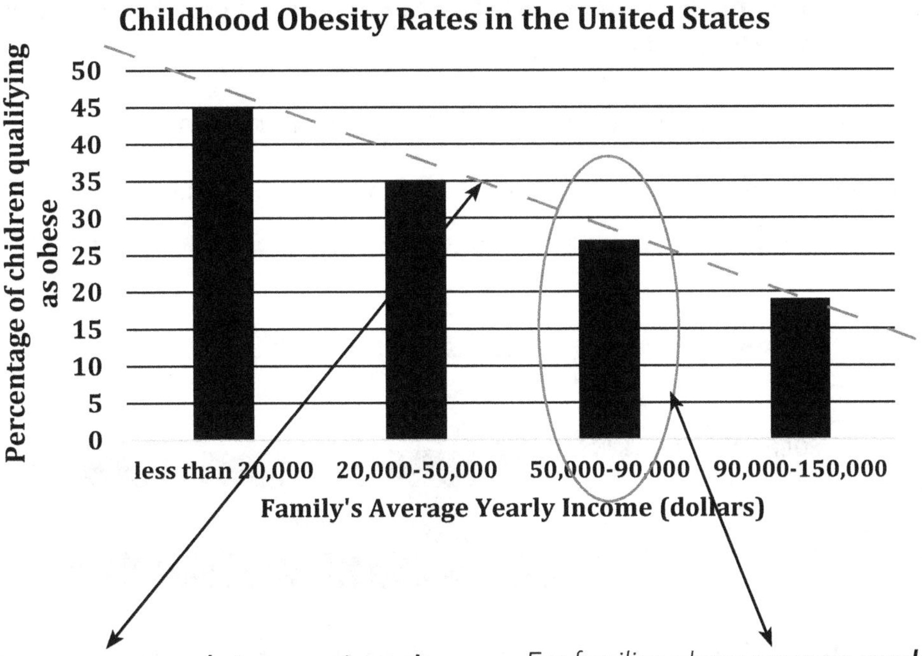

It appears that as ***average yearly*** ***<u>income rises</u>*****, the percent of children qualifying as** ***obese decreases***.

For families whose ***average yearly income*** *is* ***between 50,000 and 90,000 dollars****, slightly over* ***25 percent of children qualify as obese***.

TIPS **Make a mental note of any obvious correlation between variables.**

Use this space to note additional ways to interpret the bar graph from this lesson.

LESSON 17.2 ANSWERING THE QUESTION

Once you understand the graphic, you are ready to revise the passage.

Be careful about the units used in the answer options. For instance, when percentages are involved, take note of the PERCENTAGE OF *WHAT (is being measured)*! There will most likely be a trap answer that uses the wrong units according the graph.

EXAMPLE MATCHING GRAPH'S UNITS TO THE UNITS OF THE ANSWER CHOICES

[**GIVEN**: the passage claims that students who eat breakfast succeed in school.]

At this point, the writer wants to add specific information that supports the main topic of the paragraph.

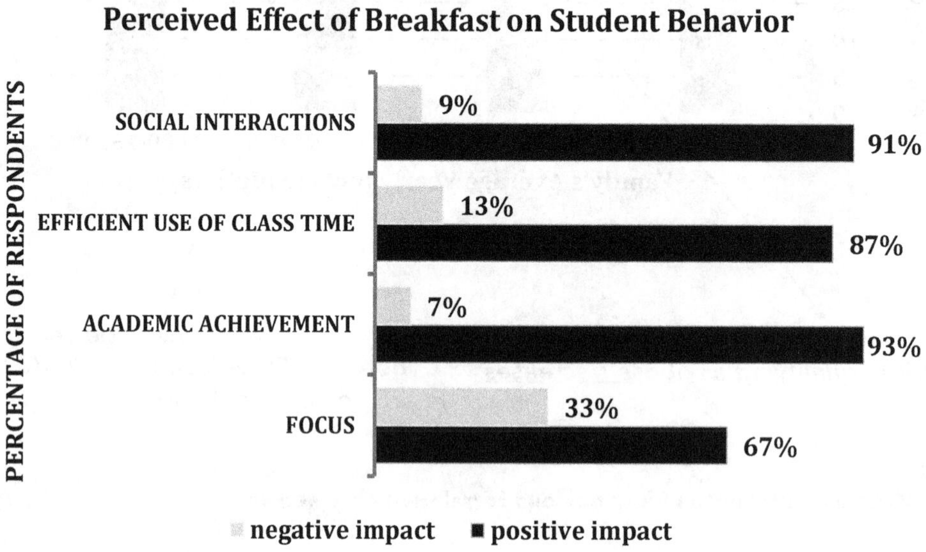

Which choice most effectively provides relevant and accurate information based on the graph above?

A) 93 percent of respondents noted that eating breakfast hindered their academic achievement. (Graph indicates that 93 percent of respondents noted a positive impact on their academic achievement.) ✕

B) Respondents credited eating breakfast with 67 percent of their focus. (Graph measures the percentage of respondents, not the percentage of focus.) ✕

C) 87 percent of respondents indicated that eating breakfast increased their efficient use of class time. ✓

D) Respondents reported that their social interactions improved by 9 percent after eating breakfast. (Graph measures percentage of respondents, not the percentage of improvement; in addition, 9 percent is associated with a negative impact.) ✕

When you are fixing an underlined portion of a sentence, the non-underlined portion will often tell you where to look in the graphic. Be sure to look in the right spot, as dictated by the sentence. There will frequently be a trap answer for those test-takers who are simply looking in the wrong spot for their answers.

EXAMPLE **MATCHING THE UNDERLINED PORTION OF THE SENTENCE TO THE GRAPH'S DATA**

As the graph shows, patients *who follow a low-cholesterol diet but do not exercise daily* experience roughly 30% fewer cases of atherosclerosis than patients *who do not follow a low-cholesterol diet and do not exercise daily.*

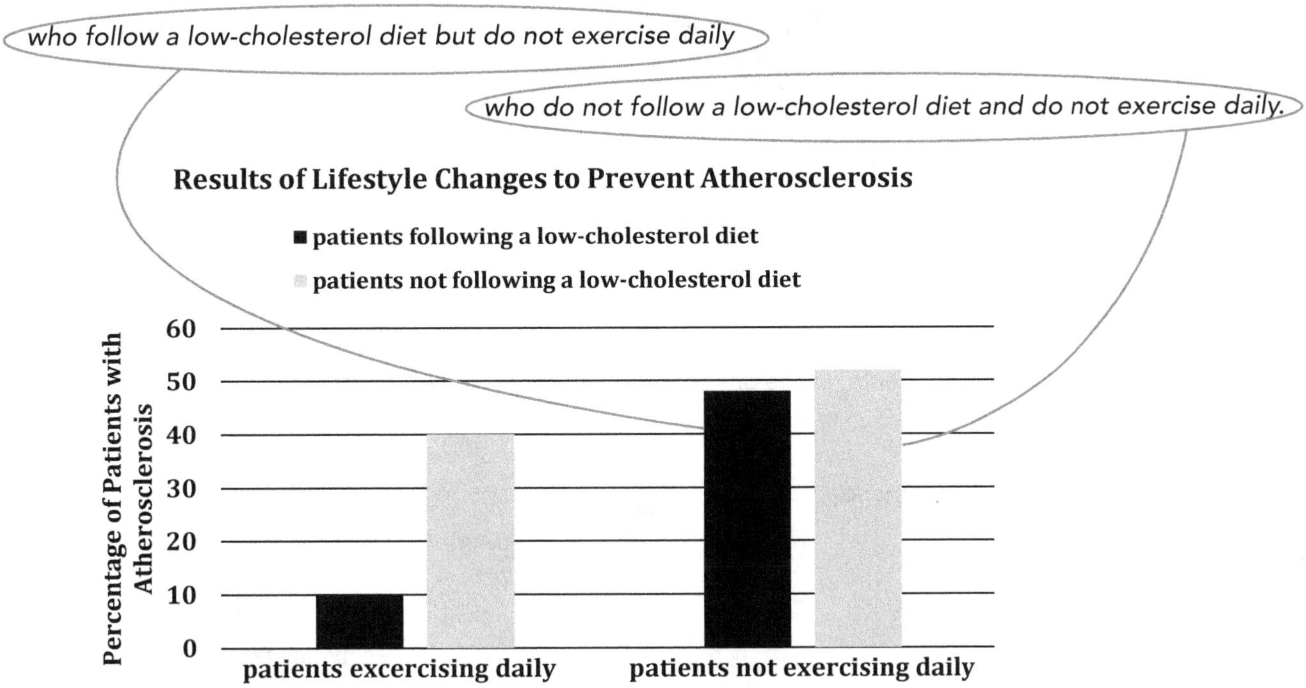

Which choice offers an accurate interpretation of the data in the chart?

A) NO CHANGE
B) a substantially lower rate of atherosclerosis than
C) four times as many cases of atherosclerosis as
D) a slightly lower rate of atherosclerosis than ✓

BE CAREFUL of key words and phrases like:.

- "roughly" (means about, not precisely)
- "slightly" (means a little bit)
- "substantially" (means a lot)
- "completely" (means entirely, absolutely)
- "as low as" and "at least" (implies no lower than)

17

EXERCISE

DIRECTIONS: Using the strategies you learned on pages 128-131, answer the following questions.

EXAMPLE:

A recent study projects that the average gas and electric bill for New York residents will increase by 10 percent every summer. ——— *12 percent every winter.*

[**GIVEN**: the passage discusses the different motivations that people have for relocating.]

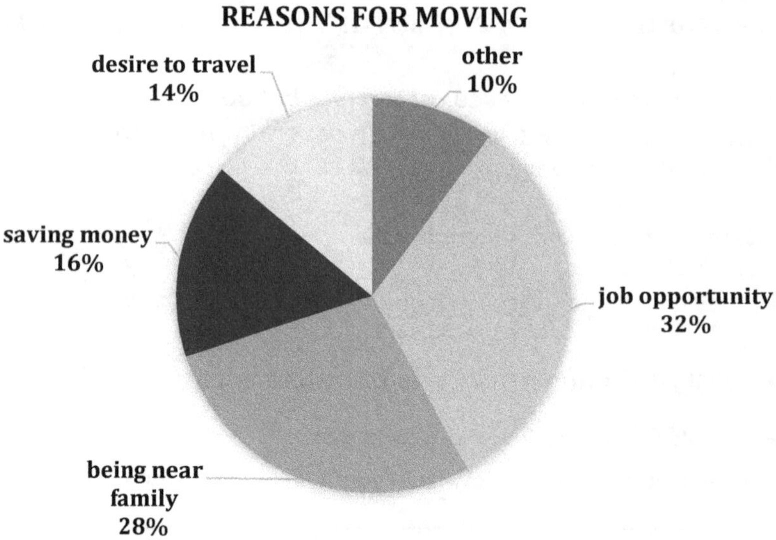

A survey asked respondents for the one major reason that caused them to move.

In fact, [1] saving money is the least significant factor causing people to relocate.

As the chart shows, saving money is [2] cited roughly 4 percent less often than job opportunity as a factor which motivates someone to move.

1

Which choice offers an accurate interpretation of the data in the chart?

A) NO CHANGE

B) 32 percent of all job opportunities cause people to relocate.

C) 28 percent of respondents cite the desire to be near family as their reason for moving.

D) people report that a desire to travel is responsible for 14 percent of their motivation to relocate.

2

Which choice offers an accurate interpretation of the data in the chart?

A) NO CHANGE

B) cited less than half as often as

C) slightly more important than

D) substantially less significant than

[**GIVEN**: the passage discusses the uses of various antibiotics.]

Effectiveness of Selected Antibiotics				
Condition	Cure rate of selected antibiotics for listed conditions			
	streptomycin (%)	gentamicin (%)	neomycin (%)	amoxicillin (%)
Tuberculosis	80	0	0	0
Eye infection	4	97	2	1
Heart valve infection	82	89	0	87
Urinary tract infection	2	92	91	99
E. coli infection	0	98	98	42
Hepatic coma	0	0	97	0
Soft tissue infection	7	95	6	93

Amoxicillin is **3** more effective than any other antibiotic in treating urinary tract infections.

3

Which choice offers an accurate interpretation of the data in the table?

A) NO CHANGE
B) slightly less effective than gentamicin
C) the least effective option
D) slightly more effective than streptomycin

The best antibiotic used for treating a heart valve infection is streptomycin; the best option for a patient suffering from a urinary tract infection is amoxicillin; the only treatment option for a patient with tuberculosis is gentamicin, and the only antibiotic that is highly effective against urinary tract infections, E. coli infections, and hepatic coma is neomycin. **4**

4

The writer wants the information in the passage to correspond as closely as possible to the information in the table. Given that goal and assuming that the rest of the sentence would remain unchanged, in which sequence should the four antibiotics be discussed?

A) NO CHANGE
B) "gentamicin," "amoxicillin," "streptomycin," "neomycin"
C) "amoxicillin," "neomycin," "gentamicin," "streptomycin"
D) "gentamicin," "neomycin," "streptomycin," "amoxicillin"

Patients suffering from soft tissue infection **5** have a slightly better chance of recovery using amoxicillin than using gentamicin.

5

Which choice offers an accurate interpretation of the data in the table?

A) NO CHANGE
B) are completely guaranteed recovery if treated with gentamicin.
C) are significantly more likely to recover using gentamicin than using neomycin.
D) have a chance of recovery if they are treated with only neomycin.

17

[**GIVEN**: the passage explains the properties of alcohols and alkanes.]

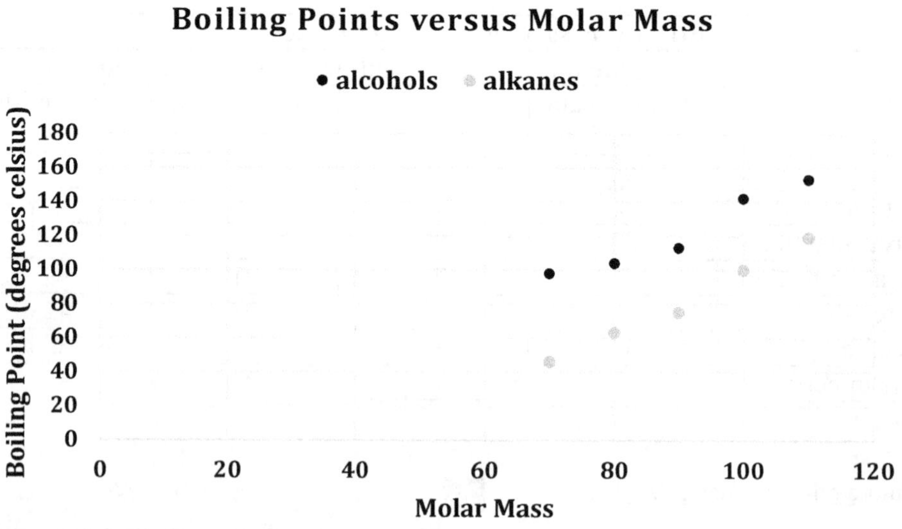

As recent observations have shown, [6] boiling points for alkanes can fall to as low as 60 degrees Celsius.

The boiling points of alkanes whose molar mass is greater than 80 [7] reach nearly 150 degrees Celsius.

6

Which choice offers an accurate interpretation of the data in the chart?

A) NO CHANGE
B) alkanes have consistently higher boiling points than alcohols.
C) as molar mass increases, boiling points increase.
D) at the molar mass of 100, alkanes and alcohols have the same boiling point.

7

Which choice offers an accurate interpretation of the data in the chart?

A) NO CHANGE
B) are at least 100 degrees Celsius.
C) are consistently higher than 60 degrees Celsius.
D) approach but do not reach 120 degrees Celsius.

[**GIVEN**: the passage discusses how the concentration of particulate matter, a type of pollutant, has changed in the United States]

Ambient Air Quality in the United States

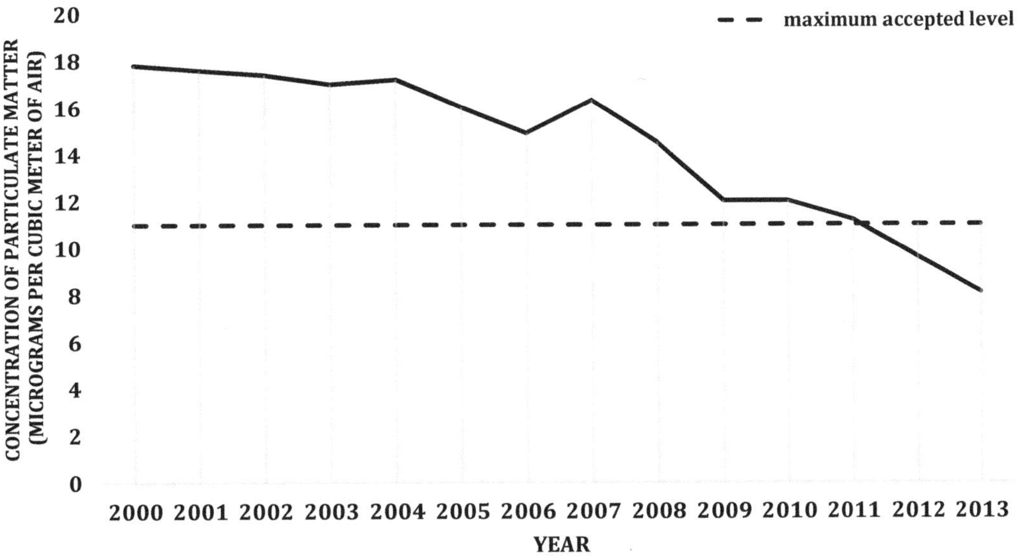

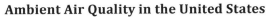

A 2013 study reveals that **8** <u>the concentration of particulate matter reached its highest point in 2007, followed by a decline in concentration.</u>

The atmosphere of the United States **9** <u>has never exhibited</u> an accepted level of particulate matter.

Since 2006, the concentration of particulate matter **10** <u>has been above the acceptable maximum each year.</u>

8

Which choice most effectively completes the sentence with relevant and accurate information based on the graph?

A) NO CHANGE

B) not until 2013 did the concentration of particulate matter fall below the accepted maximum level.

C) the concentration of particulate matter has stayed at about the same level since 2004.

D) the concentration of particulate matter has declined overall since 2000.

9

Which choice offers an accurate interpretation of the data in the graph?

A) NO CHANGE

B) from 2000 to 2011 fell within

C) for two consecutive years achieved

D) is unlikely to remain within

10

Which choice offers an accurate interpretation of the data in the graph?

A) NO CHANGE

B) has not changed noticeably from year to year.

C) greatly decreased every year.

D) rose for one year and then gradually declined.

17

ANSWER KEY

GRAPHS

LESSON 17

EXERCISE:

1. C

2. D

3. A

4. B

5. C

6. C

7. C

8. D

9. C

10. D

Chapter 18

GRAMMAR TECHNIQUE AND REVIEW

18

GRAMMAR TECHNIQUE

On the SAT, you will encounter four main question types.

Grammar

◊ Includes 13 types of grammar and punctuation rules

Tone/ Style

◊ Revising words, thesis, topic sentences; adding and omitting content

◊ Understanding main idea, tone, and supporting claims

◊ Precision, conclusion, style, and syntax revisions

Placement

◊ Adding, omitting, organizing; logical sequences and conclusions

Graphs

◊ Applying quantitative information from a graph to the passage

GRAMMAR TECHNIQUE STEPS (S.E.E.)

SAT Grammar is not difficult, though it is very easy to make a mistake. Often, these mistakes come from colloquial speech and things that we "hear" in acceptable daily conversation. However, for SAT Grammar, DO NOT use your ears.

Use your EYES and S.E.E. (Skim, Edit, Eliminate)

1 SKIM

Skim from the beginning of the passage and into Question #1.

Option: Some test-takers are fine with only reading a couple of sentences before the question and will go back and read extensively only as needed. Your GOAL is always to assess the author's overall point and tone.

NOTE: If you see a paragraph in which every sentence is numbered with brackets [#], you should read the entire paragraph because this indicates that a placement question will be imminent:

[1]

[2]

[3]

1

1

The writer plans to add the following sentence to this paragraph.

2 EDIT

Make an initial edit ON THE PASSAGE (yes, write on the passage!) before looking at answer choices. An EDIT is a change made to the underlined portion of the passage that adheres to the question types and grammar rules.

NOTE: This EDIT may seem daunting at first. Yet the more you get used to the question types and grammar rules, the easier it will be to make precise edits.

EXAMPLE 1

A practiced test-taker will see the following sentence and know to EDIT for **parallelism** list and **punctuation** rules.

These ideas are known to water filter manufacturers, food scientists; and elected officials.

scientists, and

A) NO CHANGE
B) scientists—and
C) scientists, and
D) scientists, but

EXAMPLE 2

A practiced test-taker will see the following sentence and know to EDIT for **subject/pronoun agreement** and the **difference between it/its/it's**.

Scientists have long known that dirt particles hasten melting by darkening snow and obstructing it's ability to absorb the sun's rays efficiently.

its

S *P*

A) NO CHANGE
B) its
C) its'
D) it

EXAMPLE 3

A practiced test-taker will see the following sentence and know to EDIT for aptness of word choice while keeping style in mind. Remember, when you are dealing with concision, style, and word usage, your EDIT may be notes that help you choose the best answer.

Given these solutions as well as the many health benefits of clean air, the advantages of air filters outdo the drawbacks of their expensive production.

to be better than

Advantages are more important than drawbacks. They are NOT competing with each other.

A) NO CHANGE
B) outmaneuver — *to move better than*
C) outperform — *to do better than*
D) outweigh — *to be more important than*

NOTE: If the EDIT seems difficult, you may require a greater area of reading in order to understand important context clues. Broaden your reading area while keeping in mind the exact question.

EXAMPLE

A practiced test-taker will see context clues in the paragraph and know to EDIT for aptness of word choice while keeping style in mind.

personal pronoun

While you may not realize this at first, calories in a fruit or vegetable are actually forms of solar energy. *(personal pronoun)* Your fruits and vegetables undergo a chemical reaction known as photosynthesis, which converts air, water, and other nutrients by using the sun's rays. Because calories measure energy, *(not a personal pronoun)* one <u>can say</u> that eating fruits and vegetables is indeed inherently solar.

A) NO CHANGE
B) you can say
C) it can be stated
D) DELETE the underlined portion.

3 ELIMINATE

Now, use your EDIT to perform a Process of Elimination (**POE**). This process involves eliminating any choice that does not fall within your initial edit.

EXAMPLE

If your edit for the underlined portion indicates a change from THEY to IT, go through and cross out THEY and any plural pronouns in the answer choices.

<u>they will be remembered.</u>

it

A) NO CHANGE
B) ~~their~~ memories will live on.
C) ~~them~~ remembering.
D) it will not be forgotten.

TIPS

◊ Do not substitute all choices into the sentence. Trust your edit!

◊ Control the test by using your edit to eliminate.

◊ Cross out the wrong answer choices for quick and accurate POE.

! BEWARE (PITFALLS AND COMMON MISTAKES)

1. STYLE CHANGES

Changing an answer to what YOU think sounds better WITHOUT using grammar and rules of logic.

2. NOT USING A CONTEXTUAL EDIT

Editing a sentence for style but NOT using surrounding sentences and context to determine this edit. REMEMBER: your answer may be correct for the line, but NOT correct when read in context.

3. "IT SOUNDS FINE"

Choosing an answer because you trust your ear. Always apply the rules of grammar and context by looking at both the rest of the sentence and the surrounding sentences. **Remember S.E.E. !**

18 GRAMMAR TECHNIQUE

Before proceeding to the practice tests, correct and/or identify the errors in the following chosen grammar types.

GRAMMAR LESSON	EXERCISE
1. SUBJECT/VERB AGREEMENT	Neither of the girls are coming to the party.
2. PARALLELISM	I went walking, hiking, and I went swimming. Her happiness was equal to his being clever.
3. COMPARISON	I prefer the reading of classic fiction to non-fiction. They want to be a lifeguard. I have less dollars than you. Between Jack, Mary, and I things are good. Jack is the best of the two of us.
4. SUBJECT/PRONOUN	Everyone wants their way.
5. PRONOUN CASE	John and me went to the store. John, Steve, and Ken went to the park and he fell. I did better than him.
6. DANGLING MODIFIER	Having driven all night, the bed looked so inviting to John.
7. ADJECTIVE/ADVERB	The girl runs quick. The girl is quick.
8. IRREGULAR VERB	He swum all afternoon. She would have wrote the letter if she had had time.
9. VERB TENSE	In 1969, she is happy to have met him.
10. IDIOM	Listening at the music relaxes me. We all agreed to seeing the same movie.
11. DICTION	She was reticent to ride the huge roller coaster. I alluded the cops after robbing the bank.
12. SENTENCE STRUCTURE	I was very happy, I loved life. She was not only a good musician, and a good tennis player. She was neither happy or sad. He was very angry but she was very mad too. I put sugar in my coffee: I like long books. Every two weeks, I receive my bi-weekly paycheck. His shirt is too short in length.
13. SUBJUNCTIVE MOOD/ HYPOTHETICAL	If she was finished cleaning the house, she would have relaxed. I suggest that Austin wears his seatbelt.

ANSWERS ON NEXT PAGE

GRAMMAR LESSON	ANSWER KEY
1. SUBJECT/VERB	Neither of the girls **is** coming to the party.
2. PARALLELISM	I went walking, hiking, and ~~I went~~ swimming. **(omit "I went")** Her happiness was equal to his **cleverness**.
3. COMPARISON	I prefer the reading of classic fiction to **that of** non-fiction. They want to be **lifeguards**. I have **fewer** dollars than you. **Among** Jack, Mary, and **me** things are good. Jack is the **better** of the two of us.
4. SUBJECT/PRONOUN	Everyone wants **his or her** way.
5. PRONOUN CASE	John and **I** went to the store. John, Steve, and Ken went to the park and **he** fell. **(ambiguous)** I did better than **he**.
6. DANGLING MODIFIER	Having driven all night, **John found the bed so inviting.**
7. ADJECTIVE/ADVERB	The girl runs **quickly**. The girl is quick. **(no error)**
8. IRREGULAR VERB	He **swam** all afternoon. She would have **written** the letter if she had had time.
9. VERB TENSE	In 1969, she **was** happy to have met him.
10. IDIOM	Listening **to** the music relaxed me. We all agreed **on** seeing the same movie.
11. DICTION	She was **reluctant** to ride the huge roller coaster. I **eluded** the cops after robbing the bank.
12. SENTENCE STRUCTURE	I was very happy, **and** I loved life. She was not only a good musician, **but also** a good tennis player. She was neither happy **nor** sad. He was very angry **and** she was very mad too. I put sugar in my coffee: ~~I like long books.~~ **(colon requires explanation)** Every two weeks, I receive my ~~bi-weekly~~ paycheck. **(redundancy)** His shirt is too short ~~in length~~. **(redundancy; *short* already implies length)**
13. SUBJUNCTIVE MOOD/ HYPOTHETICAL	If she **had** finished cleaning the house, she would have relaxed. I suggest that Austin **wear** his seatbelt.

TIPS

How did you do? If you missed any of the review exercises, consider re-reading the lessons before attempting the practice tests. It is vital that you know all grammar lessons in order to effectively increase your accuracy, speed, and efficient use of technique.

Practice Tests

Test 1

Test 1

Writing Test

35 MINUTES, 44 QUESTIONS

Turn to Section 2 of your answer sheet to answer the questions in this section.

DIRECTIONS

Each passage below is accompanied by a number of questions. For some questions, you will consider how the passage might be revised to improve the expression of ideas. For other questions, you will consider how the passage might be edited to correct errors in sentence structure, usage, or punctuation. A passage or a question may be accompanied by one or more graphics (such as a table or graph) that you will consider as you make revising and editing decisions.

Some questions will direct you to an underlined portion of a passage. Other questions will direct you to a location in a passage or ask you to think about the passage as a whole.

After reading each passage, choose the answer to each question that most effectively improves the quality of writing in the passage or that makes the passage conform to the conventions of standard written English. Many questions include a "NO CHANGE" option. Choose that option if you think the best choice is to leave the relevant portion of the passage as it is.

Questions 1-11 are based on the following passage.

The Diva's in the Details

Divas are no longer what they used to be. Originally, the term "diva" (from a Latin word for "goddess") was used only in the circles of classical opera, [1] and was applied to the leading female singer in an opera company. Later, it was used as a term to separate the really thrilling stars of this genre from the merely good performers of leading roles. However, the word is now more generally applied to any highly visible performer and refers not only to her onstage performing ability, [2] but also for her temperamental, headline-grabbing performances away from the theater. Such a "diva" often behaves in a manner at best imperious, at worst spoiled. In the course of everyday life, a diva can act very much like a selfish

1

The writer is considering deleting the underlined portion (ending the sentence with a period). Should the writer make this deletion?

A) Yes, because the information in the underlined portion is provided earlier in the sentence.
B) Yes, because the underlined portion detracts from the paragraph's focus on the origin of the term "diva."
C) No, because the underlined portion provides information about a term important to the passage.
D) No, because the underlined portion gives an example of a particular kind of diva.

2

A) NO CHANGE
B) and also to her
C) but also to her
D) but also because of her

CONTINUE

child.

In fairness, it should be said that the life of a diva is not easy. The operatic diva is aware that the success of a show **3** is rested on the quality of her voice in every single performance. She has no microphone to help her voice soar above the orchestra and reach the highest circles of the opera house. **4** An operatic aria demands a wide vocal range and (sometimes more importantly) a wide emotional range of acting as well. Working in harmony (in all senses of that word) is **5** very much mattering to a successful diva performance, **6** although many divas are not regarded as amiable collaborators.

3

A) NO CHANGE
B) rests
C) resting
D) had been resting

4

At this point, the writer is considering adding the following sentence.

> Often, a diva refuses to perform a certain role because she deems it beneath her skill level.

Should the writer make this addition here?

A) Yes, because it gives an example of the situation described in the previous sentence.
B) Yes, because it further explains how divas make their lives more difficult than is necessary.
C) No, because it indicates that some divas hold their fellow performers to unfair standards.
D) No, because it detracts from the paragraph's main point that the life of a diva is difficult.

5

A) NO CHANGE
B) huge in
C) key to
D) an intrinsic facet of

6

Which choice provides supporting examples that reinforce the main point of the sentence?

A) NO CHANGE
B) since the typical diva relies on the leading tenor, the orchestra pit, and her fellow castmates for support onstage.
C) since most opera singers aspire to become divas and undertake grueling training with precisely this goal in mind.
D) which can prove difficult for even the most cooperative singers.

CONTINUE

[1] A diva, in demand all around the world, travels from one venue to another: she must develop the ability to **7** adapt to new companies and singers. [2] She needs not only to cultivate her voice but also to attain the stamina of a trained athlete. [3] It is, therefore, not surprising that a true diva has a low tolerance for **8** other's incompetence and can lash out and make startling demands, especially when others do not live up to her high expectations. [4] She is only too aware of what her audience requires: only the best, every night. [5] It is an exhausting life. **9**

7

A) NO CHANGE
B) adept to
C) adept in
D) adapt by

8

A) NO CHANGE
B) others incompetence
C) others' incompetence
D) other incompetence

9

The writer plans to add the following sentence to the paragraph.

> She is required to sing in alien languages.

To make this paragraph most logical, the sentence should be placed

A) before sentence 1.
B) before sentence 2.
C) before sentence 4.
D) before sentence 5.

CONTINUE

10 She has now been dead for almost fifty years. However Maria Callas is still regarded as the greatest diva in the realm of opera. She could succeed resoundingly in traditional romantic soprano roles, but she was also able to lift her voice into the higher octaves required by Gioachino Rossini's famed musical compositions. No soprano was expected to do that; indeed, no soprano before Callas had ever tried. **11** Some argue that the mythic persona surrounding Callas was completely out of proportion to her actual talents.

10

Which choice most effectively combines the two sentences at the underlined portion?

A) NO CHANGE
B) Although Maria Callas has now been dead for almost fifty years, she
C) Having been dead for almost fifty years, Maria Callas, she
D) She has now been dead for almost fifty years, Maria Callas

11

The writer wants a concluding sentence that restates the main point of the paragraph. Which choice best accomplishes this goal?

A) NO CHANGE
B) Although the contemporary usage of the word "diva" is vastly different from its usage years ago, the term is still significant in the world of opera.
C) Despite Callas' distinction as the world's most renowned soprano, many mezzo-sopranos and altos have earned equally admirable, if not more impressive, reputations.
D) Callas revolutionized the expectations of operatic sopranos from then on and naturally became the embodiment of our modern idea of the supremely critical, yet supremely talented, "diva."

Test 1

Questions 12-22 are based on the following passage.

Juliet and Romeo: A Classic Revisited

Most people think that they know everything about Shakespeare's famed play about the "star-crossed lovers," since it is very difficult to avoid this couple—whether in a Literature 101 course, at the movies, or within an actual theater. With the possible exception of *Hamlet*, **12** *Romeo and Juliet* is the most performed of all of Shakespeare's plays. We can all picture Juliet leaning over the balcony, or preparing to swallow the lethal contents of the vial given to her by the Friar, or **13** her lover in the tomb dead beside her, just before thrusting the dagger into her breast.

Poor Romeo! His name comes first in the title, but it is Juliet who gets all the attention. Why should this be so? After all, it is he who is onstage for the majority of the scenes. **14** The play's tragic hero appears before his audience quite frequently.

12

A) NO CHANGE

B) people perform *Romeo and Juliet* the most of all of Shakespeare's plays.

C) *Romeo and Juliet* probably being the most performed of all of Shakespeare's plays.

D) Shakespeare's most performed play is that of *Romeo and Juliet*.

13

Which choice most closely matches the stylistic pattern established earlier in the sentence?

A) NO CHANGE

B) when she wakes in the tomb to find her lover

C) waking in the tomb, or to find her lover

D) waking in the tomb to find her lover

14

At this point, the writer is considering deleting the underlined sentence. Should the sentence be kept or deleted?

A) Kept, because it appropriately contextualizes the paragraph's central question.

B) Kept, because it sets up the main topic of the paragraph that follows.

C) Deleted, because it repeats information provided in the previous sentence.

D) Deleted, because it neglects to quantify how often Romeo appears.

[1] 15 The biggest reason is why Shakespeare was a man who knew the make-up of his company and who wrote to 16 their strengths. [2] For example, at the time when he was writing the great comedies, there must have been a glut of talented boy players; 17 in Shakespeare's time, boys always played female roles. [3] *Twelfth Night* has three hefty female roles, as does *As You Like It*. [4] However, *Romeo and Juliet* involves only two prominent female roles, Juliet and Juliet's Nurse. [5] On the evidence of Shakespeare's script, the boy actor assigned to Juliet was a good-enough but certainly not great performer. 18

15

A) NO CHANGE
B) Most likely because
C) The answer being
D) The answer is that

16

A) NO CHANGE
B) its
C) it's
D) they're

17

Which choice provides evidence in support of the main argument of the paragraph?

A) NO CHANGE
B) evidence indicates that there were many boy actors who appeared at the Globe Theater during Shakespeare's tenure.
C) the most well-reviewed boy actors often grew up to become the highest regarded adult actors.
D) it is, of course, impossible to know for certain whether or not this is true.

18

The writer plans to add the following sentence to this paragraph.

> The ridiculous Nurse would have been played not by a boy actor, but by a character actor, a comedian.

To make this paragraph most logical, the sentence should be placed

A) before sentence 3.
B) before sentence 4.
C) before sentence 5.
D) after sentence 5.

CONTINUE

[19] Examine the two roles of Juliet and Romeo, it is Romeo who develops as the play progresses. He changes from a boy more interested in playing with words and emotions into a man overwhelmed by real passion; he defies the rules and kills in an attempt to capture the eternity of love. [20] His verse is an intricate, aggressive whirl of different emotions. [21] Similarly, Juliet is a one-note part. She reacts only to what is placed before her, and her language is uncomplicated and direct. Even her climactic speech, though cleverly written, is not difficult in terms of acting technique: it merely requires a steadily rising inflection that communicates Juliet's increasing agitation.

To achieve his effects, Shakespeare masterfully catered to what his players could and couldn't do. It's no wonder today's actresses enjoy playing Shakespeare's heroine: they receive rave reviews for expending far less energy [22] than the actors who play Romeo do.

19

A) NO CHANGE
B) Examining the two roles of Juliet and Romeo, Romeo develops as the play progresses.
C) Upon examining the two roles of Juliet and Romeo; it is Romeo who develops as the play progresses.
D) If you examine the two roles of Juliet and Romeo, you will see that it is Romeo who develops as the play progresses.

20

In context, which choice provides the most specific information about the complexity of Romeo's character?

A) NO CHANGE
B) The historical record indicates that it took Shakespeare almost a decade to fully form the star-crossed lovers' relationship.
C) He, along with Othello, Macbeth, and King Lear, is one of Shakespeare's best-known male protagonists.
D) Some scholars argue that Romeo's actions do not make much logical sense.

21

A) NO CHANGE
B) To look at it in a different way, Juliet
C) Instead of Juliet, who
D) In contrast, Juliet

22

A) NO CHANGE
B) then those of Romeo.
C) than those of Romeo.
D) then the actors who play Romeo do.

CONTINUE

Questions 23-33 are based on the following passage.

Our "Always Connected" World

Years ago, there was a complicated, delicate etiquette that governed telephone conversation. **23** Because one avoided using the telephone at meal times. Early in the morning, the person **24** you were contacting might still be in bed: late at night, the same person might have already gone to bed. Certainly, one never used the telephone after 10 P.M., except in the case of an emergency. Indeed, if the phone rang in the middle of the night, one felt **25** quite nervous because one intuited that something awful must have happened.

Nor was the telephone regarded as a substitute for writing a letter. Even at Christmas, when I was allowed to telephone my Grandma and Grandpa to wish them a Merry Christmas and thank them for the card they had sent me, I was still expected to write a letter of thanks and to post it later in the week. Fortunately, I could write the letter and post it in the mailbox somewhat at leisure, since the Post Office could be depended on to deliver it **26** around a day.

23

A) NO CHANGE
B) Thereafter
C) Despite this,
D) For instance,

24

A) NO CHANGE
B) they were
C) one was
D) one is

25

A) NO CHANGE
B) on the edge of your seat
C) very high-strung
D) replete with trepidation

26

A) NO CHANGE
B) within
C) under
D) about

CONTINUE

Well, times have changed. Nowadays, communication has become a matter of sending texts and posting about your life on Facebook, Twitter, and Instagram. [27] You walk down any street and weave through an army of iPhone users marching steadfastly and blindly towards you. With dexterous thumbs, they flick their way through recently-posted messages and then [28] precede in tapping out replies. Others stare fixedly ahead, ear-buds nestled in their heads, apparently chanting madly to themselves—until you realize that they are talking to their mobile connections. [29] Who knows what new gadget will appear on the market in the next decade?

27

The writer is considering deleting the underlined sentence. Should the writer make this deletion?

A) Yes, because the underlined sentence contradicts the main point of the paragraph.
B) Yes, because the underlined sentence restates information from the previous sentence.
C) No, because the underlined sentence provides the main argument of the passage.
D) No, because the underlined sentence provides an example supporting the main point of the paragraph.

28

A) NO CHANGE
B) precede to tap
C) proceed in tapping
D) proceed to tap

29

The writer would like a concluding sentence that summarizes the main point of the paragraph. Which choice best accomplishes this goal?

A) NO CHANGE
B) This strong attachment to technological devices is tangential to our well being.
C) Today, it seems that instant thought needs to be transmitted into instant contact.
D) After all, mobile phones require a different infrastructure than landlines do.

CONTINUE

[1] However, friendship is about much more than accessibility. [2] When two people are in a relationship, they need to heed both a need for privacy **30** and a need to share. [3] My true love does not need me to be constantly in contact so that I can tell him that I am on the train or pass on to him every wild thought that passes through my head every second of the day. [4] **31** However, he does not need me to send him photos of the ice cream I am eating, **32** or for me to visit him at work to say hello, for that matter. **33**

30

A) NO CHANGE
B) yet
C) or
D) plus

31

A) NO CHANGE
B) Likewise, he does not need me to
C) Instead, he does not need me to
D) Additionally, not needing me to

32

Which choice most effectively captures the writer's main point about communication in this paragraph?

A) NO CHANGE
B) with the latest model of cell phone that will very soon become obsolete.
C) giving him a much-needed reminder that I am thinking of him.
D) accompanied by text and emoticons and all the usual social media gibberish.

33

The writer plans to add the following sentence to this paragraph.

> This is true even in the case of romantic bonds.

To make this paragraph most logical, the sentence should be placed

A) before sentence 1.
B) before sentence 3.
C) before sentence 4.
D) after sentence 4.

CONTINUE

Questions 34-44 are based on the following passage and supplementary material.

Measuring the Afterlife

Does the human consciousness simply self-extinguish at the point of death? This is a question that [34] has interested scientists, theologians, baffled occultists and, philosophers throughout the ages. The Greek philosopher Aristotle made clear links between two concepts that can help to answer this question, the "existence" and the "essence," in his *Metaphysics*. These ideas had a profound influence not only on the Greeks but also on subsequent [35] civilizations, the Romans, Arabs, and Medieval Europeans. Notions surrounding the concept of "existence" [36] has remained largely unchanged over time: in most Western religions, "existence" is the state of physical being—flesh and blood.

Unlike the canonical views of life and consciousness that originate with Aristotle, the views of occultists are usually considered heretical. [37] Many occultists seek to harmonize and manipulate a quality that recalls Aristotle's "essence"—the soul or spirit, as commonly understood—in order to benefit the "existence." A focus on "essence" is, arguably, especially prevalent in Asian intellectual history; such a focus is [38] as bound up with inquires involving the supernatural.

34

A) NO CHANGE
B) is interesting to scientists and theologians as well as baffles occultists and philosophers.
C) has interested and is baffling to scientists and theologians, occultists and, philosophers.
D) has interested and baffled scientists, theologians, occultists, and philosophers.

35

A) NO CHANGE
B) civilizations. The
C) civilizations; the
D) civilizations: the

36

A) NO CHANGE
B) has been remaining
C) have been remaining
D) have remained

37

At this point, the writer is considering adding the following sentence.

> The term "occultist" dates back to sixteenth-century France.

Should the writer make this addition?

A) Yes, because it provides information necessary for the reader's understanding of a key term.
B) Yes, because it supports the main argument of the passage.
C) No, because it would be better placed elsewhere in the passage.
D) No, because it provides information unrelated to the paragraph's main point.

38

A) NO CHANGE
B) also
C) yet
D) consequently

CONTINUE

How, then, do scientists make sense of all these different beliefs? Early scientific examinations of "existence" and "essence" involved the ability of the human body to project **39** it's consciousness in the form of electrical impulses that linger on in inanimate objects. **40** These impulses can be then transferred in a finite quantity, they are subject to the laws of conservation of energy. A less skeptical interpretation of such a phenomenon would point to an explanation of the existence of ghosts or supernatural entities. There is no doubt that our bodies are constantly emitting radiation over a wide range of frequencies, most of which radiation is in the form of non-visible photons or infrared heat. On very rare occasions, the radiation can overlap into the region of visible light. This could explain sightings of the human aura, a luminous glow around a person. Although these apparitions have yet to be scientifically verified, compelling evidence supports the possibility of their existence: **41** after all, vampire bats are known to hunt their prey by seeking out infrared wavelength traces.

39

A) NO CHANGE
B) its
C) there
D) their

40

A) NO CHANGE
B) Then, these impulses can be transferred in a finite quantity; subject to the laws of conservation of energy.
C) These impulses can be then transferred in a finite quantity, although it is subject to the laws of conservation of energy.
D) These impulses can be then transferred in a finite quantity, subject to the laws of conservation of energy.

41

Which choice provides the best support for the main point of the sentence?

A) NO CHANGE
B) after all, scientists have been interested in the subject for years.
C) after all, humans have made many unprovable claims in the past.
D) after all, plants have not been observed to emit radiation.

CONTINUE

Test 1

A recent series of experiments at the University of Hertfordshire in the U.K. suggests the existence of low frequency sound waves (or "infrasound") which can produce the phenomena that people typically associate with ghosts. **42** When exposed to sound frequencies higher than 15Hz, many people begin to report a variety of noticeable sensations. These include feelings of nervousness and discomfort as well as the sense of a "presence" in the room. The sound waves may also cause vibration in the human eye, causing people to see things that are not there. Usually, **43** waves below 40Hz are too low-pitched for people to actually perceive; rather than noticing the sound itself, people notice its effects. Whether there are in fact "ghosts" behind these phenomena or whether these occurrences coincidentally fit our wildest imaginings **44** remain an open question.

42

Which of the following is an accurate interpretation of the data in the chart?

A) NO CHANGE
B) When exposed to sound frequencies higher than 10Hz,
C) When exposed to sound frequencies lower than 15Hz,
D) When exposed to sound frequencies lower than 10Hz,

43

Which choice is the best interpretation of the data in the chart?

A) NO CHANGE
B) waves below 20Hz
C) waves above 15Hz
D) waves between 10Hz and 30Hz

44

A) NO CHANGE
B) remaining open questions.
C) remains an open question.
D) remain to be open questions.

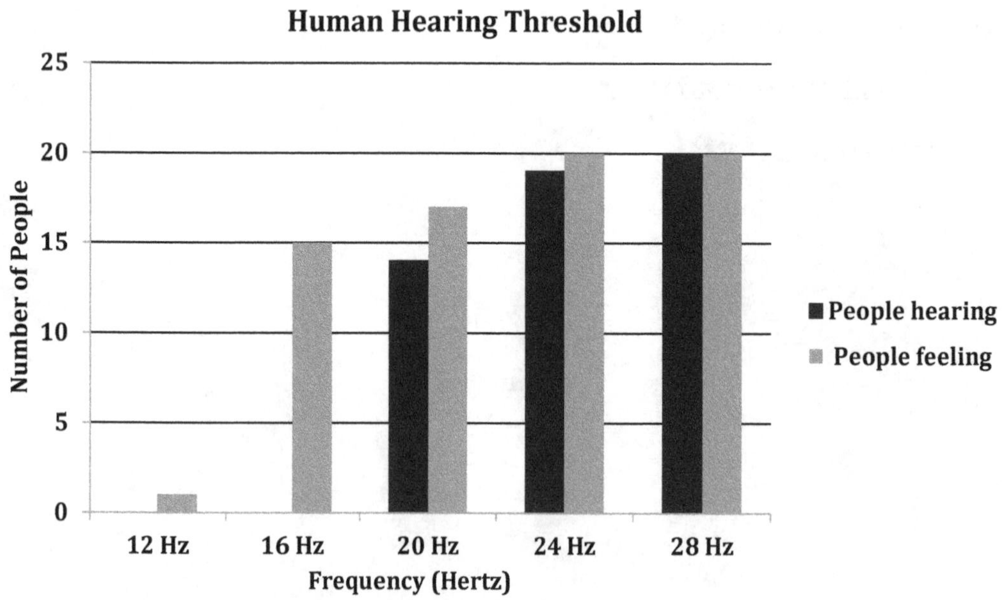

STOP

If you finish before time is called, you may check your work on this section only.

Do not turn to any other section.

No Test Material On This Page

Answer Key

TEST 1

PASSAGE 1

The Diva's in the Details

1.	C
2.	C
3.	B
4.	D
5.	C
6.	B
7.	A
8.	C
9.	B
10.	B
11.	D

PASSAGE 2

Juliet and Romeo: A Classic Revisited

12.	A
13.	D
14.	C
15.	D
16.	B
17.	A
18.	C
19.	D
20.	A
21.	D
22.	A

PASSAGE 3

Our "Always Connected" World

23.	D
24.	C
25.	A
26.	B
27.	D
28.	D
29.	C
30.	A
31.	B
32.	D
33.	B

PASSAGE 4

Measuring the Afterlife

34.	D
35.	D
36.	D
37.	D
38.	B
39.	B
40.	D
41.	A
42.	A
43.	B
44.	C

Post-Test Analysis

This post-test analysis is essential if you want to see an improvement on your next test. Possible reasons for errors on the four passages in this section are listed here. Place check marks next to the types of errors that pertain to you, or write your own types of errors in the blank spaces.

TIMING AND ACCURACY

◇ Spent too long reading individual passages
◇ Spent too long answering each question
◇ Spent too long on a few difficult questions
◇ Felt rushed and made silly mistakes or random errors
◇ Unable to work quickly using error types and POE
Other: ______________________________

APPROACHING THE PASSAGES AND QUESTIONS

◇ Unable to effectively grasp the passage's tone or style
◇ Unable to effectively grasp the passage's topic or stance
◇ Did not understand the context of underlined portions
◇ Did not eliminate false answers using error types
◇ Answered questions using first impressions instead of POE
◇ Answered questions without slotting in and checking final answer
◇ Eliminated NO CHANGE and chose a trap answer
◇ Eliminated correct answer during POE
Other: ______________________________

Use this form to better analyze your performance. If you don't understand why you made errors, there is no way that you can correct them!

GRAMMAR AND SENTENCE STRUCTURE

◇ Did not test sentence for subject-verb agreement
◇ Did not identify proper verb form and verb tense
◇ Did not test sentence for pronoun agreement
◇ Did not identify proper pronoun form (subject/object, who/which/when/where/why)
◇ Did not test for proper comparison phrasing (amount/number, between/among) and number agreement
◇ Did not test phrase for correct adverb/adjective usage
◇ Did not see broader sentence structure (parallelism, misplaced modifier)
◇ Did not see flaws in punctuation (colon, semicolon, comma splice, misplaced commas)
◇ Did not see tricky possessives or contractions (its/it's, your/you're)
◇ Did not identify flaws in standard phrases (either . . . or, not only . . . but also, etc.)
◇ Did not use proper phrasing in sentences requiring the subjunctive
Other: ______________________________

STYLE, ORGANIZATION, AND WORKING WITH EVIDENCE

◇ Did not notice cases of redundancy and wordiness
◇ Misidentified an expression as redundant or wordy
◇ Did not notice flaws in essay style or excessively informal expressions
◇ Misidentified an expression as stylistically inconsistent or informal
◇ Created the wrong relationship between two sentences
◇ Created the wrong relationship between two paragraphs
◇ Created the wrong placement for an out-of-order paragraph
◇ Did not eliminate faulty or improper English idioms
◇ Did not properly read or analyze an insertion/deletion question
◇ Did not properly read or analyze the information in a graphic
◇ Understood a graphic, but could not identify the correct passage content
Other: ______________________________

Test 2

Test 2

Writing Test

35 MINUTES, 44 QUESTIONS

Turn to Section 2 of your answer sheet to answer the questions in this section.

DIRECTIONS

Each passage below is accompanied by a number of questions. For some questions, you will consider how the passage might be revised to improve the expression of ideas. For other questions, you will consider how the passage might be edited to correct errors in sentence structure, usage, or punctuation. A passage or a question may be accompanied by one or more graphics (such as a table or graph) that you will consider as you make revising and editing decisions.

Some questions will direct you to an underlined portion of a passage. Other questions will direct you to a location in a passage or ask you to think about the passage as a whole.

After reading each passage, choose the answer to each question that most effectively improves the quality of writing in the passage or that makes the passage conform to the conventions of standard written English. Many questions include a "NO CHANGE" option. Choose that option if you think the best choice is to leave the relevant portion of the passage as it is.

Questions 1-11 are based on the following passage.

Rationality in the Golden Age of Greece

The cultures of the classical world, around the sixth century B.C.E., leaned [1] heavy on belief in gods. Yet after years of telling themselves that the storms and the sunshine and the seas were all the gods' doing, [2] the forces of nature were determined by some Greek philosophers to be no more divine than the forces of man. These thinkers began to hypothesize based on empirical data, no longer believing that Greece was prosperous because of a god's favor. The Greeks, instead, maintained that they were prosperous because of [3] his or her own merits. Contradicting all other major cultural religious traditions of the time, the civilization at large decided to pursue

1

A) NO CHANGE
B) heavy on the belief of gods.
C) heavily on belief in gods.
D) on the belief in heavy gods

2

A) NO CHANGE
B) some Greek philosophers determined that the forces of nature were
C) some Greek philosophers have determined that the forces of nature were
D) the forces of nature had been determined by some Greek philosophers to be

3

A) NO CHANGE
B) it's
C) they're
D) their

CONTINUE

reason as a primary value.

The incentives for such a change were obvious: Athens was flourishing in its art and trade after its recent victory over the Persians; Sparta was well known for its military might and moral pragmatism. It was the perfect time for Democritus of Abdera and Pythagoras of Samos to join math and science and fuel an entire society with the tenets of reason. All of a sudden, Empedocles forged the first thoughts on [4] natural selection, Plato brewed up new ideas for a society founded on equal education. The Greeks wanted the world to be understood, to have order—an order that would transcend myths of ancestors and gods. [5] They no longer found ancient stories to be a sufficient means of understanding their world and instead sought a different ordering method. [6] Though many citizens retained their mythological stories as important cultural artifacts, almost all eventually rejected the status of such stories as immutable truth.

4

A) NO CHANGE
B) natural selection; but Plato brewed up
C) natural selection, however Plato brewed up
D) natural selection as Plato brewed up

5

At this point, the writer is considering deleting the underlined sentence. Should the writer make this deletion?

A) Yes, because the underlined sentence repeats information presented in the previous sentence.
B) Yes, because the information in the underlined sentence is unrelated to the main point of the paragraph.
C) No, because the underlined sentence provides a counterargument to the point made in the previous sentence.
D) No, because the underlined sentence provides background information necessary for the main point presented in the paragraph.

6

The writer wants a concluding sentence that indicates why the Greeks preferred reason to mythology. Which choice best accomplishes this goal?

A) NO CHANGE
B) They found that compared to ancient myths, the physical principles of nature were harder to understand.
C) The philosophical principles developed by Plato and his contemporaries are still studied and, in many cases, followed today.
D) Nature, they found, operated under immutable laws and forces rather than according to the whims and caprices of the divine.

[1] Perhaps this was radical thinking, and perhaps it was questioned by **7** some, however the rest of world supported, or even downright envied, the Greeks. [2] The Greek alliance was the principal power of the Mediterranean after the Persian Wars, and power over the Mediterranean meant power over the whole of Western Europe. [3] How could an entire civilization be so decentralized in daily life, yet so unified when threatened by outside forces? [4] **8** The big reason for that was because the Greeks were the only classical civilization to pursue reason and logic, so that, regardless of their differences, they would find ways to band together in times of crisis. [5] In the words of Plato, “philosophy begins when you learn to doubt,” and doubt in disunity they did. **9**

7

A) NO CHANGE
B) some, moreover the rest of the world supported, or even downright envied, the Greeks.
C) some; however, the rest of the world supported, or even downright envied, the Greeks.
D) some, but the rest of the world, supporting or even downright envying, the Greeks.

8

A) NO CHANGE
B) The answer is because Greeks
C) The biggest reason being that the Greeks
D) The answer is that the Greeks

9

The writer plans to add the following sentence to this paragraph.

> The Eastern world could not comprehend the effectiveness of Greece’s form of governance based on rival city-states.

To make this paragraph most logical, the sentence should be placed

A) before sentence 1.
B) before sentence 3.
C) after sentence 4.
D) after sentence 5.

CONTINUE

10 For the Greeks at least, such regional hegemony was also an item of logic. Logically speaking, the "reasonable" ones are the deserving ones. Logically speaking, to keep commerce and trade alive, the Greek people needed to believe that they were on top of the world 11 because they were the smarter people, the "philosophic" people. These beliefs may grate against modern sensibilities, yet they were at the core of the Greek world view.

10

Which choice most smoothly and effectively introduces this paragraph?

A) NO CHANGE
B) Such regional hegemony were also an item of logic for the Greeks at least.
C) For the Greeks at least, such regional hegemony were also an item of logic.
D) Such regional hegemonies was also a logic item for the Greeks at least.

11

The writer is considering deleting the underlined portion (ending the sentence with a period). Should the writer make this deletion?

A) Yes, because the underlined portion contradicts the main argument of the paragraph.
B) Yes, because the underlined portion should be placed somewhere else in the paragraph.
C) No, because the underlined portion further explains the main point of the sentence.
D) No, because the underlined portion introduces a key term discussed in the following sentence.

CONTINUE

Test 2

Questions 12-22 are based on the following passage.

Making Poetry Matter

Poetry is a thing both revered and hated. These disparate reactions to poetry can be explained by **12** its disorienting quality, since a poem is a place where all you thought you knew in daily life ceases to exist—a place that is equivocal, convoluted, foreign, and inspiring. **13** Poetry is not only soothing, but also challenging, too.

14 Poet James Dickey, winner of the National Book Award, offering some timeless and articulate advice: "The first thing to understand about poetry is that it comes to you from outside you, in books or in words, but that for it to live, something from within you must come to it and meet it and complete it." **15** You cannot approach writing or reading poetry **16** with the same logic, convention, and by following rules like you do other forms of communication. As Dickey further explains, "Your response with your own mind and body and memory and emotions gives a poem its ability to work its magic; if you give to it, it will give to you and give plenty."

12

A) NO CHANGE
B) it's
C) their
D) its'

13

A) NO CHANGE
B) Poetry not only soothes but also challenges.
C) Poetry are both challenging and soothing.
D) Soothing but a challenge, many people read poetry.

14

Which choice most effectively introduces this paragraph?

A) NO CHANGE
B) Poet James Dickey is the winner of the National Book Award and offering advice timelessly and articulately
C) Offering timeless and articulate advice, poet James Dickey, winner of the National Book Award
D) Poet James Dickey, winner of the National Book Award, offers timeless and articulate advice

15

At this point, the writer is considering adding the following sentence.

> Despite earning such a prestigious award, Dickey is not unanimously praised for his work.

Should the writer make this addition here?

A) Yes, because it explains how people often disagree over the quality of poetry.
B) Yes, because it provides more information about Dickey, the passage's central subject.
C) No, because it calls into question the authority of Dickey.
D) No, because it detracts from the writer's argument that analyzing poetry requires a unique mentality.

16

A) NO CHANGE
B) with the same logic, convention, and rules as you do
C) with the same logic and conventions as well as rules, following like you might do with
D) with the same logic, convention, and rules like

CONTINUE

Poetry involves [17] <u>both objective awareness but also</u> a deep subjective understanding that comes from the very essence of daily reflection and human experience. If you read a poem today it means one thing. If you read the same poem in ten years it means another. [18] <u>If you read it every day, you will likely start to memorize its contents without even trying.</u> Was your analysis wrong or immature the first time around? Not at all. [19] <u>While many disagree about the quality of some poets, T.S. Eliot, Robert Frost, and Emily Dickinson are universally regarded as among the best English-language word-smiths in history.</u>

17

A) NO CHANGE
B) both an objective awareness and
C) not only an objective awareness and also
D) both objective awareness plus

18

Which choice best reinforces the point made in the previous two sentences about interpreting poetry?

A) NO CHANGE
B) If you then read it to your friend, he or she might have an interpretation completely different from yours.
C) If you read it either while falling in love or amidst the horror of a war, you may again have two entirely different outcomes.
D) If you expend too much effort trying to interpret a poem, the work may very well lose its intrinsic beauty.

19

The writer wants to conclude by reiterating the main point of the paragraph. Which choice best accomplishes this goal?

A) NO CHANGE
B) The poem's beauty is such that the words float freely, unattached, only coming to ground through the momentary viewpoint of the reader.
C) It is true that some readers are stronger analysts than others, a fact that often discourages people from even so much as picking up a collection of poems.
D) Books, however, tend to follow linear plot lines, providing the reader with clear character arcs and overarching themes.

CONTINUE

Speaking of such beauty, Dickey has argued that "the beginning of your true encounter with poetry should be simple. It should bypass all classrooms, textbooks, causes, examinations, and libraries and go straight to things that make your existence exist." The fact is that the university classroom may not be the best place to introduce yourself to poetry. **20** Currently, many academic institutions include poetry among their required curricula.

21 Being introduced to poetry, it is seen by young children and teenagers instead as a form of expression rather than as an aspect of a required course laden with facts, dates, and terminology. **22** The more you're encounter with poetry deepens, the more you're experience of life deepens. As novelist Leo Tolstoy most poetically stated, "If you see that some aspect of your society is bad, and you want to improve it, there is only one way to do so: you have to improve people. And in order to improve people, you begin with only one thing: you become better yourself."

20

The writer wants to conclude the paragraph with an example that supports the main point of the previous sentence. Which choice best accomplishes this goal?

A) NO CHANGE
B) The "right and wrong" atmosphere propagated in academia often discourages valuable personal reactions.
C) Many students enjoy reading poetry during their free time; however, some do not.
D) Dickey, moreover has spent many years working as an adjunct professor.

21

Which choice most effectively introduces this paragraph?

A) NO CHANGE
B) On the other hand, maybe poetry should be introduced to young children and teenagers
C) Furthermore, young children and teenagers should have been introduced to poetry
D) Instead, maybe poetry should be introduced to young children and teenagers

22

A) NO CHANGE
B) The more a person's encounter with poetry deepens, the more their experience of life deepens.
C) The more your encounter with poetry deepens, the more one's experience of life deepens.
D) The more a person's encounter with poetry deepens, the more his or her experience of life deepens.

CONTINUE

Test 2

Questions 23-33 are based on the following passage and supplementary material.

The Fascinations of the Peregrine Falcon

It is commonly known that the peregrine falcon is able to achieve the highest flight speed of any bird, clocking in at velocities around and over 200 miles per hour during a dive. **23** Unlike the peregrine, the closely-related American kestrel prefers to hover rather than dive. The peregrine falcon is an omnivorous hunter, preferring the meat of small or medium-sized **24** birds but willing to devour bats (though only at night) and small mammals. The more foolhardy of the breed have been known to hunt the larger ibis and stork, and many falcons will feast upon various insect varieties—though the falcon will do so only in times when other food is scarce. **25** A fierce predator, it is not even out of the question for a peregrine to dive into a group of four or five hundred starlings and come out with one in each talon.

23

The writer is considering deleting the underlined sentence. Should the writer make this deletion?

A) Yes, because the underlined sentence detracts from the paragraph's main focus.
B) Yes, because the underlined sentence provides information contradictory to the previous sentence.
C) No, because the underlined sentence provides the reader with an important example of a diving bird.
D) No, because the underlined sentence provides additional information about the paragraph's main subject.

24

A) NO CHANGE
B) birds; however, willing
C) birds, and willing
D) birds. But also willing

25

A) NO CHANGE
B) Fierce predators, it is not even out of the question for the peregrine to dive into a group of four or five hundred starlings
C) It is not even out of the question for the peregrine, a fierce predator, to dive into a group of four or five hundred starlings
D) Diving into a group of four or five hundred starlings, the peregrine is a fierce predator

CONTINUE

[1] Perhaps one of the most recognizable qualities of the peregrine falcon is the reverse sexual dimorphism that it exhibits across genders. [2] 26 Females tend to be much larger and much more aggressive than males, traits common in insects but seldom seen in the avian world. [3] It is not uncommon to see the female of the species chasing a male, particularly when there is a conflict over hunting or resting territory. [4] When determining sex, pay attention to wingspan from roughly 13 to 20 months of age: 27 the average female's wings will measure 19-23 inches while the average male's will measure roughly 25-41 inches. 28

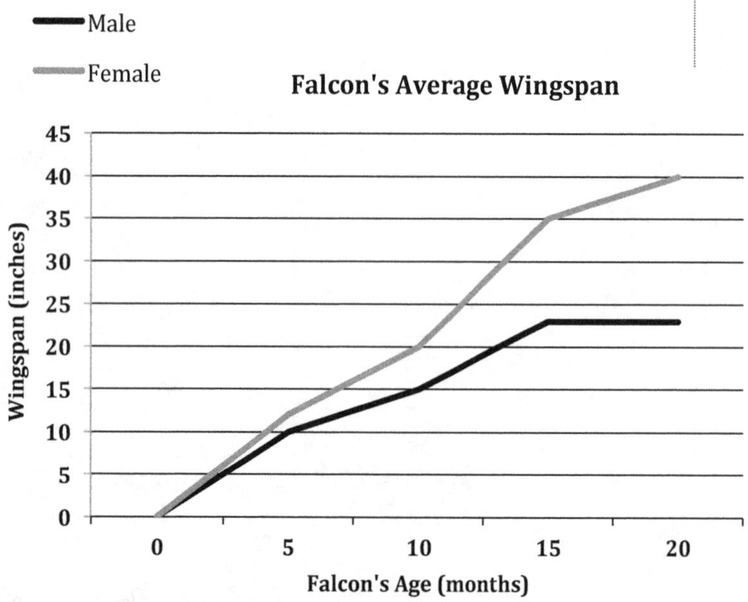

26

Which choice best interprets the data in the graph?

A) NO CHANGE
B) Females tend to be much smaller and
C) Females are more territorial as well as
D) Females are often roughly the same size but are

27

Which choice is an accurate interpretation of the data in the graph?

A) NO CHANGE
B) the average female's wingspan will measure an inch or two more than the average male's wingspan.
C) the average male's wingspan will measure exactly 25-41 inches while the average female's wingspan will measure exactly 19-23 inches.
D) the average female's wingspan will measure roughly 25-41 inches while the average male's will measure roughly 19-23 inches.

28

The writer plans to add the following sentence to this paragraph.

> Although this sexually dimorphic peculiarity is rare among birds, it is a trait that the peregrine falcon shares with most other raptors.

To make this paragraph most logical, the sentence should be placed

A) after sentence 1.
B) after sentence 2.
C) after sentence 3.
D) after sentence 4.

CONTINUE

Another remarkable trait of the peregrine is the nature of its nesting **29** structures, they are usually dug into cliff edges and are usually lined with down, fragments of old eggshells, and small rocks. Padding of this sort keeps falcon eggs from rolling out. Many falcons have even managed **30** to adapt to city life, **31** and even giant metropolises such as New York City have been known to see peregrines.

32 The peregrine falcon, although it adapts to human cities, the strategic locations of its nests, and the breathtaking speeds it can reach when diving make this swift hawk a nearly perfect hunter. Ian Coestgar, a pioneer in avian study, has recorded over 150 peregrine attacks, **33** calling "stoops" by field biologists. "I'd wager," Coestgar wrote in his field diary, "that the peregrine is capable of catching any bird, raptor or not. So fast is its dive and so formidable is its instinct. There are many great hunters in the animal kingdom," Coestgar continues. "I just consider myself lucky that I'm as large as I am, and that the falcons are as small as they are."

29

A) NO CHANGE
B) structures, some are
C) structures, which are
D) structures, some structures are

30

A) NO CHANGE
B) to adopt to
C) to adept with
D) in adapting with

31

Which choice give a supporting example describing how falcons can adjust to city life?

A) NO CHANGE
B) although most prefer to stay away from areas densely populated by humans.
C) nesting high above street level in the arches and divots of skyscrapers and churches.
D) especially in the summer months.

32

A) NO CHANGE
B) The peregrine falcon's adaptability to human cities and its strategic nesting locations as well as speeding breathtakingly when diving
C) The peregrine falcon adapting to human cities, strategically locating its nests, and the breathtaking speeds it can reach when diving
D) The peregrine falcon's adaptability to human cities, the strategic locations of its nests, and the breathtaking speeds it can reach when diving

33

A) NO CHANGE
B) called
C) having called
D) they are called

CONTINUE

Test 2

Questions 34-44 are based on the following passage.

France's Historic Vacation

[1] Unlike many other Europeans, the French are not noted for [34] its eagerness to work long hours. [2] The British are startled by the French readiness to rest from work not only on Sunday but also on Monday and Wednesday afternoons. [3] The Germans and the Swiss are less naïve but, nevertheless, are scornful of the fact that the whole of France appears to shut down for three weeks in August so that French citizens can rush to the Côte d'Azur and squash together on the narrow strips of Mediterranean beach. [4] Consequently, most of Northern Europe dismisses France as an [35] idol nation. [5] The French retort that at least they have gotten their priorities right. [6] The summer is a time for relaxation. [36]

[37] Every year, the 14th of July annually marks the start of what the French call "the great escape." July 14th is Bastille Day, the celebration of a 1790 attempt to liberate French political prisoners. (It turned out that there were only seven old men held in the Bastille prison, and their escape was plodding and drawn out.) In any case, this event marked the beginning of modern France, [38] and it was for this reason that, in 1880, Bastille Day was named a national holiday—rather like Independence Day in the United States.

34

A) NO CHANGE
B) it's
C) their
D) there

35

A) NO CHANGE
B) idling
C) idle
D) idolizing

36

The writer plans to add the following sentence to this paragraph.

> Thus, the citizens desert Paris and other large cities, leaving the streets empty during this "annual vacation."

To make this paragraph most logical, the sentence should be placed

A) before sentence 1.
B) before sentence 2.
C) before sentence 4.
D) before sentence 6.

37

A) NO CHANGE
B) Annually, the 14th of July marks the start
C) Annually, the 14th of July each year marks the start
D) The 14th of July each year, marking the start

38

A) NO CHANGE
B) moreover,
C) however
D) but

CONTINUE

The center of the celebration is the Champs-Élysées in Paris. An enormous tricolor French flag hangs from the Arc de Triomphe, a nearby monument. The broad avenue itself is lined with flags of blue, white, and red, **39** <u>and smaller versions fluttering from every possible vantage point.</u> With great pomp, the President of France progresses along the Champs-Élysées, which is lined with police officers and applauding Parisians. **40** <u>He receives the salute of the largest military parade in Europe, with cavalry and tanks and weapons not only from France but also from its many overseas territories.</u> In the most modern of these displays of power, **41** <u>jets fly low over the crowds under them with cheering.</u>

39

A) NO CHANGE
B) and from every possible vantage point, smaller versions flutter.
C) meanwhile smaller versions flutter from every possible vantage point.
D) fluttering from every possible vantage point, however, are smaller versions.

40

The writer is considering deleting the underlined sentence. Should the sentence be kept or deleted?

A) Kept, because it provides important information about the events of the French Revolution.
B) Kept, because it presents relevant and important information about the parade.
C) Deleted, because it detracts from the discussion of what the parade looked like in 1790.
D) Deleted, because it fails to specify the name of France's current president.

41

A) NO CHANGE
B) jets fly low over the cheering crowds.
C) the cheering crowds under them, low jets fly over.
D) jets fly low over the cheering crowds under them.

CONTINUE

42 After the parade, the president has more work to do. Later, the president meets with the media and talks informally about what had been achieved in the previous year, how France had fared, how she stands presently, and how she will advance. It is rather like the American President's State of the Union Address; 43 however, this speech generally occurs in January and is not associated with any national holiday. Bastille Day ends with dancing and concerts and parties and, of 44 course—a huge fireworks display centered on the Eiffel Tower. The streets are crowded and alive with people calling out to one another, gossiping, examining, buying, laughing, smiling, and reveling in being French.

42

Which choice most effectively and smoothly introduces this paragraph's discussion of the president's informal speech?

A) NO CHANGE
B) Every year, the same thing happens.
C) The parade inevitably concludes and the president must address his contingent, or at least he should.
D) DELETE the underlined sentence.

43

The writer is considering deleting the underlined portion (ending the sentence with a period). Should the writer make this deletion?

A) Yes, because the underlined portion contradicts information presented previously in the sentence.
B) Yes, because the underlined portion detracts from the discussion of the passage's main subject.
C) No, because the underlined portion provides additional information about important speeches throughout the world.
D) No, because the underlined portion explains how the two speeches differ.

44

A) NO CHANGE
B) course, a huge fireworks display
C) course; a huge fireworks display
D) course a huge fireworks display

STOP

If you finish before time is called, you may check your work on this section only.
Do not turn to any other section.

No Test Material On This Page

Answer Key

TEST 2

PASSAGE 1

Rationality in the Golden Age of Greece

1.	C
2.	B
3.	D
4.	D
5.	A
6.	D
7.	C
8.	D
9.	B
10.	A
11.	C

PASSAGE 2

Making Poetry Matter

12.	A
13.	B
14.	D
15.	D
16.	B
17.	B
18.	C
19.	B
20.	B
21.	D
22.	D

PASSAGE 3

The Fascinations of the Peregrine Falcon

23.	A
24.	A
25.	C
26.	A
27.	D
28.	B
29.	C
30.	A
31.	C
32.	D
33.	B

PASSAGE 4

France's Historic Vacation

34.	C
35.	C
36.	C
37.	B
38.	A
39.	B
40.	B
41.	B
42.	D
43.	B
44.	B

Post-Test Analysis

This post-test analysis is essential if you want to see an improvement on your next test. Possible reasons for errors on the four passages in this section are listed here. Place check marks next to the types of errors that pertain to you, or write your own types of errors in the blank spaces.

TIMING AND ACCURACY

◇ Spent too long reading individual passages
◇ Spent too long answering each question
◇ Spent too long on a few difficult questions
◇ Felt rushed and made silly mistakes or random errors
◇ Unable to work quickly using error types and POE
Other: ______________________________

APPROACHING THE PASSAGES AND QUESTIONS

◇ Unable to effectively grasp the passage's tone or style
◇ Unable to effectively grasp the passage's topic or stance
◇ Did not understand the context of underlined portions
◇ Did not eliminate false answers using error types
◇ Answered questions using first impressions instead of POE
◇ Answered questions without slotting in and checking final answer
◇ Eliminated NO CHANGE and chose a trap answer
◇ Eliminated correct answer during POE
Other: ______________________________

Use this form to better analyze your performance. If you don't understand why you made errors, there is no way that you can correct them!

GRAMMAR AND SENTENCE STRUCTURE

◇ Did not test sentence for subject-verb agreement
◇ Did not identify proper verb form and verb tense
◇ Did not test sentence for pronoun agreement
◇ Did not identify proper pronoun form (subject/object, who/which/when/where/why)
◇ Did not test for proper comparison phrasing (amount/number, between/among) and number agreement
◇ Did not test phrase for correct adverb/adjective usage
◇ Did not see broader sentence structure (parallelism, misplaced modifier)
◇ Did not see flaws in punctuation (colon, semicolon, comma splice, misplaced commas)
◇ Did not see tricky possessives or contractions (its/it's, your/you're)
◇ Did not identify flaws in standard phrases (either . . . or, not only . . . but also, etc.)
◇ Did not use proper phrasing in sentences requiring the subjunctive
Other: ______________________________

STYLE, ORGANIZATION, AND WORKING WITH EVIDENCE

◇ Did not notice cases of redundancy and wordiness
◇ Misidentified an expression as redundant or wordy
◇ Did not notice flaws in essay style or excessively informal expressions
◇ Misidentified an expression as stylistically inconsistent or informal
◇ Created the wrong relationship between two sentences
◇ Created the wrong relationship between two paragraphs
◇ Created the wrong placement for an out-of-order paragraph
◇ Did not eliminate faulty or improper English idioms
◇ Did not properly read or analyze an insertion/deletion question
◇ Did not properly read or analyze the information in a graphic
◇ Understood a graphic, but could not identify the correct passage content
Other: ______________________________

Test 3

Test 3

Writing Test

35 MINUTES, 44 QUESTIONS

Turn to Section 2 of your answer sheet to answer the questions in this section.

DIRECTIONS

Each passage below is accompanied by a number of questions. For some questions, you will consider how the passage might be revised to improve the expression of ideas. For other questions, you will consider how the passage might be edited to correct errors in sentence structure, usage, or punctuation. A passage or a question may be accompanied by one or more graphics (such as a table or graph) that you will consider as you make revising and editing decisions.

Some questions will direct you to an underlined portion of a passage. Other questions will direct you to a location in a passage or ask you to think about the passage as a whole.

After reading each passage, choose the answer to each question that most effectively improves the quality of writing in the passage or that makes the passage conform to the conventions of standard written English. Many questions include a "NO CHANGE" option. Choose that option if you think the best choice is to leave the relevant portion of the passage as it is.

Questions 1-11 are based on the following passage.

Relatively Speaking: Einstein's Theory of Experience

Albert Einstein, in his work *The Meaning of Relativity*, explains that what we individually experience is arranged in a series of events. In this series, the single moments that we remember are arranged as happening either "earlier" or "later," two time signatures which we cannot break down **[1]** further, these words do not have concrete, universal definitions. Therefore, each of us as an individual experiences an "I-time," or subjective time: what is considered earlier to me might be different **[2]** over what is considered earlier to you.

1

A) NO CHANGE
B) further, and because these
C) further, but because these
D) further because these

2

A) NO CHANGE
B) from
C) about
D) than

CONTINUE

[3] Unfortunately for us, Einstein suggests trying to associate numbers with the events, so that a greater number [4] being associated with a later event and a smaller number with an earlier one (e.g. the 27th event in my day was dinner, while the 3rd event was breakfast). However, he ultimately concludes that the "nature of this association may be quite meaningless." This is because the number associations would be different for different people. [5] For example, dinner might be the 34th thing you do in a day, or, if you are less inclined to be active, the 7th thing.

3

Which choice most smoothly and effectively introduces the discussion of Einstein's ideas about understanding time?

A) NO CHANGE
B) Because who knows why, Einstein suggests trying to associate numbers with the events
C) In an attempt to understand time more objectively, Einstein suggests trying to associate numbers with the events
D) He found this issue to be bothersome, and so Einstein suggests trying to associate numbers with the events

4

A) NO CHANGE
B) is
C) are
D) are being

5

The writer is considering deleting the underlined sentence. Should the writer make this deletion?

A) Yes, because it provides an example that contradicts the previous sentence.
B) Yes, because it provides an example that is unrelated to the previous sentence.
C) No, because it provides an example that further explicates the previous sentence.
D) No, because it provides an example that is a necessary counterargument to the previous sentence.

CONTINUE

Thus, we have highly individuated experiences. Through talking to each other we can, to a certain extent, compare them. We can come to understand that some of our "sense perceptions," as Einstein calls them (which are what we feel and what we experience), can correspond to others' perceptions. But some don't match up quite so well. We tend to believe in shared experiences **6** easier, and believe that common feeling is more real than differentiated feelings. This tendency **7** makes a given sensation or emotion feel more impersonal, more scientific. Einstein suggests that we envision life experience as a clock: we can all experience and relate to the mathematical, scientific turning of seconds into minutes, minutes into hours, and hours into days. **8** However, how we actually feel time passing us by is a matter of completely unique experience, not of science.

6

A) NO CHANGE
B) easy
C) more easily
D) more easy

7

A) NO CHANGE
B) make a given sensation or emotion feels
C) makes given sensations or emotions feel like
D) makes a given sensation or emotion feel like

8

The writer would like to conclude the paragraph by suggesting that time may not be as definite as Einstein described. Which choice best accomplishes this goal?

A) NO CHANGE
B) Time is measurable, immutable, and shared by everyone across the world.
C) However, time is also important to other scientific fields: geology, archeology, and meteorology, just to name a few.
D) Unfortunately, many cultures are resistant to adhering to rigidly timed schedules.

CONTINUE

[1] The clock, then, represents for Einstein the "epitome of our experiences." [2] It can describe our shared experience, but it can go no further. [3] He states that he is "convinced that the philosophers have had a harmful effect upon the progress of scientific thinking in removing certain fundamental concepts from the domain of empiricism, where they are under our control, where we can observe and determine them." [4] Granted, by philosophizing, we lose **9** whats real and in front of our faces. [5] We want to rationalize what we find and apply it to our lives. [6] We want our experiences to be made **10** not only into rigid structures, and into a seemingly irrational bank of feelings. [7] We are human, after all. **11**

9

A) NO CHANGE
B) whats'
C) what's being
D) what's

10

A) NO CHANGE
B) not only into rigid structure; however, also into
C) not into rigid structures only but also into
D) not only into rigid structures, but also into

11

The writer plans to add the following sentence to this paragraph.

> But what good is science without philosophical thought?

To make this paragraph most logical, the sentence should be placed

A) after sentence 1.
B) after sentence 2.
C) after sentence 4.
D) after sentence 7.

Test 3

Questions 12-22 are based on the following passage and supplementary material.

No Exam Left Behind

Life today is littered with exams. From the day we are born, our progress is measured at nearly regular intervals, moments when we find ourselves trapped in a chilly hall, our bodies tense with nervousness, mouths rigidly tight, hearts beating fast. We sit at desks, closed booklets before us, pens gripped in our hands. For many of [12] we, an exam is a torture far worse than anything invented by the Spanish Inquisition.

Thankfully, the Inquisition [13] comprises a relatively brief part of history. This contemporary form of institutionally-sanctioned torture, however, refuses to go away. A recent study indicates that the average number of exams taken since 2005 has [14] increased steadily and will continue to rise in 2020. Social scientists and educators alike condemn this trend, critically citing government programs such as former president George W. Bush's "No Child Left Behind" Act of 2001, [15] which resulted in a marked increase in the number of standardized tests administered.

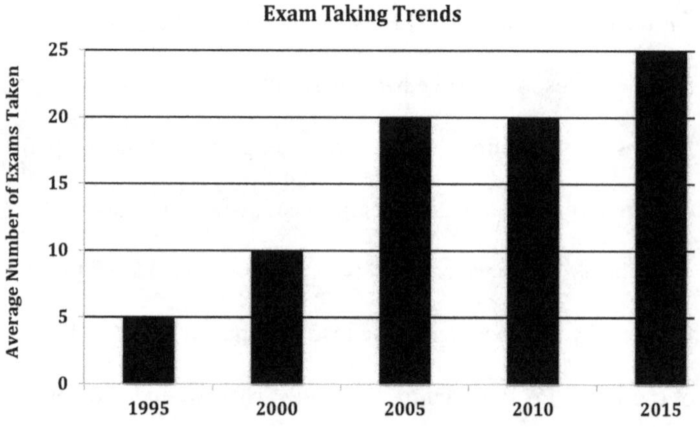

12

A) NO CHANGE
B) them
C) us
D) him or her

13

A) NO CHANGE
B) is comprising
C) had comprised
D) comprise

14

Which choice best interprets the data in the graph?

A) NO CHANGE
B) plateaued but
C) decreased but
D) steadily risen and

15

Which choice most accurately interprets the data in the graph?

A) NO CHANGE
B) which resulted in a slight increase in the number of standardized tests administered.
C) which resulted in a marked decrease in the number of standardized tests administered.
D) which resulted in no net change in the number of standardized tests administered.

CONTINUE

In this vein, author Michael Morpurgo has asserted that "One of the great failings of our education system is that we tend to focus on those who are succeeding on exams, and there are plenty of them. But the students we should be looking at—and a lot more urgently—are those who fail." He **16** puts his finger accurate on the limitation of any examination system. If you pass an exam, you are eligible for the next step in life: if you fail, then too bad! You're finished, and your future is apparently terminated.

Of course, that is a sweeping statement. We all know and admire people who have been successful in life, despite **17** their failures in the exam hall. For example, many of our best actors left school without any success in the exam stakes. As revered actress Edith Evans once said, "You don't take exams for acting: you take courage." She is right. One of life's major ironies **18** are that many of the great actors, and businessmen, and authors, and pop singers, who never made it into universities because they failed **19** exams—are offered honorary degrees by universities in recognition of their successes. **20** Do they despise exams as much as I do?

16

A) NO CHANGE
B) accurately puts his finger
C) is accurate and putting
D) is putting his finger accurate

17

A) NO CHANGE
B) his or her
C) they're
D) its

18

A) NO CHANGE
B) will be
C) being
D) is

19

A) NO CHANGE
B) exams: are
C) exams, are
D) exams are

20

The writer wants to conclude the paragraph by suggesting that the practice of bestowing these honorary degrees is flawed. Which choice best accomplishes this goal?

A) NO CHANGE
B) Do they despise academia as much as I do?
C) Would these people perhaps do better on exams if they retook them today?
D) Am I alone in thinking that this is a rather condescending gesture?

CONTINUE

[1] Whether intended or not, there is often an elitism implied in this system of exams that we enforce at every step of life. [2] To some people, letters before or after one's name suggest that one has arrived at a level which somehow implies that one is better **21** intellectually, economically, socially, and even, morally, than those who have not made the grade. [3] Common sense should tell us that it isn't necessarily so. [4] We should not feel bullied and dragooned by a system that insists that we either conform to a set pattern or be dismissed. **22**

21

A) NO CHANGE
B) intellectually, economically, socially, and even morally
C) intellectually, economically, socially and, even, morally
D) intellectually, economically, and socially, and even morally

22

The writer plans to add the following sentence to this paragraph.

> We are individuals, and each one of us approaches life in a different manner.

To make this paragraph most logical, the sentence should be placed

A) before sentence 1.
B) before sentence 2.
C) before sentence 3.
D) before sentence 4.

CONTINUE

Questions 23-33 are based on the following passage.

More than Meets the Eye: Excellence in Detective Fiction

Not every nation knows how to [23] convincing create detective fiction. American detectives are often far too energetic in their pursuit of the killer, forever racing along those mean streets at high speeds, firing off guns erratically and, in periods of less physical exertion, confronting their emotional neuroses. Swedish detectives are extremely fashionable but unbearably gloomy—not their fault, of course: it is difficult to be cheerful and positive when one spends half a year waist-deep in snow and darkness. [24] On the other hand, Italian detectives view corruption with a shrug of the shoulders; apparently, [25] he or she spends most of their time making small talk with attractive young women and being fed large meals by their mothers.

[26] Regardless of these bad examples, the English manage to master it time and time again. Despite the claim by the French that they were the first nation to produce a book that had as its hero a detective (a fellow by the name of Arsène Lupin), the first detectives to appear widely in popular literature were actually

23

A) NO CHANGE
B) create convincing
C) create a convincingly
D) creatively convince

24

A) NO CHANGE
B) But
C) Instead,
D) DELETE the underlined portion

25

A) NO CHANGE
B) it spends
C) they spend
D) one spends

26

Which choice most smoothly and effectively introduces the discussion of English detective fiction?

A) NO CHANGE
B) In truth, the English are the only writers who are masters of this kind of fiction.
C) American detective fiction and also Swedish stories pale in comparison to English ones.
D) The only writers who are masters of this kind of fiction are, truthfully, English writers.

English. [27] After the appearance of Sherlock Holmes in the 1887 story "A Study in Scarlet," the English [28] pioneered the development of this kind of writing. In the early part of the 20th century, English [29] author's dominated the genre, beginning with Dorothy L. Sayers, creator of a rather pretentious amateur detective, Lord Peter Wimsey.

The best writers of the English detective novel have been, for the most part, women. [30] Its perhaps surprising then that, regardless of the sex of the novelist, almost every detective Britain has created is male. In British detective novels, we have male inspectors heading the various divisions of the police force, men who are sometimes aided by the intelligence of great male detectives such as Sherlock Holmes and Hercule Poirot.

27

At this point, the writer is considering adding the following sentence.

> Additionally, American writer Edgar Allan Poe's detective C. Auguste Dupin appeared in "The Murders in the Rue Morgue" prior to the publication of the first Lupin story.

Should the writer make this addition here?

A) Yes, because it provides further evidence invalidating the claim that Arsène Lupin was the first detective in literature.
B) Yes, because it introduces a name that will become important later in the passage.
C) No, because it provides information that detracts from the discussion of English detective fiction.
D) No, because it supports the claim that Arsène Lupin was the first detective in literature.

28

A) NO CHANGE
B) took the lead on
C) were cutting edge in
D) were on the forefront in

29

A) NO CHANGE
B) authors
C) authors'
D) author

30

A) NO CHANGE
B) They're
C) Its'
D) It's

CONTINUE

Test 3

[1] **31** Probably the most famous and successful of all crime writers after Conan Doyle, Poirot was created by Agatha Christie. [2] However, another of Christie's detectives, Miss Marple, was the *coup de grâce* against the male domination of crime narratives. [3] Not the typically adventurous detective, she is a modest, elderly spinster who lives in the English village of St. Mary Mead, where she knits and gardens and precisely observes human nature. [4] Miss Marple travels not by Aston Martin* but by British Rail. [5] Yet she understands how people act, react, and think; gently but relentlessly, she always solves the crimes that baffle England's elite crime bureau, Scotland Yard. [6] She is the embodiment of the quiet and forceful intelligence of early twentieth-century women **32** and perhaps the single smartest fictional detective in the canon's history. **33**

*a British manufacturer of luxury cars popularized by the *James Bond* series of movies

31

A) NO CHANGE
B) Poirot was created by Agatha Christie, probably the most famous and successful of all crime writers after Conan Doyle.
C) Agatha Christie created Poirot, probably the most famous and successful of all crime writers after Conan Doyle.
D) Poirot, created by Agatha Christie, probably the most famous and successful of all crime writers after Conan Doyle.

32

The writer wants to conclude by reiterating the main point of the paragraph. Which choice best accomplishes this goal?

A) NO CHANGE
B) and an indispensable addition to a canon historically monopolized by male characters.
C) and exponentially more interesting than Lupin and even Holmes.
D) and notable for being so sharp and strong despite her advanced age.

33

The writer plans to add the following sentence to this paragraph.

> Miss Marple appears in only nine novels and a few short stories, but her impact was—and is—enormous.

To make this paragraph most logical, the sentence should be placed

A) after sentence 1.
B) after sentence 2.
C) after sentence 4.
D) after sentence 5.

CONTINUE

Test 3

Questions 34-44 are based on the following passage.

Here, There, Everywhere: A Brief History of Travel

"To travel hopefully is a better thing than to arrive," wrote Robert Louis Stevenson. Of course, he was referring to the nineteenth century, when the idea of moving freely about the world or even a single country was a rather new and wondrous thing. [34] Before the year 1800, if you wanted to get from one place to another, you walked along muddy tracks if you were poor, or, if you were wealthy, you rode on horseback or in a coach pulled by horses. It did not matter much which mode you used: the journey was [35] excruciating long, exhausting, and uncomfortable.

[36] Conversely, the Industrial Revolution altered everything. [37] John Loudon Macadam set about creating improvements to roads, something that had not been achieved since the days of the Roman Empire. Robert Stephenson drew up plans for his Rocket, which introduced the idea of steam rail traffic [38] by increasing the speed with which the distance between towns and cities could be covered. It had become imperative to be able to move smoothly and safely from factory to city to port. Market forces were already at work.

34

A) NO CHANGE
B) Any time the year 1800
C) In any year before 1800
D) Before 1800

35

A) NO CHANGE
B) excruciatingly long and exhausting and uncomfortable.
C) excruciating, long and exhausting and uncomfortable.
D) excruciatingly long, exhausting, and uncomfortable.

36

A) NO CHANGE
B) Regardless
C) So
D) Then

37

Which choice provides the most specific information regarding how the Industrial Revolution changed transportation?

A) NO CHANGE
B) John Loudon Macadam set about paving dirt roads and making them more traversable
C) John Loudon Macadam set about solving the problems presented by dirt roads
D) John Loudon Macadam set about inventing ways to improve current infrastructure

38

A) NO CHANGE
B) thus increasing
C) and increased
D) and then also increased

CONTINUE

39 The new inventions were not confined to the land. Port-to-port traffic of goods and workers 40 were aided by the new steam-driven vessels. Inevitably, the idea of empire-building followed. Equally inevitably, empires had to give way to 41 new, independent states. This probably explains why, if the nineteenth century can be 42 regarded for a century of industry and progression, the twentieth century can be regarded as a century of destruction and war.

Yet the wars of the twentieth century led to the development of the aeroplane. The jet age arrived, ensuring that travel between countries—indeed, between continents—was achieved in the shortest time possible: have lunch in Paris and see a show on Broadway that evening. After all, the flight time from Paris to New York is now approximately six hours.

39

Which choice best introduces the paragraph?

A) NO CHANGE
B) Old inventions were replaced by new ones.
C) The new inventions also took to the sky.
D) DELETE the underlined sentence and begin the paragraph with the following one.

40

A) NO CHANGE
B) is
C) have been
D) was

41

A) NO CHANGE
B) new: independent.
C) new—independent.
D) new; independent.

42

A) NO CHANGE
B) regarded to be
C) regarded as being
D) regarded as

[1] Yet practical contingencies can get in the way, since speed in the air is one thing, while speed on the ground is another. [2] Although the trip only lasts six hours in theory, to move from Paris to New York actually takes **43** a considerably more time longer. [3] The passenger is advised to be at the airport three hours before the flight takes off. [4] This time is taken up with the examination of baggage, followed by the removal of coat, shoes, belt, and any metal objects, before passengers are shunted through a detector that scans the entire body. [5] Finally, exhausted, they will be allowed to board the plane. [6] Once the plane ride is over, they will walk wearily to passport control, and will then trek further to collect their luggage. [7] Travel technology has certainly evolved, but has not saved us from everyday aggravations. **44**

43

A) NO CHANGE
B) a considerable amount more in time.
C) considerably longer.
D) considerably more time longer.

44

The writer plans to add the following sentence to this paragraph.

Arriving at the destination is no better.

To make this paragraph most logical, the sentence should be placed

A) after sentence 2.
B) after sentence 4.
C) after sentence 5.
D) after sentence 6.

STOP

If you finish before time is called, you may check your work on this section only.
Do not turn to any other section.

No Test Material On This Page

Answer Key

TEST 3

PASSAGE 1

Relatively Speaking: Einstein's Theory of Experience

1.	D
2.	B
3.	C
4.	B
5.	C
6.	C
7.	A
8.	A
9.	D
10.	D
11.	C

PASSAGE 2

No Exam Left Behind

12.	C
13.	A
14.	B
15.	A
16.	B
17.	A
18.	D
19.	C
20.	D
21.	B
22.	D

PASSAGE 3

More than Meets the Eye: Excellence in Detective Fiction

23.	B
24.	D
25.	C
26.	B
27.	C
28.	A
29.	B
30.	D
31.	B
32.	B
33.	D

PASSAGE 4

Here, There, Everywhere: A Brief History of Travel

34.	D
35.	D
36.	D
37.	B
38.	C
39.	A
40.	D
41.	A
42.	D
43.	C
44.	C

Post-Test Analysis

This post-test analysis is essential if you want to see an improvement on your next test. Possible reasons for errors on the four passages in this section are listed here. Place check marks next to the types of errors that pertain to you, or write your own types of errors in the blank spaces.

TIMING AND ACCURACY

◇ Spent too long reading individual passages
◇ Spent too long answering each question
◇ Spent too long on a few difficult questions
◇ Felt rushed and made silly mistakes or random errors
◇ Unable to work quickly using error types and POE
Other: ____________________

APPROACHING THE PASSAGES AND QUESTIONS

◇ Unable to effectively grasp the passage's tone or style
◇ Unable to effectively grasp the passage's topic or stance
◇ Did not understand the context of underlined portions
◇ Did not eliminate false answers using error types
◇ Answered questions using first impressions instead of POE
◇ Answered questions without slotting in and checking final answer
◇ Eliminated NO CHANGE and chose a trap answer
◇ Eliminated correct answer during POE
Other: ____________________

Use this form to better analyze your performance. If you don't understand why you made errors, there is no way that you can correct them!

GRAMMAR AND SENTENCE STRUCTURE

◇ Did not test sentence for subject-verb agreement
◇ Did not identify proper verb form and verb tense
◇ Did not test sentence for pronoun agreement
◇ Did not identify proper pronoun form (subject/object, who/which/when/where/why)
◇ Did not test for proper comparison phrasing (amount/number, between/among) and number agreement
◇ Did not test phrase for correct adverb/adjective usage
◇ Did not see broader sentence structure (parallelism, misplaced modifier)
◇ Did not see flaws in punctuation (colon, semicolon, comma splice, misplaced commas)
◇ Did not see tricky possessives or contractions (its/it's, your/you're)
◇ Did not identify flaws in standard phrases (either . . . or, not only . . . but also, etc.)
◇ Did not use proper phrasing in sentences requiring the subjunctive
Other: ____________________

STYLE, ORGANIZATION, AND WORKING WITH EVIDENCE

◇ Did not notice cases of redundancy and wordiness
◇ Misidentified an expression as redundant or wordy
◇ Did not notice flaws in essay style or excessively informal expressions
◇ Misidentified an expression as stylistically inconsistent or informal
◇ Created the wrong relationship between two sentences
◇ Created the wrong relationship between two paragraphs
◇ Created the wrong placement for an out-of-order paragraph
◇ Did not eliminate faulty or improper English idioms
◇ Did not properly read or analyze an insertion/deletion question
◇ Did not properly read or analyze the information in a graphic
◇ Understood a graphic, but could not identify the correct passage content
Other: ____________________

Test 4

Test 4

Writing Test

35 MINUTES, 44 QUESTIONS

Turn to Section 2 of your answer sheet to answer the questions in this section.

DIRECTIONS

Each passage below is accompanied by a number of questions. For some questions, you will consider how the passage might be revised to improve the expression of ideas. For other questions, you will consider how the passage might be edited to correct errors in sentence structure, usage, or punctuation. A passage or a question may be accompanied by one or more graphics (such as a table or graph) that you will consider as you make revising and editing decisions.

Some questions will direct you to an underlined portion of a passage. Other questions will direct you to a location in a passage or ask you to think about the passage as a whole.

After reading each passage, choose the answer to each question that most effectively improves the quality of writing in the passage or that makes the passage conform to the conventions of standard written English. Many questions include a "NO CHANGE" option. Choose that option if you think the best choice is to leave the relevant portion of the passage as it is.

Questions 1-11 are based on the following passage.

Show Me the Sports Money!

[1] Everyone should put in hard work for some goal. You have to reallocate the time [2] you otherwise spend doing schoolwork, playing, or simply relaxing to practicing and improving your skills. Some say only the affluent have the free time needed to become our greatest competitors. But claiming that only children from wealthy households can become successful athletes is, ultimately, a misunderstanding of the aptitudes that athletes really require.

1

Which choice best introduces the paragraph?

A) NO CHANGE
B) Becoming an athlete requires great sacrifice.
C) Becoming an athlete might not be worth it.
D) Athletes work harder than anyone.

2

A) NO CHANGE
B) you will otherwise spend on schoolwork, playing, and relaxing for the purpose of practicing and improving your skills.
C) you had been spending on schoolwork, playing, and simply relaxing to practicing and improving your skills.
D) you would otherwise spend doing schoolwork, playing, or simply relaxing to practicing and improving your skills.

CONTINUE

Test 4

Talent isn't something that can be bought, no matter how much money you **3** have, the same goes for love and passion. Rather, the athletic ability **4** that can be seen in every famous athlete are intrinsic. This doesn't mean that such athletes could have gotten where they are today without practice, of course, though nobody can achieve all that much through routine practice alone.

With so many children clambering to improve, it's impossible for the coaches and trainers to turn all these aspiring athletes into champions. Some children just don't have either the talent or the motivation to overcome the hurdles that block many competitors from entering professional sports. **5** It's natural for coaches to focus their attention on those young people who show that they are capable of going through the hardships of defeat and injury and are nonetheless able to pick themselves up and work even harder.

3

A) NO CHANGE
B) have; the
C) have; and the
D) have, furthermore, the

4

A) NO CHANGE
B) that you had seen in every famous athlete is intrinsic.
C) that you might see in every famous athlete is being intrinsic.
D) that can be seen in every famous athlete is intrinsic.

5

A) NO CHANGE
B) Its
C) They're
D) Its'

CONTINUE

[1] Stating that money makes a successful athlete is 6 both insulting but also inaccurate. [2] Olympic gymnastics gold-medalist Gabby Douglas has admitted that one of the hurdles she had to clear was a period of homelessness. [3] Gabby was raised by a single mother, who struggled with financial deprivation for years and still provided Gabby with the best athletic training available. 7 [4] Douglas's story of gain after loss is 8 one between many that shows us that money doesn't define ability. 9

6

A) NO CHANGE
B) insulting but also inaccurate, too.
C) not only insulting and also inaccurate.
D) both insulting and inaccurate.

7

At this point, the writer is considering adding the following sentence.

> Gabby became not only an Olympic athlete but also a gold medalist.

Should the writer make this addition here?

A) Yes, because it provides information regarding the extent of Gabby Douglas's success.
B) Yes, because it explains how difficult a struggle Douglas endured.
C) No, because it provides information already established in the paragraph.
D) No, because it should be placed elsewhere in the passage.

8

A) NO CHANGE
B) one among many
C) one between others
D) one of them

9

The writer plans to add the following sentence to this paragraph.

> There have been hundreds of athletes who have come from humble beginnings and charted unique courses to the very summit of success.

To make this paragraph most logical, the sentence should be placed

A) after sentence 1.
B) after sentence 2.
C) after sentence 3.
D) after sentence 4.

10 The threat of homelessness is a serious concern for many in America; however, a willingness to sacrifice is important above all else. **11** No matter how much dollars you pour into hunting down the best coaches, the best training environment, and the best equipment, if you don't have the skills or passion for the sport, your efforts will never bear fruit. As Tae Kwon Do master Kerry Roy puts it, "If you really want something badly enough, you'll find a way to get it."

10

Which choice best introduces the paragraph?

A) NO CHANGE
B) Strong teachers certainly help to foster athletes' success
C) It is difficult to quantify how many people could be better athletes with proper training
D) Granted, money does factor into the education of an athlete

11

A) NO CHANGE
B) No matter how much money
C) No mater how many money
D) No matter how many the amount of dollars

CONTINUE

Test 4

Questions 12-22 are based on the following passage.

Mapping Khartoum, Past and Present

[1] I lived and worked in Khartoum for four years. [2] One afternoon, about a month after my arrival in [12] the city: a friend took me to Shambart Bridge. [3] On the Eastern bank was the administrative and business capital of Khartoum, the great Mosque, and the Hilton Hotel. [4] On the Western bank sprawled the traditional Arab city of Omdurman with its palm-shaded gardens and white-walled traditional buildings. [5] Between these two cities and below our feet flowed the Nile River, which [13] split into two branches, both spanned by the Shambart Bridge. [14]

The two stretches of the river may meet here, but they do little more than shrug shoulders together. [15] There will be no mingling until they have flowed, side by side, for many miles northwards. It is bizarre to realize that although there is some cultivated land on each bank of the river, it is no more than a verdant strip of just under five hundred meters in width. The fertile land terminates with no warning. [16] The poorly pruned shrubs and untamed vines on these banks are often thought to be sacred. [17] Thereafter, they are replaced abruptly by unremittingly hard, flat, gray-brown, baked earth that stretches endlessly away into the anonymous blaze of the heat-hazed horizon. Nothing lives out there; indeed, that bleakness could never have held life.

12

A) NO CHANGE
B) the city—a
C) the city, a
D) the city. A

13

A) NO CHANGE
B) splits
C) is splitting
D) had split

14

To make this paragraph most logical, sentence 1 should be placed

A) where it is now.
B) after sentence 2.
C) after sentence 4.
D) after sentence 5.

15

A) NO CHANGE
B) Both will never mingle until the time when
C) They do not mingle until
D) Neither will be mingling until the place where

16

Which choice best reinforces the point of the previous sentence?

A) NO CHANGE
B) The poorly pruned shrubs and untamed vines in this stretch are eerily serene.
C) Though the shrubs are poorly pruned and the vines untamed, this stretch along the river is an undeniably gorgeous sight to behold.
D) It is as though the poorly pruned shrubs and untamed vines hit an invisible wall, unable to pass through to the other side.

17

A) NO CHANGE
B) Fortunately,
C) Sometimes,
D) Without,

CONTINUE

Test 4

There is a road that goes directly from North Khartoum to **18** Port Said. Port Said is in the North Eastern corner of Sudan. Although there are no traffic signs, now and again one comes **19** around a small courtyard of dusty buildings, an antique petrol pump, and large urns containing water for the refreshment of passing camels and their herders. **20** No other sign of habitation or life are visible. To the east, the land appears to be rising, and one becomes aware of barren rock and drifting sand. In the far distance there appear to be man-made shapes: it is hard to tell. As they come closer, these shapes resolve themselves in to a wall against which the sand has drifted. Behind this wall, there appear to be stunted pyramids, a myriad of them.

This is Meroe, although there is no printed sign to tell the visitor that this is all that is left of this ancient city of the **21** Kush, the Kush civilization came before the Pharaohs of Egypt. There is nothing else here, only two hundred small pyramids, each windowless but with an entrance porch facing east, away from the Nile. This is the burial ground of the Kushite kings, deserted and decaying. The visitor shudders a little at the eeriness of the place. For how many eons have these edifices stood here, alone with **22** their secrets?

18

Which choice most effectively combines the sentences at the underlined portion?

A) Port Said, which is to be found in
B) Port Said that you find in
C) Port Said, which one might find if looking in
D) Port Said in

19

A) NO CHANGE
B) within
C) across
D) out

20

A) NO CHANGE
B) No other sign of habitation or life is visible.
C) There is no other signs of habitation or life visible.
D) There are no other habitation or a life sign to be found.

21

A) NO CHANGE
B) Kush, and the civilization came before the Pharaohs of Egypt.
C) Kush; however, the civilization came before the Pharaohs of Egypt.
D) Kush, a civilization that came before the Pharaohs of Egypt.

22

A) NO CHANGE
B) there
C) they're
D) its

CONTINUE

Questions 23-33 are based on the following passage and supplementary material.

Raised for Weakness: Against "Purebred" Animals

Pedigree. The word alone [23] illicits notions of distinction, aristocracy, and grandeur; even cats and dogs now assume ideal, "pedigreed" forms. Thousands of years of domestication have given us remarkable variations in the attributes of these animals, and some feline and canine qualities are now more sought-after than others. Yet appearance and personality, two of the major considerations for [24] breeding—can often only be stabilized through restrictive measures. In order to maintain, say, even-tempered blue-eyed kittens, one must breed cats that possess these qualities to keep the wanted traits in circulation within a relatively small group.

[25] Though time-honored, major health concerns often arise from such inbreeding practices; animal welfare groups are trying to spread awareness of these problems and thus change the breeding system. These [26] iconoclasts, disdaining the standards of perfection delineated by breed registries such as the American Kennel Club. The goal is to prevent the creation of shortsighted and unhealthy extremes by protecting animal health before the relationship between man and animal becomes [27] hopelessly skewed.

23

A) NO CHANGE
B) elicit
C) illicit
D) elicits

24

A) NO CHANGE
B) breeding, can
C) breeding can
D) breeding; can

25

A) NO CHANGE
B) Such inbreeding practices entail major health concerns, though time-honored
C) Though time-honored, such inbreeding practices entail major health concerns
D) Such inbreeding practices are time-honored, creating major health concerns

26

A) NO CHANGE
B) disdaining iconoclasts
C) iconoclasts disdaining
D) iconoclasts disdain

27

A) NO CHANGE
B) hopeless skewed.
C) skewed to a degree that becomes hopeless.
D) without hope, skewed.

CONTINUE

For example, a registry-qualifying German Shepherd looks nothing like the German Shepherds you typically see at a dog park. These real-life specimens are long-bodied with low, bushy tails. But the most striking difference between the idealized Shepherd and the actual animal involves poise and stature. Continuous inbreeding to capture the "correct" posture configuration has given the Shepherd hind leg bones that are bowed into a permanent hunch. A lap around the show track highlights the typical Shepherd's awkward stride, which hinders the dog's ability to perform **28** intense acrobatics and is a far cry from the progenitor Shepherd's steady gait.

The German Shepherd is not the only breed that has suffered inbreeding-related afflictions. In fact, a recent study of over twenty dog breeds shows that, on the whole, purebreds are more likely to suffer from **29** blindness, high cholesterol, and arthritis than their mixed breed counterparts. Furthermore, the research indicates that **30** purebred dogs suffer from arthritis sixty percent of the time.

28

A) NO CHANGE
B) fierce
C) deep
D) vivid

29

Which choice most accurately interprets the information provided in the chart?

A) NO CHANGE
B) blindness and high cholesterol
C) arthritis
D) blindness and arthritis

30

Which choice is an accurate interpretation of the data in the chart?

A) NO CHANGE
B) sixty percent of arthritic ailments inflict mixed breed dogs.
C) sixty percent of purebred dogs suffer from arthritis.
D) purebred dogs can withstand sixty percent of arthritic pain.

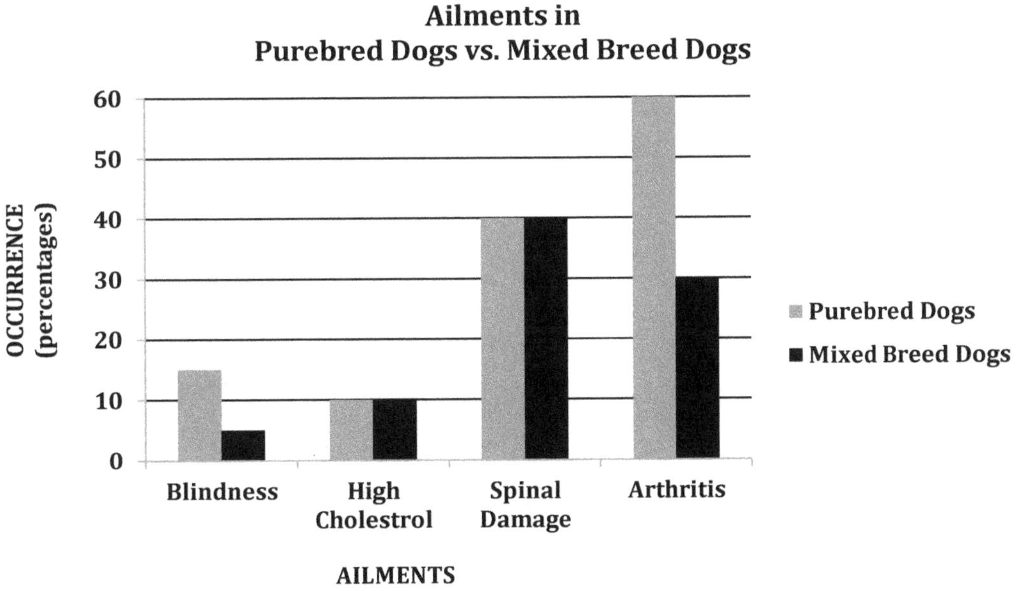

[31] This problem is not limited to our canine companions: for instance, the hairless Sphinx cat has been bred for its suede-like touch but—because there is nothing to protect this animal from the environment—is vulnerable to ailments such as skin cancer and hypothermia. [32] Similarly, clipping the wings of household birds is considered to be a cruel and unnecessary practice.

Anti-inbreeding activists may be advocating for too much change too [33] fast. Their ethics are fundamentally right. How much longer will breed supersede quality of life for dogs and cats? Not long, let us hope. After all, excruciating fashions such as foot-binding in Imperial China and tight corsets in medieval Europe fell into near-complete disuse as the centuries progressed. If history repeats itself, maybe the animals will also get a reprieve.

31

Which choice most smoothly and effectively transitions between paragraphs?

A) NO CHANGE
B) Cats have troubles
C) This problem extends beyond the realm of dogs into the realm of cats and most likely other domestic animals as well
D) Our canine companions suffer from this problem, but others are suffering and we shouldn't forget it

32

At this point, the writer would like to add a concluding sentence that reinforces that in-breeding can lead to medical problems for other animals. Which choice best accomplishes this?

A) NO CHANGE
B) Moreover, selective breeding of livestock has halted evolution by genetic variation.
C) Likewise, the Himalayan cat's meticulously bred squatty nose predisposes it to pneumonia and other respiratory ailments.
D) Systematic inbreeding of laboratory mice is of great importance to biomedical research.

33

Which choice most effectively combines the sentences at the underlined portion?

A) NO CHANGE
B) fast; however, their
C) fast, and their
D) fast because their

CONTINUE

Test 4

Questions 34-44 are based on the following passage.

David Lean, Epic Filmmaker

[1] David Lean was born in London in 1908. [2] His move into full-scale directing came in 1942 when he worked on *In Which We Serve* with Noel Coward. [3] He started his working life in a chartered accountant's office, where he was bored; consequently, he left and took a temporary job as a tea-boy at Gaumont Studios. [4] He graduated to the role of clapper-boy and from there to the heights of Third Assistant Director. [5] This led to a real promotion: for several years, he worked as a film editor. [6] Lean went on to direct fifteen films in forty-nine years, often also taking on writing and editing responsibilities. [7] That may seem like a surprisingly small number of **34** films, and he was nominated for an Academy Award for Best Director for seven of his films and won twice. [8] In **35** their list of the best British films ever made, the British Film Institute includes eleven of his films. **36**

34

A) NO CHANGE
B) films because
C) films; however,
D) film, so

35

A) NO CHANGE
B) there
C) they're
D) its

36

To make this paragraph most logical, sentence 2 should be placed

A) where it is now.
B) after sentence 3.
C) after sentence 5.
D) after sentence 8.

CONTINUE

A film directed by David Lean has a sense of place, whether the film is set in the deserts of Arabia or the workhouses of Dickens' London. Lean makes us understand the [37] effects these places have on the people who inhabit them. There is a shot early in *Lawrence of Arabia* that illustrates this [38] clearly, Lawrence is making his first foray on camel into the Arabian Desert. His guide is his with him. As the two move on, Lean allows the camera to rise gently. [39] During the time in which Lean was shooting the film, such nuanced camera maneuvers could only be performed by the most skilled technicians. This tiny movement transforms what could be simply a narrative link or an observation of the dwarfing quality of the desert into a comment about the central character. Lawrence is entering into his milieu, calmly and acceptingly.

37

A) NO CHANGE
B) affects these places have
C) affects this place has
D) effects this place has

38

A) NO CHANGE
B) clearly: Lawrence
C) clearly, and Lawrence
D) clearly because Lawrence

39

The writer is considering deleting the underlined sentence. Should the sentence be kept or deleted?

A) Kept, because it contains information essential to the discussion of the sense of place Lean creates in his work.
B) Kept, because it provides necessary information explaining why Lean was so adored by the British Film Institute.
C) Deleted, because it detracts from the discussion of the sense of place Lean creates in his work.
D) Deleted, because it contains information that invalidates other information in the paragraph.

CONTINUE

[40] Later in the film, another character—the commanding Sherif Ali—makes his stunning first appearance at a watering hole. For almost a minute of screen time, the camera, like Lawrence himself, stares into the shimmering distance as what at first appears to be a mirage steadily [41] coming closer. There is no sound beyond the padding of the camel. Then, a sudden flurry of cuts brings about the death of Lawrence's guide and leaves Lawrence gazing up into the face of Sherif Ali, who is practical and unmoved. No other director would have had the courage to hold that entrance for [42] so long an amount of time.

Lean's career reached a pinnacle with the spectacular triumphs of *The Bridge over the River Kwai*, *Lawrence of Arabia*, *Doctor Zhivago*, and *A Passage to India*. [43] Instead, his real triumph was a black-and-white British film he made in 1945 and titled *Brief Encounter*. It is a quiet examination of a married woman and a stranger whom she briefly meets in the refreshment bar of a local train station. [44] Lean is truly an unparalleled director.

40

Which choice most specifically introduces the discussion of the scene examined in the paragraph?

A) NO CHANGE
B) Other scenes in the movie have excellent dialogue that reveals the stoic temperaments of Lean's characters.
C) Sherif Ali is a character who appears later in the film, arriving at a watering hole.
D) This is not Lean's only impressive film, even though *Lawrence of Arabia* ably captures vastness of its desert setting.

41

A) NO CHANGE
B) come
C) comes
D) came

42

A) NO CHANGE
B) an amount of time so long.
C) so long.
D) that much.

43

A) NO CHANGE
B) However,
C) Although,
D) Really,

44

The writer wants to conclude the passage by explaining why *Brief Encounter* stands out. Which choice best accomplishes this goal?

A) NO CHANGE
B) Most of his films were shot in color.
C) It may not be my favorite film of all time, but some adore it.
D) It is truly a piece of classic cinema, full of silent observation and understatement.

STOP

If you finish before time is called, you may check your work on this section only.
Do not turn to any other section.

Answer Key

TEST 4

PASSAGE 1

Show Me the Sports Money!

1.	B
2.	D
3.	B
4.	D
5.	A
6.	D
7.	C
8.	B
9.	A
10.	D
11.	B

PASSAGE 2

Mapping Khartoum, Past and Present

12.	C
13.	B
14.	A
15.	C
16.	D
17.	A
18.	D
19.	C
20.	B
21.	D
22.	A

PASSAGE 3

Raised for Weakness: Against "Purebred" Animals

23.	D
24.	B
25.	C
26.	D
27.	A
28.	A
29.	D
30.	C
31.	A
32.	C
33.	B

PASSAGE 4

David Lean, Epic Filmmaker

34.	C
35.	D
36.	C
37.	A
38.	B
39.	C
40.	A
41.	C
42.	C
43.	B
44.	D

Post-Test Analysis

This post-test analysis is essential if you want to see an improvement on your next test. Possible reasons for errors on the four passages in this section are listed here. Place check marks next to the types of errors that pertain to you, or write your own types of errors in the blank spaces.

TIMING AND ACCURACY

◇ Spent too long reading individual passages
◇ Spent too long answering each question
◇ Spent too long on a few difficult questions
◇ Felt rushed and made silly mistakes or random errors
◇ Unable to work quickly using error types and POE
Other: ______________________________

APPROACHING THE PASSAGES AND QUESTIONS

◇ Unable to effectively grasp the passage's tone or style
◇ Unable to effectively grasp the passage's topic or stance
◇ Did not understand the context of underlined portions
◇ Did not eliminate false answers using error types
◇ Answered questions using first impressions instead of POE
◇ Answered questions without slotting in and checking final answer
◇ Eliminated NO CHANGE and chose a trap answer
◇ Eliminated correct answer during POE
Other: ______________________________

Use this form to better analyze your performance. If you don't understand why you made errors, there is no way that you can correct them!

GRAMMAR AND SENTENCE STRUCTURE

◇ Did not test sentence for subject-verb agreement
◇ Did not identify proper verb form and verb tense
◇ Did not test sentence for pronoun agreement
◇ Did not identify proper pronoun form (subject/object, who/which/when/where/why)
◇ Did not test for proper comparison phrasing (amount/number, between/among) and number agreement
◇ Did not test phrase for correct adverb/adjective usage
◇ Did not see broader sentence structure (parallelism, misplaced modifier)
◇ Did not see flaws in punctuation (colon, semicolon, comma splice, misplaced commas)
◇ Did not see tricky possessives or contractions (its/it's, your/you're)
◇ Did not identify flaws in standard phrases (either . . . or, not only . . . but also, etc.)
◇ Did not use proper phrasing in sentences requiring the subjunctive
Other: ______________________________

STYLE, ORGANIZATION, AND WORKING WITH EVIDENCE

◇ Did not notice cases of redundancy and wordiness
◇ Misidentified an expression as redundant or wordy
◇ Did not notice flaws in essay style or excessively informal expressions
◇ Misidentified an expression as stylistically inconsistent or informal
◇ Created the wrong relationship between two sentences
◇ Created the wrong relationship between two paragraphs
◇ Created the wrong placement for an out-of-order paragraph
◇ Did not eliminate faulty or improper English idioms
◇ Did not properly read or analyze an insertion/deletion question
◇ Did not properly read or analyze the information in a graphic
◇ Understood a graphic, but could not identify the correct passage content
Other: ______________________________

Test 5

Test 5

Writing Test

35 MINUTES, 44 QUESTIONS

Turn to Section 2 of your answer sheet to answer the questions in this section.

DIRECTIONS

Each passage below is accompanied by a number of questions. For some questions, you will consider how the passage might be revised to improve the expression of ideas. For other questions, you will consider how the passage might be edited to correct errors in sentence structure, usage, or punctuation. A passage or a question may be accompanied by one or more graphics (such as a table or graph) that you will consider as you make revising and editing decisions.

Some questions will direct you to an underlined portion of a passage. Other questions will direct you to a location in a passage or ask you to think about the passage as a whole.

After reading each passage, choose the answer to each question that most effectively improves the quality of writing in the passage or that makes the passage conform to the conventions of standard written English. Many questions include a "NO CHANGE" option. Choose that option if you think the best choice is to leave the relevant portion of the passage as it is.

Questions 1-11 are based on the following passage.

America the Diverse: First-Generation Lifestyles

— 1 —

Today, when you walk into a supermarket, above the normal humming of the air conditioning, the harsh scraping of shopping cart wheels, and the soft lilting of songs on the radio, you can hear occasional snippets of dialogue from places all over the world. After **1** one turns into the cereal aisle, maybe you'll walk past a cheerful greeting from India. Roll your cart past the dairy section and you'll hear easy banter from China. As you meander through the store, you'll pass a smile from Brazil, a question from Kenya, and perhaps an apology from France.

1

A) NO CHANGE
B) you turn
C) they turn
D) you will turn

CONTINUE

—2—

Ironically, works of fiction offer some of the clearest perspectives on these real-life first-generation tensions. Perhaps Amy Tan, author of *The Joy Luck Club* (a novel featuring four Chinese immigrant mothers and their American-born daughters), **2** say it best. As one of the daughters remarks about her mother, "I think how to explain this, recalling the words Harold and I have used with each other in the past . . . But these are words she could never understand." For first-generation Americans, the biggest struggle is deciding on a cultural identity. These children are born American, are members of distant cultures, are educated in American schools, and are instructed at home in the values of their ancestors. **3** Due largely to its popularity, *The Joy Luck Club* was turned into a movie in 1993.

2

A) NO CHANGE
B) has said
C) is saying
D) says

3

The writer is considering deleting the underlined sentence. Should the writer make this deletion?

A) Yes, because the underlined sentence includes information that contradicts the main argument of the paragraph.
B) Yes, because the underlined sentence presents information that does not help the main argument of the paragraph.
C) No, because the underlined sentence presents information necessary for the main argument of the paragraph.
D) No, because the underlined sentence further defines a key term important to the passage.

CONTINUE

— 3 —

[1] 4 Some call America the melting pot; I think that they likely have good reason. [2] Since 5 their first colonization in the fifteenth century, the New World has attracted all types of people, from the tight-lipped Puritans who settled in New England to the debt-laden criminals who were sent to Georgia. [3] With immigrants from 6 everywhere flocking to the country from all corners of the world, America's melting pot now contains more ingredients than anyone can count. 7

4

Which choice best introduces the paragraph?

A) NO CHANGE
B) America isn't known as the melting pot for nothing.
C) The melting pot is a thing people call America, and they mean it.
D) The melting pot is a weird term but not used to describe America for no reason.

5

A) NO CHANGE
B) its
C) it's
D) it has been

6

A) NO CHANGE
B) everywhere, flocking to the country from all corners of the world
C) all corners of the world flocking to the country
D) all corners of the world that flock from everywhere to the country

7

The writer plans to add the following sentence to this paragraph.

> Today, America's diversity has risen far beyond the sole distinction of religion.

To make this paragraph most logical, the sentence should be placed

A) before sentence 1.
B) before sentence 2.
C) before sentence 3.
D) after sentence 3.

— 4 —

The children of [8] immigrants—known as "first-generation Americans," have centuries of their home cultures pumping through their veins, yet these relative newcomers must try to comprehend what is shaping them on the outside. These children are caught between two worlds: that of their well-remembered ancestors and [9] an alluring American culture. With parents who had to risk all in order to get an education and have the opportunity to find a new life in America, first-generation children face enormous expectations. In the eyes of many immigrant parents, a person without an education is a person without a future. [10] However, many second- and third-generation Americans also face strong pressure to do well in school.

— 5 —

It's true that first-generation Americans have many advantages that seem to float them to the top, but first they have to balance the two cultures that are trying to shape them. Nevertheless, once these issues of identity have been addressed, a new story begins, maybe even one that can be told perfectly in many languages.

Question [11] asks about the previous passage as a whole.

8

A) NO CHANGE
B) immigrants, known
C) immigrants; known
D) immigrants known

9

A) NO CHANGE
B) an alluringly American culture.
C) that of a culture alluringly American in its nature.
D) that of an alluring American culture.

10

The writer wants to conclude the paragraph by suggesting that first-generation Americans face many difficulties. Which choice best accomplishes this goal?

A) NO CHANGE
B) However, the pressure of getting the best grades isn't the only burden these first-generation Americans carry.
C) However, this pressure to do well in school is often paired with strong familial support.
D) However, the burden of getting the best grades isn't unique to people living in America.

Think about the previous passage as a whole as you answer question 11.

11

To make the passage most logical, paragraph 2 should be placed

A) where it is now.
B) after paragraph 3.
C) after paragraph 4.
D) after paragraph 5.

CONTINUE

Questions 12-22 are based on the following passage.

Oh Give Me a Home, Where the Mountain Sheep Roam

The mountain ranges of the American West rise far above the zone of life and have summits that are deeply overladen with ancient snow and ice. Yet the upper slopes and summits of the Rocky Mountains of Colorado and of the Sierra of California [12] is not barren and lifeless, even though these highest reaches stand far above the timber-line. There are no other mountain ranges in the world [13] where they show such varied and vigorous arrays of life above the tree-line. How different are the climatic conditions in the Rocky Mountains and in the Sierra, where the timber-line is at approximately eleven thousand, five hundred feet, or a vertical mile higher than it is in the Alps!

The range is distinguished by a spate of lakes. Glaciers the world over have been the chief makers of lake-basins, large and small. These basins were formed in darkness, and hundreds and even thousands of years may have been required for the glaciers to carve and set the gem-like [14] ponds' whose presence now adds so much to the light and beauty of the rugged mountain ranges. In descending from the mountain-summits, ponderous glaciers and ice rivers came down steep slopes and precipitous walls with such momentum that their great weight [15] bared irresistibly against the earth. [16] Concurrently, on the lakes and tarns lie fields of grass and meadows of luminous flowers.

12

A) NO CHANGE
B) are
C) were
D) was

13

A) NO CHANGE
B) who
C) when
D) that

14

A) NO CHANGE
B) ponds whose
C) pond's whose
D) ponds' who's

15

A) NO CHANGE
B) bore
C) bear
D) bears

16

A) NO CHANGE
B) Moreover,
C) Now,
D) However,

CONTINUE

These idyllic pastures are the home **17** where many mountain sheep live. Large numbers of these animals like to rest comfortably **18** within the shattered shoulder of granite between Long's Peak and Mt. Meeker. Imagine the patriarchal ram—heavy and proud—in the mountain heights. Above the limits of tree growth and just over two miles above the surface of the sea, numerous wild sheep reside. **19** Here the lambs are born, and from this place the herd makes spring foraging excursions far down the slopes into warmer zones, seeking out greenstuffs not yet in season on the heights.

17

A) NO CHANGE
B) of many mountain sheep who live there.
C) of many mountain sheep.
D) where you can find many mountain sheep.

18

A) NO CHANGE
B) among
C) despite
D) without

19

At this point, the writer is considering adding the following sentence.

Many flocks reside at an altitude of twelve thousand feet.

Should the writer make this addition here?

A) Yes, because it provides an example supporting the main point of the paragraph.
B) Yes, because it contradicts a faulty assumption likely to be made by many readers.
C) No, because it simply restates information provided in the previous sentence.
D) No, because it presents information that is unrelated to the paragraph's main subject.

CONTINUE

[20] <u>However, the sheep might do better to stay at lower altitudes.</u> Warm coverings of soft hair protect these animals from the coldest blasts. Winter quarters appear to be mostly in localities from which winds regularly sweep the snow. This sweeping completed naturally by the elements prevents the snow from burying food beyond reach, and lessens the danger that these short-legged mountaineers will become snowbound. The sheep commonly [21] <u>endure</u> wind-storms by crowding closely against the lee side of a ledge. Now and then the sheep are so deeply drifted over with snow that many of the weaker ones perish, unable to wallow out. The snow-slide, the white terror of the heights, occasionally carries off an entire flock of these bold animals. [22] <u>Amidst the snow, these majestic creatures stick together to withstand their eternal winter.</u>

20

Which choice provides the best introduction to the paragraph?

A) NO CHANGE
B) Indeed, the sheep have adapted to the mountain climate.
C) Indeed, I don't know how these sheep endure such extreme conditions.
D) However, the sheep are not the only mammals to live in these mountains.

21

A) NO CHANGE
B) carry on
C) preserve
D) maintain

22

The writer wants to conclude by suggesting that, despite the accompanying dangers, living above the tree-line is a preferable option for the sheep. Which choice best accomplishes this goal?

A) NO CHANGE
B) Still, most of these sheep steadfastly spend their lives high in the Rockies, looking down at the world below.
C) However, the risk of residing at lower altitudes among mountain lions and other predators would prove far greater.
D) Regardless, none of these sheep could manage to live in the highest altitudes of the Himalayas and other taller mountain ranges.

CONTINUE

Questions 23-33 are based on the following passage.

To Act, or Not to Act?

[1] Acting is more than mere craft. [2] 23 To categorize acting as a craft is to liken actors to plumbers: they are certainly adept in what they do, but there is no genuine production of art. [3] In this view, the actor is the mere transposition of the playwright's words from page to presence, from vision to visage, from ideas to identity. [4] In actuality, he is an artist who adds universal depth to a specific character. [5] Whether others want to accept this reality or not, an actor is the bridge into the 24 dramatists world, and part of that connection lies within a basic human need to relate to something concrete: the actor is the touchstone. 25

26 An actor's physical attributes, inflecting his voice deliberately, and even his smallest gestures fuse into someone that the audience can identify and place in a specific context. And the viewers, despite the dramatist's abstract intentions, also supply an exceedingly indispensable characteristic of live performance: interpretation. Without actors, a playwright would never be able to 27 effective communicate his or her intentions to the audience.

23

A) NO CHANGE
B) Categorizing acting as a craft is like if you liken actors to plumbers
C) To categorize acting as a craft, you must also liken them to plumbers
D) To categorize acting as a craft is for you to liken actors to plumbers

24

A) NO CHANGE
B) dramatist's
C) dramatists'
D) dramatist

25

The writer plans to add the following sentence to this paragraph.

> However, the actor is not a dumb instrument used to implement a playwright's work.

To make this paragraph most logical, the sentence should be placed

A) after sentence 1.
B) after sentence 2.
C) after sentence 3.
D) after sentence 4.

26

A) NO CHANGE
B) An actor's physical attributes, deliberate vocal inflection, and even his smallest gestures fusing
C) An actor attributing physically, inflecting deliberately, and gesturing precisely fuses
D) An actor's physical attributes, his deliberate vocal inflections, and even his smallest gestures fuse

27

A) NO CHANGE
B) effectively communicate
C) with great effect communicate
D) communicate effective

28 Reading a script is okay, but part of a full theatrical experience is to witness the physical manifestation of the playwright's characters. Actors bring in their own experiences, skills, and training to fully embody unique stage personalities. Although performed many times, the character of Troy Maxson in August Wilson's *Fences* will always be inextricably tied to any given **29** actor's portrayal, each performer provides a new vantage from which to view and interpret Wilson's character.

28

Which choice best introduces the paragraph?

A) NO CHANGE
B) Go ahead and read a script, but
C) It is surely possible to read a playwright's script, but
D) Scripts are available to read if you want, but

29

A) NO CHANGE
B) actor's portrayal, each performer providing a new vantage from which to view and interpret Wilson's character.
C) actor's portrayal and each performer provides a new vantage from which to view and interpret Wilson's character.
D) actor's portrayal; and each performer provides a new vantage from which to view and interpret Wilson's character.

CONTINUE

[30] Just like all the other kinds, it is difficult to perceive and judge what is truly defined as art, but defining what isn't may be even more important. The truth is that [31] acting, like all art—is an intangible concept because its merit is governed by a system that is primarily subjective, meaning that there is no standardized and indisputable method for distinguishing an outstanding performance from an inept one. Rather, a meaningful critique of acting depends on considerations of delivery and execution in a given moment. [32] To put it plainly, acting is like figure skating. The actor can be trained and versed in his craft, [33] since at the end of it all, the performance itself is the art, not the mere presence of the actor.

Should all of this mean that acting is definitely an art form? The concept of "art" is perhaps too ill-defined to provide any clear answer. But it is unmistakable that acting, at the very least, is a mode of expression that transcends simple showmanship and performance by offering access to profound, universal truths.

30

A) NO CHANGE
B) Just because all art forms share one important attribute
C) Since acting is like other types of art
D) As with any mode of art

31

A) NO CHANGE
B) acting—like all art
C) acting; like all art
D) acting like all art

32

The writer is considering deleting the underlined sentence. Should the sentence be kept or deleted?

A) Kept, because it provides a useful point of comparison for the passage's main subject.
B) Kept, because it introduces a key term that will become important for the remainder of the passage.
C) Deleted, because it contradicts the paragraph's discussion of the subjectivity of art.
D) Deleted, because it introduces a comparison that is irrelevant to the paragraph's main subject.

33

A) NO CHANGE
B) but
C) and
D) nor

CONTINUE

Test 5

Questions 34-44 are based on the following passage and supplementary material.

A New Horizon for 3D Film

[1] Contrary to common misconceptions, 3D films really aren't entirely new. [2] In fact, 3D film has existed for nearly a century now. [3] [34] Additionally, the format's fame is a much newer phenomenon. [4] It doesn't matter in what genre a given movie resides, whether [35] it's animated or filmed with red carpet actors; if a film wants to join the "it" crowd, it must carry the 3D label. [36]

34

A) NO CHANGE
B) Furthermore,
C) However,
D) On the one hand,

35

A) NO CHANGE
B) its
C) they're
D) their

36

The writer plans to add the following sentence to this paragraph.

> If you walk into a cinema today, you will find that at least half of the showings are in 3D.

To make this paragraph most logical, the sentence should be placed

A) before sentence 1.
B) after sentence 1.
C) before sentence 3.
D) after sentence 3.

CONTINUE

[37] Recent statistics indicate that people enjoy 3D and 2D film showings equally. [38] Comparing the revenues for the same movie shown in 3D and 2D show that, in almost every scenario, [39] the 3D version out-earns the 2D version by millions of dollars. Moreover, the number of 3D screen installations in theaters around the country more than doubled in 2011,

37

Which choice best interprets the data in the chart?

A) NO CHANGE
B) Recent statistics indicate that 3D showings earn better critical reviews than do 2D showings.
C) Recent statistics indicate that 3D showings do comparatively better at the box office than 2D showings.
D) Recent statistics indicate that 3D film showings are becoming less popular.

38

A) NO CHANGE
B) Comparing the revenues for the same movie shown in both 3D and 2D show
C) Comparing the 3D and 2D revenues for the same movie shows
D) To compare the revenues for the same movie in 2D and 3D is showing

39

Which choice most accurately interprets the data in the chart?

A) NO CHANGE
B) the 2D version out-earns the 3D version by millions of dollars.
C) the 3D version out-earns the 2D version by hundreds of millions of dollars.
D) the two versions earn nearly equal revenues.

2D vs. 3D Film Revenues

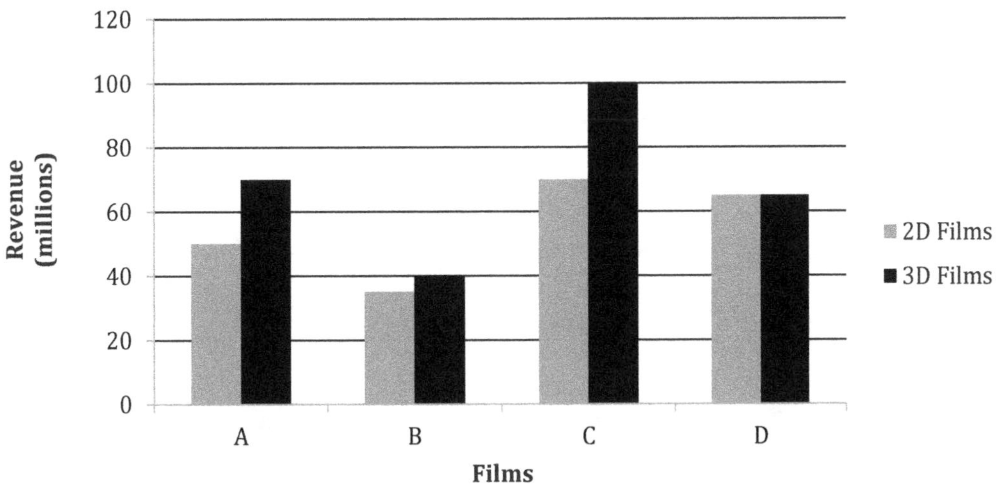

CONTINUE

according to *Box Office Pro* Magazine. **40** Not only do people seem to flock to the concept of 3D film, and directors also see this fad as a chance to cash in.

Philip Bowcock, Cineworld financial director, dubs 3D film "a fad with legs . . . The right films will do well. 3D will keep going." However, the most recent surveys of the rising generation may prove otherwise. **41** This fact is evident in the data. 3D film has become prosaic, so viewers are more likely to complain about the resulting motion sickness than to focus on the attractions of this film type. **42** With new technological breakthroughs appearing every day and with film viewers demanding higher stakes than a series of once-impressive three-dimensional effects.

40

A) NO CHANGE

B) Not only do people seem to flock to the concept of 3D film; but directors also see this fad as a chance to cash in.

C) Not only do people seem to flock to the concept of 3D film, but also directors see this fad as a chance to cash in.

D) Not only are people seeming to flock to the concept of 3D film; however, directors are seeing this fad as a chance to cash in.

41

Which choice provides the most specific example that reinforces the previous sentence?

A) NO CHANGE

B) Many people provided insightful and even unexpected responses to the different survey questions.

C) The surveys reveal very useful information for film studios.

D) Most respondents indicated that they are becoming less impressed with the novelty of 3D films.

42

A) NO CHANGE

B) With new technological breakthroughs appearing every day and film viewers demand higher stakes

C) With new technological breakthroughs appearing every day, film viewers demanding higher stakes

D) With new technological breakthroughs appearing every day, film viewers demand higher stakes

CONTINUE

Headache aside, the overwhelming cry from the opposition is that 3D film requires emotional and narrative substance to be a truly worthwhile form of entertainment. **43** Basically, once the preliminary awe of 3D wears off, the viewers go back to square one: the actual movie plot. Most viewers see the rise of 3D for every movie as an attempt to cover up poorly written screenplays. Who cares if the story itself isn't exciting? The visual effects will surely make up for that!

In this day and age, no technological innovation can stay fresh forever; however, 3D cinema may yet hang on. Technicians are currently working on adding new perks to the idea of 3D viewing. According to CNN, South Korean researchers are developing a way to create the 3D environment without glasses. Famed director Steven Spielberg even remarked, "I'm certainly hoping that 3D gets to the point where people do not notice it, because then it becomes another tool." If the technical quality of 3D cinema can continue to improve without significantly compromising artistry or increasing **44** prices; one day 3D film may no longer be just a fad.

43

A) NO CHANGE
B) Concurrently,
C) Without further ado,
D) Previously,

44

A) NO CHANGE
B) prices, and one
C) prices: one
D) prices, one

STOP

If you finish before time is called, you may check your work on this section only.
Do not turn to any other section.

Answer Key

TEST 5

PASSAGE 1

America the Diverse: First-Generation Lifestyles

1. B
2. D
3. B
4. B
5. B
6. C
7. C
8. B
9. D
10. B
11. C

PASSAGE 2

Oh Give Me a Home, Where the Mountain Sheep Roam

12. B
13. D
14. B
15. B
16. C
17. C
18. A
19. C
20. B
21. A
22. C

PASSAGE 3

To Act, or Not to Act?

23. A
24. B
25. C
26. D
27. B
28. C
29. B
30. D
31. B
32. A
33. B

PASSAGE 4

A New Horizon for 3D Film

34. C
35. A
36. D
37. C
38. C
39. A
40. C
41. D
42. D
43. A
44. D

Post-Test Analysis

This post-test analysis is essential if you want to see an improvement on your next test. Possible reasons for errors on the four passages in this section are listed here. Place check marks next to the types of errors that pertain to you, or write your own types of errors in the blank spaces.

TIMING AND ACCURACY

◇ Spent too long reading individual passages
◇ Spent too long answering each question
◇ Spent too long on a few difficult questions
◇ Felt rushed and made silly mistakes or random errors
◇ Unable to work quickly using error types and POE
Other: ____

APPROACHING THE PASSAGES AND QUESTIONS

◇ Unable to effectively grasp the passage's tone or style
◇ Unable to effectively grasp the passage's topic or stance
◇ Did not understand the context of underlined portions
◇ Did not eliminate false answers using error types
◇ Answered questions using first impressions instead of POE
◇ Answered questions without slotting in and checking final answer
◇ Eliminated NO CHANGE and chose a trap answer
◇ Eliminated correct answer during POE
Other: ____

Use this form to better analyze your performance. If you don't understand why you made errors, there is no way that you can correct them!

GRAMMAR AND SENTENCE STRUCTURE

◇ Did not test sentence for subject-verb agreement
◇ Did not identify proper verb form and verb tense
◇ Did not test sentence for pronoun agreement
◇ Did not identify proper pronoun form (subject/object, who/which/when/where/why)
◇ Did not test for proper comparison phrasing (amount/number, between/among) and number agreement
◇ Did not test phrase for correct adverb/adjective usage
◇ Did not see broader sentence structure (parallelism, misplaced modifier)
◇ Did not see flaws in punctuation (colon, semicolon, comma splice, misplaced commas)
◇ Did not see tricky possessives or contractions (its/it's, your/you're)
◇ Did not identify flaws in standard phrases (either . . . or, not only . . . but also, etc.)
◇ Did not use proper phrasing in sentences requiring the subjunctive
Other: ____

STYLE, ORGANIZATION, AND WORKING WITH EVIDENCE

◇ Did not notice cases of redundancy and wordiness
◇ Misidentified an expression as redundant or wordy
◇ Did not notice flaws in essay style or excessively informal expressions
◇ Misidentified an expression as stylistically inconsistent or informal
◇ Created the wrong relationship between two sentences
◇ Created the wrong relationship between two paragraphs
◇ Created the wrong placement for an out-of-order paragraph
◇ Did not eliminate faulty or improper English idioms
◇ Did not properly read or analyze an insertion/deletion question
◇ Did not properly read or analyze the information in a graphic
◇ Understood a graphic, but could not identify the correct passage content
Other: ____

Test 6

Test 6

Writing Test

35 MINUTES, 44 QUESTIONS

Turn to Section 2 of your answer sheet to answer the questions in this section.

DIRECTIONS

Each passage below is accompanied by a number of questions. For some questions, you will consider how the passage might be revised to improve the expression of ideas. For other questions, you will consider how the passage might be edited to correct errors in sentence structure, usage, or punctuation. A passage or a question may be accompanied by one or more graphics (such as a table or graph) that you will consider as you make revising and editing decisions.

Some questions will direct you to an underlined portion of a passage. Other questions will direct you to a location in a passage or ask you to think about the passage as a whole.

After reading each passage, choose the answer to each question that most effectively improves the quality of writing in the passage or that makes the passage conform to the conventions of standard written English. Many questions include a "NO CHANGE" option. Choose that option if you think the best choice is to leave the relevant portion of the passage as it is.

Questions 1-11 are based on the following passage.

Origami for Engineers

If you fold a square of paper in half, then fold the sides to the middle and again once more, you will then hold in your hands a crude, but functional, paper airplane. We all made toys like this when we were **[1]** young. Some of these toys were paper airplanes, paper footballs, paper cranes, or paper boxes.

1

Which choice most effectively combines the sentences at the underlined portion?

A) young, likened to
B) young, such as
C) young; some of which were
D) young, some were

CONTINUE

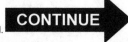

Test 6

Simple? Today, mathematicians and scientists say otherwise. In recent years, [2] origami; or the art of sculpturally folded paper, has become a crucial factor in many fields of mathematics and science, including research involving space equipment and medical technology. For hundreds of years, origami was just an art form. Now, with the astounding speed of technological advancement that marked the turn of the 21st century, origami [3] had become an application that may one day save lives.

Robert J. Lang, a physicist and origami artist, tells us in his recent TED talk that origami has much more to do with mathematics than one would think. He explains that he can turn a single square sheet of paper into virtually any shape. [4] In contrast to this, Lang has created a computer program that is able to turn a basic stick figure into a pattern of circular creases that you can fold into a base for your origami figure. However, the relation between origami and math doesn't stop at flaps and circles. [5] Origami dates back to approximately 100 A.D., and has certainly come a long way since. What scientists have realized over the years is that origami can be used to reshape designs to fit size constraints.

2

A) NO CHANGE
B) origami, or
C) origami—or
D) origami or

3

A) NO CHANGE
B) becomes
C) did become
D) has become

4

A) NO CHANGE
B) On the other hand,
C) In fact,
D) Regardless,

5

The writer is considering deleting the underlined sentence. Should the writer make this deletion?

A) Yes, because the underlined sentence detracts from the discussion of Robert Lang's TED Talk.
B) Yes, because the underlined sentence contradicts information presented in Robert Lang's TED Talk.
C) No, because the underlined sentence provides information necessary to understanding Robert Lang's TED Talk.
D) No, because the underlined sentence provides information from Robert Lang's TED Talk.

CONTINUE

Test 6

[1] When scientists at the Lawrence Livermore National Laboratory decided to send a telescope with a lens 100 meters in diameter into space, **6** it was met with an obvious stumbling block. [2] How on Earth (or in space) were they going to fit such a large telescope into such a small rocket? [3] **7** They dividing the glass lens into separate parts that could fold and unfold was one possibility. [4] However, even after folding the circular lens numerous times, the scientists were left with a result that was not nearly small enough. [5] The National Laboratory engineers were able to collaborate with origami artists to come up with a pattern for folding the lens down until it was only five meters in diameter—still the largest lens in the world, but **8** many more manageable. **9**

6

A) NO CHANGE
B) we were
C) he or she was
D) they were

7

A) NO CHANGE
B) Dividing
C) The scientists divided
D) That the scientists divide

8

A) NO CHANGE
B) much
C) less
D) fewer

9

The writer plans to add the following sentence to this paragraph.

> The solution, though, was anything but impossible for an origami artist.

To make this paragraph most logical, the sentence should be placed

A) after sentence 1.
B) after sentence 2.
C) after sentence 3.
D) after sentence 4.

As you can see, [10] origami has a long and rich history. What wasn't possible before due to size constraints [11] can now be achieved using origami concepts. Maybe the paper airplane you folded as a child will one day take the shape of a real airplane and carry technology to new, unseen heights.

10

Which choice best introduces the passage's concluding paragraph?

A) NO CHANGE
B) origami is rich in practical applications.
C) people can get rich making origami.
D) Robert Lang has a wealth of origami knowledge.

11

A) NO CHANGE
B) is now achieved by way of the use of origami concepts.
C) is being achieved through the using of origami concepts.
D) can now be achieved by way of using origami concepts.

CONTINUE

Questions 12-22 are based on the following passage and supplementary material.

The Death of Movie-Going?

As a film critic, I attend special screenings of the latest Oscar contenders (although some are clearly everything but Oscar-worthy). Doing so is primarily a solitary experience, one that I have become accustomed to, even though there is something fantastic about watching a movie with strangers in the dark. Whether you are witnessing a laugh-out-loud comedy or a weighty drama, you share **12** raw emotional reactions, completely and utterly visceral, with persons you may never see again. It is a fleeting affair, with the highs and lows of a tryst that could never possibly endure. There is some solace in this notion of sharing profound moments without the emotional burden of having to call the other person back.

But the psychology of movie-going may not be what it once was. A recent independent survey revealed that **13** the same number of people list Netflix and going to a movie theater as their preferred viewing method. **14** Moreover, this relatively new at-home viewing company (Netflix) is rapidly changing the industry: a startling **15** 50% of viewers list the service as their method of choice. It seems that consumers are forgoing the overpriced popcorn, cramped seats, and social obligations in favor of home-made snacks, plush couches, and laptops.

12

A) NO CHANGE
B) untreated
C) coarse
D) crude

13

Which choice is an accurate interpretation of the data in the chart?

A) NO CHANGE
B) most people prefer to view movies on Netflix.
C) fewer people now use Netflix because of a recent 55% increase in cost.
D) nobody prefers to go to a movie theater anymore.

14

A) NO CHANGE
B) Unfortunately,
C) Rightly so,
D) Nevertheless,

15

Which of the following best interprets that data in the chart?

A) NO CHANGE
B) 55%
C) 45%
D) 20%

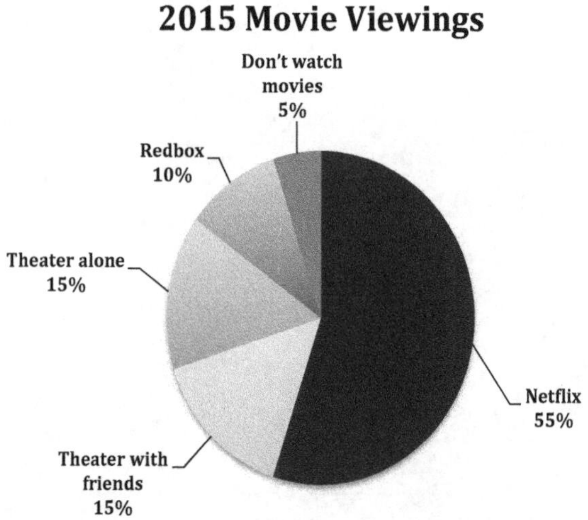

  CONTINUE

However, it is clear that movies are designed for collective experience. Have we forgotten the fun and joy **16** about to gather together to watch a new release, then—right after—of having heated coffee-shop discussions about the director's intentions? Have we forgotten the simple pleasure of sharing a laugh, remembering how the main character in a slapstick farce took an exaggerated tumble down the stairs? Now, it seems that we are relegated to keeping those moments to ourselves or, even worse, to sharing them in online blogs. **17** Certainly, such outlets are far from desirable.

Even when a film is subpar, **18** you can commiserate with your friends, who share your awareness of the movie's follies. In fact, critiquing a bad movie together can lead to deeply intellectual discussions. **19** Every year, a slew of horribly crafted, sorry excuses for movies hits big screens all over the world. But if you watch such a movie alone or leave early, you will be limited by your own constricted views—never hearing another person's viewpoint and never growing in your own perspective.

16

A) NO CHANGE
B) about to gather together to
C) of gathering together because of watching
D) of gathering together to watch

17

The writer wants a concluding sentence that explains the consequences of this new style of movie-watching. Which choice best accomplishes this goal?

A) NO CHANGE
B) As a result, we miss out on the connectivity behind a true film experience.
C) We can only guess what ill effects will come from these new film-going habits.
D) However, I will grant that some people do prefer using various social media as a means of public discourse.

18

A) NO CHANGE
B) one can commiserate with one's friends
C) they can commiserate with their friends
D) commiserating with one's friends

19

Which choice provides the most specific example in support of the previous sentence?

A) NO CHANGE
B) Oftentimes, I delight in rolling my eyes at the latest lousy film.
C) Recently, after attending a showing of the critically-panned *Transformers*, my friend and I engaged in an enlightening discussion about how the director could have more subtly employed CGI technology.
D) One afternoon last summer, my friend and I saw three films in a row (*Maleficent*, *Divergent*, and *Noah*), and we hated all of them.

CONTINUE

[20] This downside is not limited to poorly-constructed films, either. [21] An impeccable black-and-white classic, I remember watching a reshowing of Billy Wilder's *Sunset Boulevard* at an independent film event in New York City. I was attending in order to acquire some material for my blog; to my surprise, many other people had arrived there for leisure but without a single companion. It was a film event after all, and it had seemed that the proper etiquette would be to bring friends. Unfortunately, that was not the case. Instead, we all sat there with the grayscale of the screen flickering on our solitary faces, vacant seats between each of us. It was sad.

To best capture the true allure of watching a film collectively, I leave you with the [22] words departed by Norma Desmond, the main character in *Sunset Boulevard*: "It's just us. And the cameras. And those wonderful people out there in the dark."

20

Which choice provides the best transition between the two paragraphs?

A) NO CHANGE
B) I have seen a lot of films over the years.
C) Some of my favorite films are old ones.
D) Please consider the following anecdote.

21

A) NO CHANGE
B) I remember watching a reshowing of Billy Wilder's *Sunset Boulevard*, an impeccable black-and-white classic, at an independent film event in New York City.
C) I remember watching an impeccable black-and-white classic, Billy Wilder's *Sunset Boulevard*, a reshowing at an independent film even in New York City.
D) An impeccable black-and-white classic, I remember watching a reshowing of Billy Wilder's *Sunset Boulevard*; moreover, I was at an independent film event in New York City.

22

A) NO CHANGE
B) departing words of
C) words departing from the mouth of
D) words, departed by

CONTINUE

Test 6

Questions 23-33 are based on the following passage.

Life, Liberty, and Self-Reliance: Emerson's Vision

[1] Where did our obsession with and absolute insistence on having every individual **23** liberty, we can possibly imagine come from? [2] What is at the root of our preoccupation with gadgets that magnify and emphasize our own self-importance? [3] How did we justify, and pass off as a need, our desire to follow our every whim and to have the freedom to ignore any data that shows the pitfalls of choosing such radical autonomy? [4] It all began with "Self-Reliance." [5] Ralph Waldo Emerson's ever-popular and widely-taught essay can be at least partly credited with inflating our perceptions of self-worth, for better or for worse. **24**

In "Self-Reliance," Emerson writes about conformity and why it is essentially evil incarnate. Simply, conformity is not only wrong because of what one may conform to, **25** and also wrong for its own sake. We are not merely at risk of being misguided by false **26** ideas. Any inclination towards following any idea that is not our own is misguidance itself.

23

A) NO CHANGE
B) liberty, possibly imaginable
C) liberty within the realm of possible imagination
D) liberty that we can possibly imagine

24

To make this paragraph most logical, sentence 4 should be placed

A) where it is now.
B) before sentence 1.
C) before sentence 3.
D) after sentence 5.

25

A) NO CHANGE
B) but also
C) it's also
D) however,

26

Which choice most effectively combines the sentences at the underlined portion?

A) ideas, however
B) ideas, although
C) ideas, and also
D) ideas; any

CONTINUE

27 How many people ascribe to this oddly liberating notion? 28 Giving people the freedom to decide for themselves what is wrong and what is right, "Self-Reliance," and moreover depicts this self-determination as more sacred than the dictates of any social law. 29 At sixteen, after reading that part of the essay, I have felt empowered. Was I really ordained with the power to choose without limit? This idea constitutes heaven for almost any teenager. I could decide what was acceptable and what wasn't based on my own reasons. I could write my own testament and carve it in stone.

27

The writer wants to introduce the paragraph with a question. Which choice best accomplishes this goal?

A) NO CHANGE
B) What other scholars, if any, could have come up with such a forward-thinking idea?
C) When did such a radical idea first come about?
D) What, then, should we do if we do not conform?

28

A) NO CHANGE
B) "Self-Reliance," giving people the freedom to decide for themselves what is wrong and what is right,
C) "Self-Reliance" gives people the freedom to decide for themselves what is wrong and what is right,
D) "Self-Reliance": it gives people the freedom to decide for themselves what is wrong and what is right,

29

A) NO CHANGE
B) After reading that part of the essay at sixteen, I am feeling empowered.
C) At sixteen, after reading that part of the essay, feelings of empowerment followed.
D) At sixteen, I felt empowered after reading that part of the essay.

The problem with this is that what we construe as wrong or right, good or bad, [30] vary on a daily basis. This variance may guide us to wrong decisions and dangerous choices that are not beneficial for us in the long run. So what then? Emerson says that this is okay: [31] we should not let our fickle natures stop us from being true to ourselves. We should speak what we think and, if what we say today contradicts what we say tomorrow, then that's part of the process we must go through to learn who we are. And if these many changes of mind [32] causes us to be misunderstood, that's fine too. In fact, it's better than fine, because as Emerson declares in his remarks on history's greatest figures, "to be great is to be misunderstood."

Maybe it's not such a bad thing to have our own views and thoughts, and to adhere to them most of the time. But maybe listening to [33] others' views and thoughts, and being affected by them, doesn't equal conformity. After all, humility is a virtue that doesn't have to contradict self-reliance.

30

A) NO CHANGE
B) varies
C) varied
D) varying

31

A) NO CHANGE
B) we should not be letting our fickle natures stopping us from being true to ourselves.
C) our fickle natures should not be let to stop us from being true to ourselves.
D) though our natures are fickle, we should not let these natures to stop us from being true to ourselves.

32

A) NO CHANGE
B) is causing
C) has caused
D) cause

33

A) NO CHANGE
B) others
C) other's
D) that of other

Test 6

Questions 34-44 are based on the following passage.

Waiting for Absurdist Theater

The Theater of the Absurd seized the attention of the [34] public, in the 1950s. During the decade, this artistic movement [35] gained momentum with the London production of Samuel Beckett's play *Waiting for Godot* and remained highly visible as plays such as Eugène Ionesco's *The Bald Prima Donna* and *The Killer* and Jean-Paul Sartre's *No Exit* were staged [36] across Europe and in the United States. Depending on their audiences, these plays were greeted as either "brilliant" or "baffling." Even today, there is no compromise: [37] it's either Europe or the United States.

Drama scholar Martin Esslin once defined "The Theater of the Absurd" as theater "that expresses the idea that human existence has no meaning or purpose." [38] Regardless, all communication breaks down among typical Absurdist characters. The playwrights involved [39] portraying man's reaction to a world apparently without meaning, where man is a puppet controlled or menaced by invisible outside forces. This brand of theater is closely related to the branch of philosophy we know as "Existentialism," which states that there is no grand reason for our existence. We must just accept it.

34

A) NO CHANGE
B) public—in the 1950s.
C) 1950s people in public.
D) public in the 1950s.

35

A) NO CHANGE
B) grew its following
C) picked up speed
D) reached a pinnacle

36

A) NO CHANGE
B) through
C) at
D) with

37

Which choice best restates the main point of the previous sentence?

A) NO CHANGE
B) it's either the 1950s or today.
C) it's either Beckett or Ionesco.
D) you either love them or you hate them.

38

A) NO CHANGE
B) Previously,
C) On an unrelated note,
D) True to this idea,

39

A) NO CHANGE
B) portray
C) having portrayed
D) portrays

CONTINUE

For instance, [40] *Waiting for Godot* was not Beckett's first play. [41] Two tramps, Estragon and Vladimir, sit by the edge of a road. These two are apparently awaiting the arrival of someone called Godot. They are joined later by the pompous Pozzo and his companion Lucky, [42] which is mostly silent and has a rope round his neck. Throughout the play, the characters talk at random. Then a boy enters to announce that Godot will not come today. This action heralds the end of Act One. Act Two repeats the sequence, with a few variations, though for many in the original audiences one act was enough.

"It has no plot, no climax, no dénouement, no beginning, no middle, no end. It has a situation, but barely. It jettisons everything by which we recognize theater. A play, it asserts and proves, is basically a means of spending two hours in the dark without being bored," wrote Kenneth [43] Tynan. Tynan is a leading twentieth-century theater critic. Even the actors in early *Godot* productions called the play "Waiting for God Knows What," [44] this sums up the divisive nature of the Theater of the Absurd.

40

Which choice most effectively introduces the discussion of Beckett's play in the paragraph?

A) NO CHANGE
B) the two-act *Waiting for Godot* is frequently included in textbooks today.
C) *Waiting for Godot* unfolds over two incomparably confounding acts.
D) *Waiting for Godot* was first written in French.

41

A) NO CHANGE
B) Vladimir and Estragon are two tramps, they sit by the edge of the road.
C) Two tramps sitting by the edge of a road, Estragon and Vladimir.
D) By the edge of the road, two tramps, Estragon and Vladimir, sitting.

42

A) NO CHANGE
B) who
C) he
D) where

43

Which choice most effectively combines the sentences?

A) Tynan, having led as a twentieth-century theater critic.
B) Tynan, a leading twentieth-century theater critic.
C) Tynan, he is a leading twentieth-century theater critic.
D) Tynan, and he is a leading twentieth-century theater critic.

44

A) NO CHANGE
B) sums up
C) this is summing up
D) summing up

STOP

If you finish before time is called, you may check your work on this section only.
Do not turn to any other section.

Answer Key

TEST 6

PASSAGE 1

Origami for Engineers

1.	B
2.	B
3.	D
4.	C
5.	A
6.	D
7.	B
8.	B
9.	D
10.	B
11.	A

PASSAGE 2

The Death of Movie-Going?

12.	A
13.	B
14.	A
15.	B
16.	D
17.	B
18.	A
19.	C
20.	A
21.	B
22.	B

PASSAGE 3

Life, Liberty, and Self-Reliance: Emerson's Vision

23.	D
24.	A
25.	B
26.	D
27.	D
28.	C
29.	D
30.	B
31.	A
32.	D
33.	A

PASSAGE 4

Waiting for Absurdist Theater

34.	D
35.	A
36.	A
37.	D
38.	D
39.	B
40.	C
41.	A
42.	B
43.	B
44.	D

Post-Test Analysis

This post-test analysis is essential if you want to see an improvement on your next test. Possible reasons for errors on the four passages in this section are listed here. Place check marks next to the types of errors that pertain to you, or write your own types of errors in the blank spaces.

TIMING AND ACCURACY

◇ Spent too long reading individual passages
◇ Spent too long answering each question
◇ Spent too long on a few difficult questions
◇ Felt rushed and made silly mistakes or random errors
◇ Unable to work quickly using error types and POE
Other: ______________________________

APPROACHING THE PASSAGES AND QUESTIONS

◇ Unable to effectively grasp the passage's tone or style
◇ Unable to effectively grasp the passage's topic or stance
◇ Did not understand the context of underlined portions
◇ Did not eliminate false answers using error types
◇ Answered questions using first impressions instead of POE
◇ Answered questions without slotting in and checking final answer
◇ Eliminated NO CHANGE and chose a trap answer
◇ Eliminated correct answer during POE
Other: ______________________________

Use this form to better analyze your performance. If you don't understand why you made errors, there is no way that you can correct them!

GRAMMAR AND SENTENCE STRUCTURE

◇ Did not test sentence for subject-verb agreement
◇ Did not identify proper verb form and verb tense
◇ Did not test sentence for pronoun agreement
◇ Did not identify proper pronoun form (subject/object, who/which/when/where/why)
◇ Did not test for proper comparison phrasing (amount/number, between/among) and number agreement
◇ Did not test phrase for correct adverb/adjective usage
◇ Did not see broader sentence structure (parallelism, misplaced modifier)
◇ Did not see flaws in punctuation (colon, semicolon, comma splice, misplaced commas)
◇ Did not see tricky possessives or contractions (its/it's, your/you're)
◇ Did not identify flaws in standard phrases (either . . . or, not only . . . but also, etc.)
◇ Did not use proper phrasing in sentences requiring the subjunctive
Other: ______________________________

STYLE, ORGANIZATION, AND WORKING WITH EVIDENCE

◇ Did not notice cases of redundancy and wordiness
◇ Misidentified an expression as redundant or wordy
◇ Did not notice flaws in essay style or excessively informal expressions
◇ Misidentified an expression as stylistically inconsistent or informal
◇ Created the wrong relationship between two sentences
◇ Created the wrong relationship between two paragraphs
◇ Created the wrong placement for an out-of-order paragraph
◇ Did not eliminate faulty or improper English idioms
◇ Did not properly read or analyze an insertion/deletion question
◇ Did not properly read or analyze the information in a graphic
◇ Understood a graphic, but could not identify the correct passage content
Other: ______________________________

Test 7

Test 7

Writing Test

35 MINUTES, 44 QUESTIONS

Turn to Section 2 of your answer sheet to answer the questions in this section.

DIRECTIONS

Each passage below is accompanied by a number of questions. For some questions, you will consider how the passage might be revised to improve the expression of ideas. For other questions, you will consider how the passage might be edited to correct errors in sentence structure, usage, or punctuation. A passage or a question may be accompanied by one or more graphics (such as a table or graph) that you will consider as you make revising and editing decisions.

Some questions will direct you to an underlined portion of a passage. Other questions will direct you to a location in a passage or ask you to think about the passage as a whole.

After reading each passage, choose the answer to each question that most effectively improves the quality of writing in the passage or that makes the passage conform to the conventions of standard written English. Many questions include a "NO CHANGE" option. Choose that option if you think the best choice is to leave the relevant portion of the passage as it is.

Questions 1-11 are based on the following passage.

Idealizing America with *Meet Me in St. Louis*

[1] The musical feature *Meet Me in St. Louis* [1] are a film that, for middle-class Americans, depicted the quintessential goals and pleasures of family life in the wake of the Second World War. [2] At the heart of *Meet Me in St. Louis* are the dreams and unexpected realities of the Smith family, who live around the time of the 1904 St. Louis World's Fair. [3] The Smiths' greatest crisis involves a life-altering decision: whether to leave comfortable, homely St. Louis for a new life of opportunity in bustling, aggressive New York City. [4] But as the film plays out, there is really no contest. [5] Since this is a film made by M.G.M., it offers that studio's complaisant and complacent panacea for social problems: "East, West: Home is Best." [2]

1

A) NO CHANGE
B) is a film
C) being a film
D) are films

2

To make this paragraph most logical, sentence 2 should be placed

A) where it is now.
B) before sentence 1.
C) before sentence 4.
D) before sentence 5.

  CONTINUE

Test 7

Almost eighty years after it first appeared, *Meet Me in St. Louis* is still popular, **3** <u>because</u> in the United States (where it unfailingly appears on television every Christmas) but also nearly everywhere else in the Western world. The modern-day **4** <u>critic, or</u> cynic—might sneer at the movie's sentimental popularity by pointing out everything that is missing from this depiction of everyday American life. In the early twentieth century, apparently, **5** <u>life in St. Louis was very particular and unique.</u>

3

A) NO CHANGE
B) and
C) not only
D) DELETE the underlined portion.

4

A) NO CHANGE
B) critic—or
C) critic or
D) critic; or

5

Which choice offers the most specific examples of criticisms that a cynic might make?

A) NO CHANGE
B) there were many things that modern day film buffs might take issue with.
C) everyone in St. Louis was gainfully employed, financially well-off, and sickeningly sunny.
D) many of the problems we know today were not yet around.

CONTINUE

6 One big thing about the film is that it seems to epitomize the axiom that optimism knows no bounds; *Meet Me in St. Louis* even calls to mind a sentence from Voltaire's satirical work, *Candide*: "All is for the best in the best of all possible worlds." **7** Voltaire, at least on the surface level, was wary of such optimism, and implied that ill-advised beliefs lead to self-destructive impracticality. **8** Prior to Voltaire, other philosophers expressed differing opinions on the matter.

6

Which choice most smoothly and effectively introduces the paragraph?

A) NO CHANGE
B) Let's talk about how the film appears to epitomize
C) The film, contrary to its criticisms, is epitomizing
D) The film epitomizes

7

A) NO CHANGE
B) Although Voltaire was being
C) However, Voltaire was
D) And Voltaire, being

8

The writer is considering deleting the underlined sentence. Should the sentence be kept or deleted?

A) Kept, because it defines a term that is important to the passage.
B) Kept, because it sets up the argument in the following paragraph.
C) Deleted, because it detracts from the discussion of Voltaire in the paragraph.
D) Deleted, because it neglects to mention whether Voltaire watched *Meet Me in St. Louis.*

CONTINUE

It is probably true that a **9** film like *Meet* *Me in St. Louis* could not succeed in today's jaded market. Too much has happened in the intervening years for us to embrace the film's upbeat premise. **10** However, do not ridicule and dismiss the film just because some critics do because it is far more carefully crafted than its most vehement critics realize. *Meet Me in St.* **11** *Louis*, do not pretend to be a picture of 1940s life: it is set at the beginning of the 1900s, and thus places its characters in an era when America was still relatively hopeful about its future, as becomes evident during the film's cheery finale at the St. Louis World's Fair. And for all his caveats about optimism, even Voltaire ended *Candide* with a reassuring exhortation: "Let us cultivate our garden." It is up to the reader of *Candide* and the audience of *Meet Me in St. Louis* to decide whether an optimistic outlook is a viable response or merely a foolish reaction to the realities of the world.

9

A) NO CHANGE
B) film, like *Meet*
C) film like, *Meet*
D) film, like, *Meet*

10

Which choice most smoothly and effectively transitions into a discussion of the film's merits?

A) NO CHANGE
B) Furthermore, one should not ridicule and dismiss the film, it has far more careful craft than its most vehement critics want you to realize.
C) Furthermore, people should not ridicule and dismiss the film, and it has far more careful craft than its most vehement critics realize.
D) However, it is wrong to ridicule and dismiss the film, which is far more carefully crafted than its most vehement critics realize.

11

A) NO CHANGE
B) *Louis*, isn't pretending
C) *Louis*, not pretending
D) *Louis* does not pretend

Questions 12-22 are based on the following passage.

Highly Probable: Quantum Theory and Its Consequences

Even among physicists themselves, the complexities of quantum theory can prove mystifying. After all, concepts such as simultaneity—that an object can exist in two different places at the very same time— [12] is inherently befuddling. As a result of all this confusion, various misinterpretations of quantum theory have taken root outside, and even within, the scientific community. Perhaps the greatest misunderstanding of all [13] has arose over the postulation that the universe is probabilistic in nature. In order to clarify the confusion, we must ask ourselves: What does it mean for something to be probabilistic?

Consider the simple example of a coin toss, a very familiar case of probability: there is a 50% possibility that the coin will come up heads and a 50% possibility that it will come up tails. [14] Quantum probability is based on similar laws of chance but involves more complex alternatives. One of the central tenets of quantum theory is that subatomic particles are governed by probability [15] functions—mathematical equations that describe the relative likelihoods of different particle behaviors. [16] That our bodies happen to be made up of subatomic particles, some have extrapolated from this fact to conclude that we ourselves are little more than "walking slot machines," governed by nothing more than random chance.

12

A) NO CHANGE
B) being
C) are
D) has been

13

A) NO CHANGE
B) arisen
C) have arose
D) has arisen

14

The writer is considering deleting the underlined sentence. Should the writer make this deletion?

A) Yes, because it discusses a term unrelated to the topic of the paragraph.
B) Yes, because it provides information contradictory to the topic of the paragraph.
C) No, because it provides important information about a key term in the passage.
D) No, because it explains how the idea of quantum probability was developed.

15

A) NO CHANGE
B) functions, these are mathematical
C) functions. Mathematical
D) function, being mathematical

16

A) NO CHANGE
B) Instead of
C) Due in part when
D) Because

  CONTINUE

As such, our behavior is not our own, and our "choices," seemingly made of our own volition, are akin to the erratic spins of a roulette wheel. Unfortunately, such interpretations of quantum theory are the **17** product of a grossly misunderstanding—namely, that if the outcome of something is probabilistic or uncertain, then it is necessarily unpredictable. **18** However, this may or may not be the case.

19 I'm going to talk about a coin toss again. While the outcome of a single coin toss is uncertain, over the long term—say, if I were to toss the coin 1,000 times in a row—the behavior of the coin begins to fit a predictable pattern. And while human beings are certainly more complex than coins, **20** he or she are still largely creatures of habit. Observe us for a while, and our own patterns and predilections begin to emerge.

17

A) NO CHANGE
B) grossly product of a misunderstanding
C) products of a gross misunderstanding
D) product, of a gross misunderstanding

18

The writer wants to conclude by expressing strong disagreement with the interpretation of quantum theory presented in this paragraph. Which choice best accomplishes this goal?

A) NO CHANGE
B) Who can say if this is an accurate understanding of the principles?
C) However, nothing could be farther from the truth.
D) I tend to agree with only part of this interpretation.

19

Which choice most smoothly and effectively introduces the paragraph?

A) NO CHANGE
B) Consider once again the toss of a coin.
C) Once again, the coin toss is still a relevant way to think about this theory.
D) The coin toss makes sense now again.

20

A) NO CHANGE
B) it is
C) we are
D) one is

CONTINUE

21 Because, if I am feeling tired, there is a probability that I will take a nap. There is also the probability, however, that I will make myself an espresso—especially if I need to stay awake and finish writing an essay like this one. In contrast to the 50/50 probability of any coin flip, the probability for my behavior can change according to my circumstances: I am still left with an enormous measure of freedom. As it stands, 22 it is probably a better idea to take a nap.

21

A) NO CHANGE
B) Let's just say,
C) Fortunately,
D) For instance,

22

Which choice best restates the main idea of the previous sentence?

A) NO CHANGE
B) I do not have the time to toss a coin 1,000 times in a row.
C) the implications of quantum theory are far more liberating than its detractors seem to realize.
D) quantum theory is a confusing subject that can never be applied to humans in any definitive way.

Questions 23-33 are based on the following passage and supplementary material.

The Challenges of Habitat Biology

It is an utterly complicated feat to replicate an animal's natural habitat, whether that of a domesticated pet in the home, an exotic animal in the pet store, or a wild beast in the zoo. Beyond providing the basic necessities of food and water, there are other factors that must be considered: **23** mineral deficiencies being prevented, housing animals in social settings appropriate to **24** it's natures, regulating and controlling psychological or physiological behaviors, and more. A simple oversight in something that we humans would never commonly **25** consider; an addition or change that would not affect us in the least, can drastically affect quality of life for an animal.

23

A) NO CHANGE
B) to prevent mineral deficiencies
C) preventing mineral deficiencies
D) prevent mineral deficiencies

24

A) NO CHANGE
B) its
C) there
D) their

25

A) NO CHANGE
B) consider; such as
C) consider an
D) consider, an

CONTINUE

Test 7

In a study involving prairie dogs at a rehabilitation center, the mere presence of an extra fluorescent light bulb instigated **26** slower weight gain for the animals. The surplus heat emanating from the lighting fixture caused the rodents to become **27** sluggish and inert. Their physical activity decreased. A neighboring cage that housed more prairie dogs only had one bulb, which was enough to provide light without drastically altering the immediate environment. This second set did not suffer from heat exhaustion and therefore **28** maintained a healthy weight. Both groups were provided with the same diet; the **29** sole factor contributing to this anomaly was the disorientation and stress induced by the extra bulb.

26

Which choice is an accurate interpretation of the data in the chart?

A) NO CHANGE
B) no change in
C) inconsistent
D) more rapid

27

Which choice best combines the two sentences?

A) sluggish and inert, and their physical activity consequently decreased.
B) sluggish and inert because their physical activity consequently decreased.
C) sluggish and inert, thus decreasing their physical activity.
D) sluggish and inert, but their physical activity decreased.

28

Which choice best interprets the data in the chart?

A) NO CHANGE
B) lost weight.
C) gained weight.
D) their weight fluctuated.

29

A) NO CHANGE
B) soul factor
C) sole factors
D) soul factors

Prairie Dog Weight Gain Over 4 Weeks

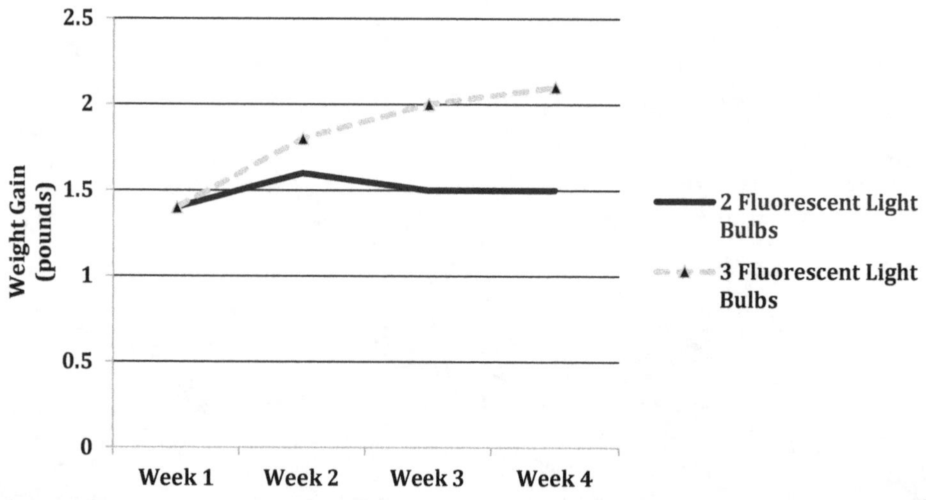

CONTINUE

[30] Prairie dogs are certainly not the only mammals to be negatively affected by the presence of artificial light. At Kruger National Park in South Africa, a reserve spanning 19,633 square kilometers, a wide assortment of animals [31] are kept in recreated biomes; however, the problem remains that not all species require the same living conditions. The elephant and the lion will keep watchful eyes on each other without much interference. However, a hyena population residing too close to a pride of lions may be thrown into a state of anxiety and fury. Caimans need hydration from bodies of water, cheetahs hunt in the arid expanse of the Savannah, and Cape Buffalo require lush vegetation to eat—all to approximate their natural habits. Not only are such different habitats expensive to create, but such measures also necessitate remarkable man-power, time, and energy.

Controlled fires are periodic occurrences at Kruger National Park and are meant to replicate the phenomenon of lightning striking the plain. The electrical energy found in lightning can separate out the nitrogen atoms in the atmosphere, and these atoms will then fall to the earth and combine with nitrates in the soil. This organic fertilization process helps to rejuvenate the [32] land, promoting succulent plant growth for herbivores and recreating processes that occur in the wild. Thus, the park rangers can [33] keep on going with the innate equilibrium between plant and animal life.

30

Which choice most smoothly and effectively introduces the paragraph?

A) NO CHANGE
B) It is often easy to discern which types of light certain animals thrive under.
C) Biologists and ecologists consider similar issues when replicating even larger habitats.
D) Improper vegetation can also detract from replicating an animal's natural habitat.

31

A) NO CHANGE
B) are being
C) have been
D) is

32

A) NO CHANGE
B) land, and promote
C) land, but promote
D) land, and promoting

33

A) NO CHANGE
B) maintain
C) outlast
D) endure

Test 7

Questions 34-44 are based on the following passage.

Everybody Steals?

Most of us have been the **34** victim of stealing by way of thieves at one time or another. **35** The act provokes multiple reactions within us: **36** shock, fear, insecurity, when you sense betrayal, and anger are among the first emotions that sweep through us when we realize that something has not simply been mislaid but has been deliberately taken from us. We are outraged that someone could do anything like that, **37** thus making us incensed. The irony is that very few of us have not stolen something at least once in our lives.

34

A) NO CHANGE
B) victim of stealing thieves
C) victim of theft
D) victim when a theft stole from us

35

A) NO CHANGE
B) They act, provoking
C) It, the act, provokes
D) Provoking

36

A) NO CHANGE
B) shocking, fearing, insecurity, sensing betrayal, and getting angry
C) shock, fear and insecurity, betrayal, and anger
D) shock, fear, insecurity, a sense of betrayal, and anger

37

A) NO CHANGE
B) and incensing us.
C) incensing us.
D) DELETE the underlined portion and end the sentence with a period.

CONTINUE

Test 7

There is no use denying it, dear reader, however desperately **38** he or she tries to do so. Can you honestly raise your hand and plead "not guilty" to the charge? Can you really claim that you never put your hand into the cookie jar and swiped a cookie when your mother's back was turned? Have you never filched a coin from the jar where the family stores loose change? After all, it was only a couple of cents and will never be missed, and anyway you intended to replace it later. You can be quite honest **39** here. You are not alone. **40** How many times are we ripped off in the supermarket by believing that the label on the package is accurate, or, indeed, that a hamburger contains 100% beef with neither soy nor horse included? I know people who stay in the most expensive hotels in the world: some of them never consider leaving without purloining an ashtray, or a towel, **41** despite (or perhaps because of) the label on the item with the hotel's name and logo.

38

A) NO CHANGE
B) they try
C) you try
D) one tries

39

Which choice best combines the two sentences at the underlined portion?

A) here, and you
B) here, but you
C) here, for you
D) here, however you

40

The writer is considering deleting the underlined sentence. Should the writer make this deletion?

A) Yes, because the underlined sentence detracts from the discussion of times when the reader may have stolen things.
B) Yes, because the underlined sentence neglects to mention to what degree people are lied to.
C) No, because the underlined sentence provides an example of a time when the reader might have stolen something from a supermarket.
D) No, because the underlined sentence defines a key term that will become important later in the passage.

41

A) NO CHANGE
B) despite—or perhaps because of, the label
C) despite, or perhaps because of the label
D) despite; or, perhaps, because of, the label

Well, of course, you can claim that none of the above can really be counted as stealing. These acts cannot be considered major crimes, right? **42** Shoplifting is definitely a thing that we all know about. Of course, I know that school children today are far better behaved than they were when I was a kid; back in those dark times, the furtive theft of a chocolate bar from a candy store was a pretty common occurrence. And while we're on the subject of school, don't tell me that you have never plagiarized, even just a **43** little—in order to get an assignment done on time, and hoped that the teacher was only half reading what you handed in.

Why do we feel such turmoil and aggression when other people con us? I suspect that **44** it's because, at the bottom of our hearts, we feel rather guilty. The only thing we can do to comfort ourselves is claim innocence. We are set such bad examples by everyone around us. To quote an old piece of advice, "Don't steal, don't lie, and don't cheat. The government hates competition."

42

Which choice best introduces the paragraph's discussion of shoplifting?

A) NO CHANGE
B) Shoplifting is something that we all know, I'm sure.
C) Take shoplifting, for example.
D) For instance, shoplifting is a rather rare occurrence.

43

A) NO CHANGE
B) little: in
C) little, in
D) little in;

44

A) NO CHANGE
B) its
C) they're
D) its'

STOP

If you finish before time is called, you may check your work on this section only.
Do not turn to any other section.

No Test Material On This Page

Answer Key

TEST 7

PASSAGE 1

Idealizing America with *Meet Me in St. Louis*

1.	B
2.	A
3.	C
4.	B
5.	C
6.	D
7.	C
8.	C
9.	A
10.	D
11.	D

PASSAGE 2

Highly Probable: Quantum Theory and Its Consequences

12.	C
13.	D
14.	C
15.	A
16.	D
17.	C
18.	C
19.	B
20.	C
21.	D
22.	C

PASSAGE 3

The Challenges of Habitat Biology

23.	C
24.	D
25.	D
26.	D
27.	C
28.	A
29.	A
30.	C
31.	D
32.	A
33.	B

PASSAGE 4

Everybody Steals?

34.	C
35.	A
36.	D
37.	D
38.	C
39.	C
40.	A
41.	A
42.	C
43.	C
44.	A

Post-Test Analysis

This post-test analysis is essential if you want to see an improvement on your next test. Possible reasons for errors on the four passages in this section are listed here. Place check marks next to the types of errors that pertain to you, or write your own types of errors in the blank spaces.

Use this form to better analyze your performance. If you don't understand why you made errors, there is no way that you can correct them!

TIMING AND ACCURACY

◇ Spent too long reading individual passages
◇ Spent too long answering each question
◇ Spent too long on a few difficult questions
◇ Felt rushed and made silly mistakes or random errors
◇ Unable to work quickly using error types and POE
Other: ______________________________

APPROACHING THE PASSAGES AND QUESTIONS

◇ Unable to effectively grasp the passage's tone or style
◇ Unable to effectively grasp the passage's topic or stance
◇ Did not understand the context of underlined portions
◇ Did not eliminate false answers using error types
◇ Answered questions using first impressions instead of POE
◇ Answered questions without slotting in and checking final answer
◇ Eliminated NO CHANGE and chose a trap answer
◇ Eliminated correct answer during POE
Other: ______________________________

GRAMMAR AND SENTENCE STRUCTURE

◇ Did not test sentence for subject-verb agreement
◇ Did not identify proper verb form and verb tense
◇ Did not test sentence for pronoun agreement
◇ Did not identify proper pronoun form (subject/object, who/which/when/where/why)
◇ Did not test for proper comparison phrasing (amount/number, between/among) and number agreement
◇ Did not test phrase for correct adverb/adjective usage
◇ Did not see broader sentence structure (parallelism, misplaced modifier)
◇ Did not see flaws in punctuation (colon, semicolon, comma splice, misplaced commas)
◇ Did not see tricky possessives or contractions (its/it's, your/you're)
◇ Did not identify flaws in standard phrases (either . . . or, not only . . . but also, etc.)
◇ Did not use proper phrasing in sentences requiring the subjunctive
Other: ______________________________

STYLE, ORGANIZATION, AND WORKING WITH EVIDENCE

◇ Did not notice cases of redundancy and wordiness
◇ Misidentified an expression as redundant or wordy
◇ Did not notice flaws in essay style or excessively informal expressions
◇ Misidentified an expression as stylistically inconsistent or informal
◇ Created the wrong relationship between two sentences
◇ Created the wrong relationship between two paragraphs
◇ Created the wrong placement for an out-of-order paragraph
◇ Did not eliminate faulty or improper English idioms
◇ Did not properly read or analyze an insertion/deletion question
◇ Did not properly read or analyze the information in a graphic
◇ Understood a graphic, but could not identify the correct passage content
Other: ______________________________

Test 8

Test 8

Writing Test
35 MINUTES, 44 QUESTIONS

Turn to Section 2 of your answer sheet to answer the questions in this section.

DIRECTIONS

Each passage below is accompanied by a number of questions. For some questions, you will consider how the passage might be revised to improve the expression of ideas. For other questions, you will consider how the passage might be edited to correct errors in sentence structure, usage, or punctuation. A passage or a question may be accompanied by one or more graphics (such as a table or graph) that you will consider as you make revising and editing decisions.

Some questions will direct you to an underlined portion of a passage. Other questions will direct you to a location in a passage or ask you to think about the passage as a whole.

After reading each passage, choose the answer to each question that most effectively improves the quality of writing in the passage or that makes the passage conform to the conventions of standard written English. Many questions include a "NO CHANGE" option. Choose that option if you think the best choice is to leave the relevant portion of the passage as it is.

Questions 1-11 are based on the following passage and supplementary material.

The Power of Genomics

Since its emergence, **[1]** genomics; the science of determining what our genes are and how those genes function— has certainly made some strange philosophical and political bedfellows. It is true that genomics techniques are proving to be the most powerful tools in science since the advent of quantum mechanics. Yet, strangely, this entire field of inquiry also forces some rather **[2]** pointedly and profound questions about humanity as a species.

1

A) NO CHANGE
B) genomics; the science of determining what our genes are and how those genes function;
C) genomics (the science of determining what our genes are and how those genes function)
D) genomics—the science of determining what our genes are and how those genes function,

2

A) NO CHANGE
B) profoundly and pointedly
C) pointed and profoundly
D) pointed and profound

CONTINUE

Test 8

[3] In more ways than one, the turn of the 21st century feels like lifetimes ago: the 1990s were heralded as the Decade of the Genome. The Human Genome Project (HGP), as **[4]** they were called, emerged from the clamor of molecular biologists and biochemists from a range of backgrounds, and emerged for a good reason: decades after the discovery of DNA's double-helix geometry by Watson, Crick, and Franklin, **[5]** we humans still had a lot to figure out about science.

3

Which choice best introduces the discussion of the Decade of the Genome?

A) NO CHANGE
B) Many things happened at the turn of the millennium
C) This relatively new field of study emerged when there was still much to learn
D) The end of the 20th century was an important time not only for science, but also for social justice

4

A) NO CHANGE
B) it was
C) we were
D) it were

5

Which choice provides the most specific reason that scientists wanted to research the human genome?

A) NO CHANGE
B) other scientists decided to pick up where their predecessors had left off.
C) we humans still knew little about what makes up a gene or how many genes there even are.
D) chemists, biologists, and even physicists had motives to continue their predecessors' research.

CONTINUE

Seemingly anxious to answer these questions as quickly as possible, [6] an unconventional research format was followed by the organizers of the HGP. Structuring the Project as a data-identification competition, the administrating National Institutes of Health (NIH) decided to "let the best person win." Maverick biochemist J. Craig Venter ended up beating the competition using his unexpected "shotgun" technique: identify each base pair of genes and allow the [7] computers' and the other competitors to figure out where the delineations are and what they mean.

6

A) NO CHANGE
B) following an unconventional research format, the organizers of the HGP.
C) the HGP organizers, following an unconventional research format.
D) the HGP organizers followed an unconventional research format.

7

A) NO CHANGE
B) computers and the other competitors
C) computers' and the other competitors'
D) computer's and the other competitor's

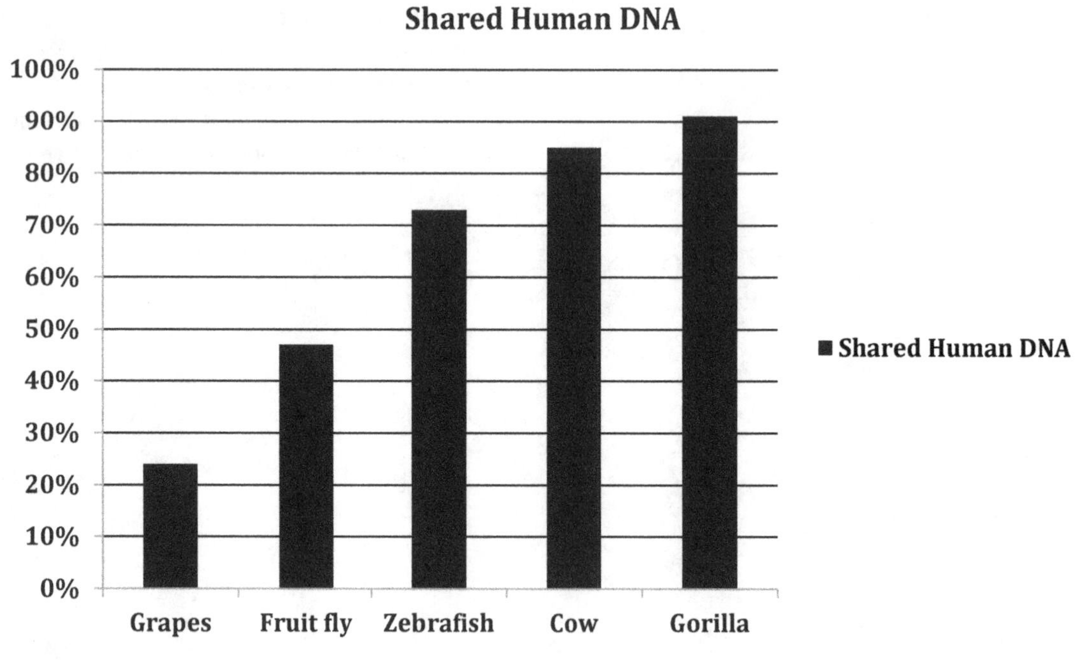

CONTINUE

Test 8

As the Decade of the Genome came to a close, we had discovered that it only takes about 25,000 genes to make a human a human: this was a striking discovery, because prior estimates went as high as 100,000 genes. We also found out that we share **8** exactly half of our DNA with fruit flies and a whopping **9** 73% with cows. **10** On the other hand, the Human Genome Project yielded the startling conclusion that junk DNA (base pairs with no function for humans) isn't junk; in many cases, such DNA is nearly identical to the active DNA of other species. On a molecular level, this may be the best possible confirmation of modern evolutionary theory.

Yet the social application of genomic research could have a transformative impact. Genomic screening has the potential to eliminate every disease known to man—every single one. Even aging, on a molecular level, is considered a form of pathological affliction. Instead of allowing evolution to run its course and humanity to gradually grow more robust, we could eliminate weakness, eradicate aging, and permanently warp human-influenced ecosystems all over the world. The Human Genome Project reminds us that every ecosystem and every organism—from a person to a fruit fly—is a delicate construct. **11** What if you could change aspects of yourself that you don't like?

8

Which choice best interprets the data in the chart?

A) NO CHANGE
B) about a quarter
C) exactly a quarter
D) about half

9

Which of the following is an accurate interpretation of the data in the chart?

A) NO CHANGE
B) 24%
C) 15%
D) 85%

10

A) NO CHANGE
B) Instead,
C) Perhaps most importantly,
D) However,

11

The writer would like to conclude the passage with a question that suggests reservations about the potential social applications discussed in the paragraph. Which choice best accomplishes this goal?

A) NO CHANGE
B) Can you imagine how wonderful this world would be without disease?
C) Has society progressed significantly since 1990?
D) Are we willing to tamper with the very foundations of biology?

Test 8

Questions 12-22 are based on the following passage.

Johnny Appleseed's Dark Side

[1] The classic tale of Johnny Appleseed, the altruistic conservationist, always pleases children in classrooms and is always a delight to tell around a lively campfire. [2] However, there are many who now believe that this folk hero's intentions, though indeed noble, may be not as suitable for children as were once thought. [3] It is true, yes, that the real-life Johnny Appleseed, named John Chapman, traveled the early United States from about 1790 to 1830, planting apple orchards. [4] Yet apples grown from **12** seeds specifically those apples left untreated and allowed to grow on their own, are known to be hard and sour. [5] These are the crabapples that Chapman was likely to have sown. **13**

Indeed, **14** entirely different factors could have explained Johnny Appleseed's initial popularity. According to Michael Pollan, author of *The Botany of Desire: A Plant's-Eye View of the World*, John Chapman could have been bringing the frontiersman something more than **15** charming and generous. "Really, what Johnny Appleseed was doing and the reason he was welcome in every cabin in Ohio and Indiana," Pollan writes, "was that he was bringing the gift of alcohol to the frontier. He was our American Dionysus."

12

A) NO CHANGE
B) seeds, specifically
C) seeds and specifically
D) seeds—specifically

13

The writer plans to add the following sentence to this paragraph.

> What may have been considered the "fruits of his labor" are now thought to have been nearly inedible.

To make this paragraph most logical, the sentence should be placed

A) before sentence 1.
B) before sentence 2.
C) after sentence 3.
D) after sentence 5.

14

Which choice best introduces the paragraph?

A) NO CHANGE
B) Johnny Appleseed would have done better to plant better quality fruit.
C) the people visited by Chapman were left with nothing more than bad fruit.
D) people today are still fascinated by the folklore surrounding Chapman.

15

A) NO CHANGE
B) charm and having generousness.
C) charming and generosity.
D) charm and generosity.

CONTINUE

Pollan's theory, [16] who is gaining clout among historians, postulates that the tart apples Chapman planted across the region were being used to make cheap, dirty alcohols such as applejack and hard cider—two brews distilled by leaving apple juice outside over harsh winter nights. [17] Applejack in particular was popular. It was a low-cost and low-maintenance product. Chapman's [18] "philanthropy" has indeed begun to appear in a more negative light: alcoholism was a common malady in the decades after the American [19] Revolution, it wrecked both the physical and mental state of those caught in its throes. [20] Many families throughout the history of the United States have been harmed in one way or another by the presence of alcohol.

16

A) NO CHANGE
B) whom
C) which
D) it

17

Which choice most effectively combines the two underlined sentences?

A) Because its low cost makes it popular, Applejack is a low-maintenance product.
B) Applejack in particular was popular because of the low cost and low required maintenance.
C) Applejack, in particular popular, was an option that was both low-cost and low-maintenance.
D) A low-cost and low-maintenance option was Applejack in particular.

18

A) NO CHANGE
B) "philanthropy," having indeed begun
C) "philanthropy" have indeed begun
D) "philanthropy" indeed have begun

19

A) NO CHANGE
B) Revolution, wrecking
C) Revolution for wrecking
D) Revolution; however, it wrecked

20

Which choice provides the most specific example regarding the effects of alcoholism during Johnny Appleseed's time?

A) NO CHANGE
B) A recent study reveals that more than half of rural Americans drink in excess at least occasionally—a figure that has increased significantly since Chapman was alive.
C) A military report from 1812 even claims that roughly 2,000 men were released from the Continental Army in one year as a result of excessive drinking and disorder.
D) Back in America's early days, most people preferred lower proof English-style beers to rum and other highly alcoholic "New World" liquors.

CONTINUE

But whatever the cultural problems of a blossoming America, the fact remains that John Chapman was a gentle man and a profound teacher. A missionary for the Swedenborgian Church, **21** he could often be seen at morning in the early dawn, sitting beside a brook, his hands clasped in his lap, his face serene in prayer. He let the children of the towns he visited shadow him while he worked, both teaching them divine lessons and instructing them in the art of apple germination. A unique product of his era, Chapman was a true pioneer, never settling into any confining trade or lifestyle, **22** often opting to sleep alone in the woods and rarely claiming any town as his true home.

21

A) NO CHANGE
B) he was seen at morning in the early dawn
C) in the morning, he was often seen early at dawn
D) he could often be seen in the early dawn

22

A) NO CHANGE
B) often he opted
C) often opted
D) opts often

CONTINUE

Test 8

Questions 23-33 are based on the following passage.

The "Virtual Reality" of Live Theater

We think of drama as a form of literature, which moves **23** its' audience to a recognition of the emotions and struggles that lie within the words of its characters. At some time in our lives, we have all—like one of Shakespeare's tragic heroes—had to consider the consequences that may follow a conflict-inducing course of action. Because of this recognition of a common situation, we listen to the dramatist's dialogue and we find ourselves agreeing with T. S. Eliot's definition of poetry: "Yes, that is exactly what I would have said, if I had had the words." It is this moment of complete communion **24** between the figure on the stage and ourselves that, perhaps, **25** crystallize the magic of theater.

Shakespeare called the theater "a mirror to **26** life." For the duration of a given play we might well agree with him. **27** However, if we think about that neat definition for a moment, we should begin to realize that, in fact, a mirror does not present an exact truth. At the fair, we have all laughed at our distorted reflections in a hall of mirrors. However, all mirrors distort to a greater or lesser degree: **28** regardless, the person we see in the mirror is not the person we know. It is the person that other people see.

23

A) NO CHANGE
B) it's
C) their
D) its

24

A) NO CHANGE
B) within
C) throughout
D) among

25

A) NO CHANGE
B) crystallizes
C) was crystallizing
D) have crystallized

26

Which choice most effectively combines the sentences at the underlined portion?

A) life," and for
B) life," for
C) life"; and for
D) life," however, for

27

A) NO CHANGE
B) For instance
C) Since
D) Likewise

28

A) NO CHANGE
B) yet,
C) fortunately,
D) DELETE the underlined portion.

CONTINUE

29 <u>Some people are more apt to enjoy theatrical productions than are others.</u> We know that the ten extras waving swords and coughing their way through the dry ice 30 <u>is</u> not really fighting a battle, no matter how much fake blood is smeared across their arms. We are aware of the trickery achieved with lighting and sound and screen-projection effects. 31 <u>However, the seats, the building, and the people in attendance are undeniably real.</u> Above all, we know that these characters we are watching are, as Shakespeare put it, "merely players, who strut and fret their time upon the stage, and then are heard no more." How is it, then, that the playwright succeeds in making us forget all that trickery?

29

Which choice best introduces the paragraph?

A) NO CHANGE
B) Shakespeare's London may very well be the most fascinating time period in history for a theater scholar.
C) Millions of people visit the theater every year, especially in large metropolitan cities like London.
D) When we visit the theater, we know that we are not in a real world.

30

A) NO CHANGE
B) was
C) are
D) were

31

The writer is considering deleting the underlined sentence. Should the sentence be kept or deleted?

A) Deleted, because it does not add to the paragraph's discussion of the artifice of theater.
B) Deleted, because it is entirely unrelated to Shakespeare's theater.
C) Kept, because it defines a term that is important to the main argument of the paragraph.
D) Kept, because it introduces the main point of the passage.

CONTINUE

Shakespeare does exactly this by touching on the half-hidden fears of his audience, by making us feel uneasy in the opening scenes of his plays. Some plays begin with what we might call "civil disobedience": a rioting mob running through the streets of a city *(Julius Caesar*, *Coriolanus*, *Romeo and Juliet)*. **32** In light of this, Shakespeare draws on our fears and superstitions concerning the evil side of life and depicts witches and ghosts (*Hamlet* or *Macbeth*). Shakespeare makes **33** us want to discover whether the disasters that lie just below the surfaces of all our lives can be countered, defeated, and dissolved. The important thing is that Shakespeare has hooked us and made us want to know what lies at the end of the play.

32

A) NO CHANGE
B) Instead,
C) So,
D) In other instances,

33

A) NO CHANGE
B) you
C) one
D) them

CONTINUE

Questions 34-44 are based on the following passage.

Gardening as a Science, Gardening as an Art

It is a characteristic of human nature to attempt to carve out a patch of nature which expresses our feelings towards the fertile earth—simply put, **34** playing with dirt. Real gardening aficionados spend hours consulting gardening catalogs, planning layouts for what are referred to as "outside rooms," creating areas for "mass planting," considering the values of sheltered arbors, establishing which areas are to be made into shaded walks and which left open to the sun, or pondering the necessity of a water fountain. **35** Mentioning a particular plant to these connoisseurs and they will immediately refer to it by its Latin name, recount the variations of the original plant now available, discuss its soil needs and positioning, explain what care and tending it requires, and determine **36** when it needs being pruned and tamed.

For others, the best thing about gardening is that **37** he or she really does not need to have any specialized knowledge or experience. (However, if you do have either of these two qualities, **38** or you can cut down on the mistakes that come from old-fashioned trial and error.) Years ago, when I lived in Africa, I had a small garden and a gardener named Kennedy. He never knew the name of any plant that he put into the ground. If I asked Kennedy what he was planting, he would reply with a shrug, "It is red (or yellow, or blue, as the case might be)." He was always right.

34

A) NO CHANGE
B) to create a garden.
C) to masterfully cultivate.
D) to produce a bountiful cornucopia.

35

A) NO CHANGE
B) Having mentioned
C) I mentioned
D) Mention

36

A) NO CHANGE
B) when it is a need to be pruned or tamed.
C) when it needs to be tamed or pruning.
D) when it needs pruning or taming.

37

A) NO CHANGE
B) it really does
C) you really do
D) we really do

38

A) NO CHANGE
B) but
C) and
D) DELETE the underlined portion.

CONTINUE

No doubt, more professional gardeners would be shocked by so nonchalant an approach to 39 nomenclature, but I always thought that Kennedy had the correct view of what a garden was all about. Color and contrast, light and shade: these are the things that pass through the eye of the beholder and bring quiet contentment to 40 his or her soul.

39

A) NO CHANGE
B) naming stuff
C) words by which to call things
D) what to refer to things that need naming

40

A) NO CHANGE
B) their
C) its
D) our

41 Of course, people cultivate gardens all over the world. The original English Cottage garden, which we admire today for its charm, calm, and cheerfulness, was actually more like a medieval pharmacy. The stunning leaves and flowers of the various plants were **42** used as anecdotes and antiseptics to ease physical and mental pain. Herbs were grown in the garden to add flavor and taste to meals. Fruits provided essential vitamins to the body—these included not only the blackberry, raspberry, and strawberry, **43** and fruits that are far less seen these days: gooseberries, black, red, and white currants, and mulberries. A small tree—apple, pear, or hazelnut—was often included. These trees provided the vitamins necessary to keep people energetic and healthy through the winter months. Vegetables too provided natural Vitamin C and antioxidants. **44** Next time you try to cultivate a garden, it might behoove you to research how best to take care of the specific types of plants you're attempting to grow.

41

Which choice best introduces this paragraph?

A) NO CHANGE
B) Some gardens, naturally, are more admirable than others.
C) Some of the best gardens can be found on the British Isles.
D) However, gardens began with a more practical intention.

42

A) NO CHANGE
B) used for anecdotes
C) used as antidotes
D) used by antidotes

43

A) NO CHANGE
B) but also
C) and also
D) but

44

The writer would like to conclude by restating the main point of the paragraph. Which choice best accomplishes this goal?

A) NO CHANGE
B) Some plants have proven to be exceedingly healthy for their human cultivators.
C) In these gardens and their modern-day successors, the technicalities and pragmatism of gardening meet the refreshment and inspiration of nature.
D) Clearly, some plants are much healthier to ingest than are others.

STOP

If you finish before time is called, you may check your work on this section only.
Do not turn to any other section.

No Test Material On This Page

Answer Key

TEST 8

PASSAGE 1

The Power of Genomics

1. C
2. D
3. C
4. B
5. C
6. D
7. B
8. D
9. D
10. C
11. D

PASSAGE 2

Johnny Appleseed's Dark Side

12. B
13. D
14. A
15. D
16. C
17. B
18. A
19. B
20. C
21. D
22. A

PASSAGE 3

The "Virtual Reality" of Live Theater

23. D
24. A
25. B
26. A
27. A
28. D
29. D
30. C
31. A
32. D
33. A

PASSAGE 4

Gardening as a Science, Gardening as an Art

34. B
35. D
36. D
37. C
38. D
39. A
40. A
41. D
42. C
43. B
44. C

Post-Test Analysis

This post-test analysis is essential if you want to see an improvement on your next test. Possible reasons for errors on the four passages in this section are listed here. Place check marks next to the types of errors that pertain to you, or write your own types of errors in the blank spaces.

TIMING AND ACCURACY

◇ Spent too long reading individual passages
◇ Spent too long answering each question
◇ Spent too long on a few difficult questions
◇ Felt rushed and made silly mistakes or random errors
◇ Unable to work quickly using error types and POE
Other: ______________________________

APPROACHING THE PASSAGES AND QUESTIONS

◇ Unable to effectively grasp the passage's tone or style
◇ Unable to effectively grasp the passage's topic or stance
◇ Did not understand the context of underlined portions
◇ Did not eliminate false answers using error types
◇ Answered questions using first impressions instead of POE
◇ Answered questions without slotting in and checking final answer
◇ Eliminated NO CHANGE and chose a trap answer
◇ Eliminated correct answer during POE
Other: ______________________________

Use this form to better analyze your performance. If you don't understand why you made errors, there is no way that you can correct them!

GRAMMAR AND SENTENCE STRUCTURE

◇ Did not test sentence for subject-verb agreement
◇ Did not identify proper verb form and verb tense
◇ Did not test sentence for pronoun agreement
◇ Did not identify proper pronoun form (subject/object, who/which/when/where/why)
◇ Did not test for proper comparison phrasing (amount/number, between/among) and number agreement
◇ Did not test phrase for correct adverb/adjective usage
◇ Did not see broader sentence structure (parallelism, misplaced modifier)
◇ Did not see flaws in punctuation (colon, semicolon, comma splice, misplaced commas)
◇ Did not see tricky possessives or contractions (its/it's, your/you're)
◇ Did not identify flaws in standard phrases (either . . . or, not only . . . but also, etc.)
◇ Did not use proper phrasing in sentences requiring the subjunctive
Other: ______________________________

STYLE, ORGANIZATION, AND WORKING WITH EVIDENCE

◇ Did not notice cases of redundancy and wordiness
◇ Misidentified an expression as redundant or wordy
◇ Did not notice flaws in essay style or excessively informal expressions
◇ Misidentified an expression as stylistically inconsistent or informal
◇ Created the wrong relationship between two sentences
◇ Created the wrong relationship between two paragraphs
◇ Created the wrong placement for an out-of-order paragraph
◇ Did not eliminate faulty or improper English idioms
◇ Did not properly read or analyze an insertion/deletion question
◇ Did not properly read or analyze the information in a graphic
◇ Understood a graphic, but could not identify the correct passage content
Other: ______________________________

Test 9

Test 9

Writing Test

35 MINUTES, 44 QUESTIONS

Turn to Section 2 of your answer sheet to answer the questions in this section.

DIRECTIONS

Each passage below is accompanied by a number of questions. For some questions, you will consider how the passage might be revised to improve the expression of ideas. For other questions, you will consider how the passage might be edited to correct errors in sentence structure, usage, or punctuation. A passage or a question may be accompanied by one or more graphics (such as a table or graph) that you will consider as you make revising and editing decisions.

Some questions will direct you to an underlined portion of a passage. Other questions will direct you to a location in a passage or ask you to think about the passage as a whole.

After reading each passage, choose the answer to each question that most effectively improves the quality of writing in the passage or that makes the passage conform to the conventions of standard written English. Many questions include a "NO CHANGE" option. Choose that option if you think the best choice is to leave the relevant portion of the passage as it is.

Questions 1-11 are based on the following passage.

Back to the Sixties

Someone once said, "If you can remember the sixties, then you weren't there." This may be a flippant remark, of course, but it does help to perpetuate the clichés of flower power, [1] Beatle-mania, and, free love. For those who regard the sixties as a piece of history, this quote conjures up a spurious picture [2] of the true experience of what it was really like to be young at the time. I was there, and I remember the period very differently.

1

A) NO CHANGE
B) Beatle-mania, and, free, love.
C) Beatle-mania, and free love.
D) Beatle-mania; and free love.

2

A) NO CHANGE
B) of what truly experiencing to be young at the time was really like.
C) of what it was really like to be young at the time.
D) of what the experience was really like at the time being young.

CONTINUE

Test 9

In 1960, I celebrated my twentieth birthday. Legally, I was still a child: in those days, [3] <u>one was</u> not regarded as an adult by society until age twenty-one. In the UK, at eighteen I could buy cigarettes and I could join the army (compulsory conscription at [4] <u>eighteen—a</u> legacy of the Second World War, had only been abolished that very year), [5] <u>yet I was not sure if I wanted to serve my country.</u> I could go to the cinema and watch any kind of film, but education on intimate relationships [6] <u>were</u> regarded as one of the duties of a parent, not as something that I would be introduced to at school.

3

A) NO CHANGE
B) they were
C) it was
D) it were

4

A) NO CHANGE
B) eighteen, a
C) eighteen a
D) eighteen; a

5

Which choice provides the most specific support for the main point of the paragraph?

A) NO CHANGE
B) yet I could not buy alcohol or vote for the government that would send me to war.
C) and I could also drive and stay out as late as I wanted.
D) but I did not smoke, even though cigarette advertising was not so harshly regulated back then.

6

A) NO CHANGE
B) is
C) have been
D) was

In retrospect, the sixties did seem to be the time when everything [7] we have been used to was galvanized into new ways of living. [8] Equally certain is the idea that the changes people today make such a fuss about were not the changes that were actually influential. People today have no concept of how isolated each part of the UK was before the sixties, before there were motorways, high-speed trains, and inexpensive air travel. In 1960, there were only two television channels in the country. Neither channel began broadcasting before the afternoon, and both closed at midnight at the latest. Above all, the channels of communication—television, radio, and print—were satellites of the government.

7

A) NO CHANGE
B) we were being used to
C) we had been used to
D) we, being used to it,

8

At this point, the writer is considering adding the following sentence.

> The 1970s, however, were different in this regard.

Should the writer make this addition here?

A) Yes, because it provides a useful point of comparison for the main point of the passage.
B) Yes, because it states the main point of the passage.
C) No, because it detracts from the paragraph's discussion of the 1960s.
D) No, because it would be better placed elsewhere in the passage.

CONTINUE

Test 9

9 Thanks to hindsight, we can see that, before the decade of the 1960s, there was some discontent. The warfare in Europe was long **10** over. People noticed that things in the UK were not developing as they were in evolving countries such as Germany, **11** for example. That did not seem right. As a teenager, I had wondered why only American films were ever in Technicolor. That did not seem right. Most representative of the times was a show that opened in London's West End in February 1960, a show that had not been rehearsed in the usual manner: this production had been improvised through impromptu sessions by the actors and musicians. It was called *Fings Ain't Wot They Used To Be,* and it embodied a spirit of rebellion that only grew stronger in the years to come.

9

Which choice most smoothly and effectively introduces the discussion of the origin of 1960s rebellion?

A) NO CHANGE
B) Hindsight is 20/20 and we can see that there had been some discontented rumbles before the decade of 1960.
C) With the benefit of hindsight, we can see that there had been rumbles of discontent before 1960.
D) Looking back, there were a lot of signs of discontent before the year 1960.

10

Which choice best combines the two sentences at the underlined portion?

A) over, also because people
B) over because people
C) over, however people
D) over, and people

11

A) NO CHANGE
B) to be specific.
C) also.
D) DELETE the underlined portion (deleting the comma after "Germany" and ending the sentence with a period).

CONTINUE

Test 9

Questions 12-22 are based on the following passage and supplementary material.

Animal Egotism: Case Studies in Survival

[1] Self-interest is what underlies human common-sense morality. [2] Our evolution does not operate on the level of a social group. [3] **12** For an action to be morally right, it is essential that the action maximize one's own well-being. [4] German philosopher Friedrich Nietzsche proclaimed in *Beyond Good and Evil* that "egoism belongs to the essence of a noble soul" and that "the noble soul accepts the fact of his egoism without question . . . as something that may have its basis in the primary law of things." [5] We are creatures dictated by our evolutionary genetics and our most basic self-interest: to continue being replicated. [6] Our evolution operates on the basis of what lingers in our genetic identities. **13**

14 Take for example the hypothetical case of a mother bear and her cub preparing for winter hibernation. In the months prior, the mother bear will consume as much sustenance as she needs to double her weight. However, **15** if she is not achieved the required weight by eating animals of other species, a mother bear will often eat her own cub in order to fulfill her nutritional needs. Unpleasant indeed, yet the mother bear is acting in the interest of her own survival. It seems that a parent ought to protect **16** it's offspring to secure reproduction, but if the entire bloodline of the organism is at stake, biological imperatives take over.

12

A) NO CHANGE
B) That an action is morally right,
C) In order that an action will be right morally,
D) An action being morally right,

13

To make this paragraph most logical, sentence 2 should be placed

A) where it is now.
B) before sentence 1.
C) before sentence 4.
D) before sentence 6.

14

Which choice best introduces the example presented in the paragraph?

A) NO CHANGE
B) One big example, hypothetically, is the case of a mother bear and her cub getting ready to hibernate in winter.
C) Here, take this example of a hypothetical case of a mother bear and her cub readying themselves for winter.
D) DELETE the underlined sentence.

15

A) NO CHANGE
B) if she had not achieved
C) she should not achieve
D) should she not achieve

16

A) NO CHANGE
B) their
C) its
D) its'

CONTINUE

Some may argue that this form of selfishness is not relevant to humans. **17** Consequently, it is the basis of all human interaction. Examine the physical makeup of a newborn baby. Proportionately, its head is **18** significantly larger than an adult's; in fact, scientists calculate that a infant's head constitutes approximately **19** eight percent of its total body weight. There are several reasons for this, **20** but there's a really big one: brain development. Over time, babies have developed larger craniums that have been genetically modified to sustain larger brains, but this requirement (along with decreased mobility) renders a human baby helpless for a long period of time. To offset this need for extensive care, larger heads were accompanied by larger eyes

17

A) NO CHANGE
B) Furthermore,
C) Subsequently,
D) Nonetheless,

18

Which choice is an accurate interpretation of the data in the chart?

A) NO CHANGE
B) only slightly smaller than
C) significantly smaller than
D) about the same size as

19

Which choice best interprets the data in the chart?

A) NO CHANGE
B) fifty-five percent
C) ten percent
D) twenty percent

20

A) NO CHANGE
B) but let's talk about the most important of all
C) but one reason in particular is most important
D) but one sticks out as being most important

Adult's Body Weight by Anatomy

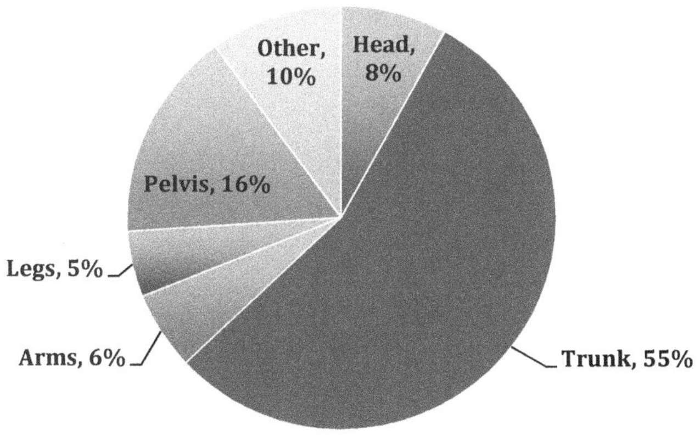

Infant's Body Weight by Anatomy

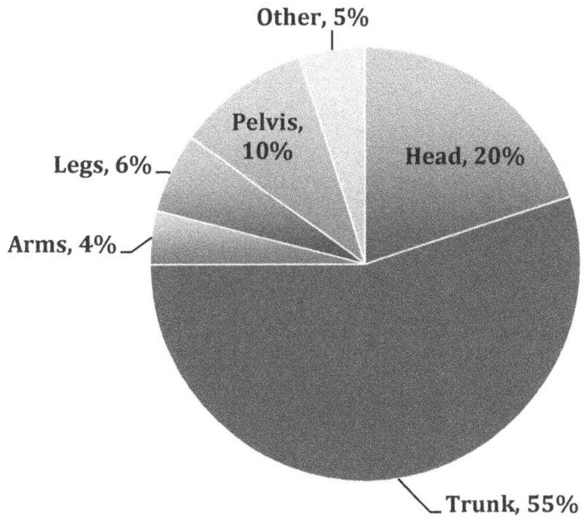

to elicit parental connection to the baby. Genetically speaking, such a trait combats a human mother's possible urge to abandon her young, **21** although some humans are more loving to their young than are others.

22 Us who rail against "egoism" are simply following a genetic predisposition. One contemplates such issues not—as many are fooled into believing—from an explicit "sense of superiority." Rather, these contemplations are the by-products of forces that we are often powerless to discern.

21

Which choice provides the most specific support for the argument made in the sentence?

A) NO CHANGE
B) and there are many different mechanisms behind this fascinating characteristic.
C) although there are differing theories regarding why such a characteristic exists.
D) as humanity's innate love of visual stimulation counteracts an instinct that may otherwise be considered "natural."

22

A) NO CHANGE
B) Those
C) He or she
D) Them

Test 9

Questions 23-33 are based on the following passage.

Literary Plunder: The Myths of *Treasure Island*

[1] 23 With no idea of the huge influence it would have thereafter, *Treasure Island* was written by Robert Louis Stevenson. [2] An adventure novel published in 1883, *Treasure Island* features pirates engaging in mutiny and assassination, plundering cape towns, and causing general mayhem. [3] Oddly enough, the book was initially written for children. [4] However, today people of all ages and all walks of life delight in its compelling drama. [5] A surreal tale of criminality, this novel gave its seafarers attributes that have had a significant impact 24 on the way pirates are perceived at present. 25

23

A) NO CHANGE
B) Having a surprisingly huge influence thereafter, Robert Louis Stevenson wrote *Treasure Island.*
C) *Treasure Island*, when written by Robert Louis Stevenson, had no idea it would have such a huge influence thereafter.
D) When Robert Louis Stevenson wrote *Treasure Island*, he had no idea of the huge influence it would have in popular culture.

24

A) NO CHANGE
B) about
C) with
D) into

25

To make this paragraph most logical, sentence 4 should be placed

A) where it is now.
B) after sentence 1.
C) after sentence 2.
D) after sentence 5.

Test 9

[26] Stevenson was a master at crafting compelling, original stories. Consider the black spot. In the novel, pirates use a piece of paper colored on one side with a menacing black spot, on the other with a message of what is to come for the recipient. [27] The recipient, then doing his best to flee from his homeland, for if one ever receives a black spot, one should never stay on to see what doom is coming. This practice was not the brainchild of Stevenson, but a modified appropriation, a custom that was already terrible in all respects and to which Stevenson added a horrific twist. It was already a [28] normal thing in the Caribbean for pirates to present a man with an ace of spades (traditionally an ominous sign, as though a man were on his last leg) to threaten him, to let him know that his treachery and deceit would not go unnoticed. The ace was not a death [29] warrant; but it was a warning message.

26

Which choice best introduces the paragraph?

A) NO CHANGE
B) Though many of his books are revered, *Treasure Island* is widely believed to contain the most captivating content.
C) The book is full of tales of mystery and intrigue.
D) Many of the plot devices in the book are based on actual pirate lore and methodology.

27

A) NO CHANGE
B) The recipient then does his best
C) The recipient, then does his best
D) The recipient then, does his best

28

A) NO CHANGE
B) common practice
C) typical thing in behavior
D) prosaic orthodoxy

29

A) NO CHANGE
B) warrant, instead
C) warrant,
D) warrant; rather,

CONTINUE

Then there are the odd traditions that Stevenson exploited, such as the eyepatch. This feature has become a standard of piratedom, but it was rarely found on a pirate of the nineteenth century. In fact, such patches were rarely found on anyone at the time, and weren't unique to any one occupation. **30** Generals and also farmers, politicians and shopkeepers may or may not have worn them; simply put, if a person lived at the time, and happened to damage **31** their eye somehow, that person would have an eyepatch. But surely, at least it was only pirates who used peg-legs, yes? No! The same logic applies to the peg-leg, which was used for all sorts of injuries and was not very piratesque at all.

I suppose I'm getting myself all riled up because Stevenson's piece of fiction has so changed the way we think about pirates, which were a real, and are still a very real, threat to **32** nations' across the world. Just the other day I saw a headline, "Somalian Pirates Attack International Cruise Liner." Pirate culture is still very much alive. And can I assure you, the guys who attacked that cruise liner weren't sporting hooks for hands or holding dusty burlap maps. **33** Clearly, some pirates are more attractive than others.

30

A) NO CHANGE
B) Generals and farmers, as well as politicians and shopkeepers
C) Generals, farmers, politicians, and shopkeepers
D) Generals, farmers, politicians, and, shopkeepers

31

A) NO CHANGE
B) its
C) your
D) his or her

32

A) NO CHANGE
B) nation's
C) nations
D) a nation

33

The writer would like to conclude by stating the main point of the paragraph. Which choice best accomplishes this goal?

A) NO CHANGE
B) Though it may be the best known, *Treasure Island* is not the only excellent work of pirate literature.
C) If Robert Louis Stevenson were alive today, he might write a new story about the terrible Somali pirates.
D) Delighting in exciting pirate literature should not discount the real life danger such criminals present.

Test 9

Questions 34-44 are based on the following passage.

Called to Teach

I wonder when the word "vocation" lost its original meeting. In grammar school, I was taught that to have a vocation in life was rather special. When "vocation" referred to a person's employment or main [34] occupation it was regarded as something worthy, and something requiring dedication. The origin of the word itself is grounded in the Christian religion, although its implications seem to be included in many other faiths. [35] The term suggests that God has created each person with gifts and talents oriented to a specific purpose and way of life, or a single vocation. This suggests that each of us should utilize these gifts in our professions, our family lives, and our involvement in society, for the sake of the greater common good.

I cannot say that I understood all this [36] very clear when I was a child, though I did believe that the things my three teachers in grammar school—Mrs. Ingle, Mrs. Senior, and Mr. Penkethman—said [37] was gospel truth. However, the very fact that I still remember their names indicates how significant they were. [38] There definition of "vocation" resonated with me since it also resonated with my mother's repeated axiom: "The world isn't all about you."

34

A) NO CHANGE
B) occupation; which
C) occupation, which
D) occupation, it

35

The writer is considering deleting the underlined sentence. Should the writer make this deletion?

A) Yes, because it provides information that contradicts the main point of the paragraph.
B) Yes, because it provides a definition unimportant to the paragraph.
C) No, because it presents an important counterargument to the main point of the paragraph.
D) No, because it explains a key term in the passage.

36

A) NO CHANGE
B) clearly very
C) clear very
D) very clearly

37

A) NO CHANGE
B) is
C) are
D) were

38

A) NO CHANGE
B) Her
C) Their
D) They're

CONTINUE

Test 9

In those [39] innocent childhood days, I wanted to be an actor on the silver screen. (As I discovered in high school, my acting ambition was strong, but my talent was worse than weak.) I guess Clint Eastwood and Sean Connery were pretty relieved [40] whenever I became a teacher instead. [41] Ultimately, I regarded teaching as something to do and to get paid for. Little by little, though, I began to realize the worth and sheer joy of this profession, the importance of doing one's best to do it well.

[42] At boarding schools outside of America is where I worked most. One was the [43] more expensiver school in all of Switzerland, a place where parents left their kids to get on with education while they got on with their high-powered lives. The others were in South America, at quite the other end of the financial scale. I felt needed in all of these schools, and I am reminded, looking back, of how much sentiments have changed. To have a profession such as that of a teacher or a doctor or a writer today too often [44] meaning that you demand a lot of money up front, irrespective of how much your skills might actually be needed. Payment before service is the rule. In contrast, and all these years later, my mother and those three teachers still seem to have gotten the idea of a vocation right.

39

A) NO CHANGE
B) green days of yore,
C) pastimes that were innocuous,
D) naive and ephemeral reminiscences,

40

A) NO CHANGE
B) how
C) that
D) where

41

A) NO CHANGE
B) Simultaneously,
C) Regardless,
D) At first,

42

Which choice most smoothly and effectively introduces this paragraph?

A) NO CHANGE
B) I worked a bunch at boarding schools outside the US.
C) For most of my career, I worked in boarding schools outside America.
D) For most of my career, you could find me at boarding schools teaching outside of America.

43

A) NO CHANGE
B) most expensive
C) expensiver
D) more expensive

44

A) NO CHANGE
B) means
C) mean
D) to mean

STOP

If you finish before time is called, you may check your work on this section only.
Do not turn to any other section.

Answer Key

TEST 9

PASSAGE 1

Back to the Sixties

1. C
2. C
3. A
4. B
5. B
6. D
7. C
8. C
9. C
10. D
11. D

PASSAGE 2

Animal Egotism: Case Studies in Survival

12. A
13. D
14. A
15. D
16. C
17. D
18. A
19. D
20. C
21. D
22. B

PASSAGE 3

Literary Plunder: The Myths of *Treasure Island*

23. D
24. A
25. A
26. D
27. B
28. B
29. D
30. C
31. D
32. C
33. D

PASSAGE 4

Called to Teach

34. D
35. D
36. D
37. D
38. C
39. A
40. C
41. D
42. C
43. B
44. B

Post-Test Analysis

This post-test analysis is essential if you want to see an improvement on your next test. Possible reasons for errors on the four passages in this section are listed here. Place check marks next to the types of errors that pertain to you, or write your own types of errors in the blank spaces.

TIMING AND ACCURACY

◇ Spent too long reading individual passages
◇ Spent too long answering each question
◇ Spent too long on a few difficult questions
◇ Felt rushed and made silly mistakes or random errors
◇ Unable to work quickly using error types and POE
Other: ____________________

APPROACHING THE PASSAGES AND QUESTIONS

◇ Unable to effectively grasp the passage's tone or style
◇ Unable to effectively grasp the passage's topic or stance
◇ Did not understand the context of underlined portions
◇ Did not eliminate false answers using error types
◇ Answered questions using first impressions instead of POE
◇ Answered questions without slotting in and checking final answer
◇ Eliminated NO CHANGE and chose a trap answer
◇ Eliminated correct answer during POE
Other: ____________________

Use this form to better analyze your performance. If you don't understand why you made errors, there is no way that you can correct them!

GRAMMAR AND SENTENCE STRUCTURE

◇ Did not test sentence for subject-verb agreement
◇ Did not identify proper verb form and verb tense
◇ Did not test sentence for pronoun agreement
◇ Did not identify proper pronoun form (subject/object, who/which/when/where/why)
◇ Did not test for proper comparison phrasing (amount/number, between/among) and number agreement
◇ Did not test phrase for correct adverb/adjective usage
◇ Did not see broader sentence structure (parallelism, misplaced modifier)
◇ Did not see flaws in punctuation (colon, semicolon, comma splice, misplaced commas)
◇ Did not see tricky possessives or contractions (its/it's, your/you're)
◇ Did not identify flaws in standard phrases (either . . . or, not only . . . but also, etc.)
◇ Did not use proper phrasing in sentences requiring the subjunctive
Other: ____________________

STYLE, ORGANIZATION, AND WORKING WITH EVIDENCE

◇ Did not notice cases of redundancy and wordiness
◇ Misidentified an expression as redundant or wordy
◇ Did not notice flaws in essay style or excessively informal expressions
◇ Misidentified an expression as stylistically inconsistent or informal
◇ Created the wrong relationship between two sentences
◇ Created the wrong relationship between two paragraphs
◇ Created the wrong placement for an out-of-order paragraph
◇ Did not eliminate faulty or improper English idioms
◇ Did not properly read or analyze an insertion/deletion question
◇ Did not properly read or analyze the information in a graphic
◇ Understood a graphic, but could not identify the correct passage content
Other: ____________________

Test 10

Test 10

Writing Test

35 MINUTES, 44 QUESTIONS

Turn to Section 2 of your answer sheet to answer the questions in this section.

DIRECTIONS

Each passage below is accompanied by a number of questions. For some questions, you will consider how the passage might be revised to improve the expression of ideas. For other questions, you will consider how the passage might be edited to correct errors in sentence structure, usage, or punctuation. A passage or a question may be accompanied by one or more graphics (such as a table or graph) that you will consider as you make revising and editing decisions.

Some questions will direct you to an underlined portion of a passage. Other questions will direct you to a location in a passage or ask you to think about the passage as a whole.

After reading each passage, choose the answer to each question that most effectively improves the quality of writing in the passage or that makes the passage conform to the conventions of standard written English. Many questions include a "NO CHANGE" option. Choose that option if you think the best choice is to leave the relevant portion of the passage as it is.

Questions 1-11 are based on the following passage.

Edward Hopper Paints America

The work of one of America's finest twentieth-century artists, Edward Hopper, [1] having been subjected to much critical discussion by art aficionados—although, significantly, not by the general public by whom he has always been venerated. [2] Hopper rarely discussed his own work as a public thing. Still, he did once remark that "the whole answer is there on the canvas."

1

A) NO CHANGE
B) have been subjected
C) has been subjected
D) were being subjected

2

A) NO CHANGE
B) It's rare that Hopper would have in public been discussing his own work.
C) Hopper rarely discussed his own work publicly.
D) In public, Hopper was rarely one to discuss work that was his own.

CONTINUE

This comment suggests that Hopper took to heart a maxim given to him by [3] Robert Henri. Henri was a teacher of his at the New York School of Art: "It isn't the subject [of a painting] that counts, but what you feel about it." Henri may well have been referring to matters of artistic inspiration: Hopper seems to have taken this advice to be equally applicable [4] by anyone who wanders into an art gallery. Hopper's paintings create within the observer a feeling of instant recognition not only of what is clearly presented in the depiction, [5] but of all the implications and questions too that lie behind what is actually shown.

3

Which choice best combines the sentences at the underlined portion?

A) Robert Henri, who was being a teacher of his
B) Robert Henri, one of his teachers
C) Robert Henri, and one of his teachers
D) Robert Henri was one of his teachers

4

A) NO CHANGE
B) with
C) to
D) of

5

A) NO CHANGE
B) and also of all the implications and questions
C) but the implications and questions that also
D) but also of all the implications and questions

CONTINUE

Test 10

At first glance, Hopper's *Automat* (1927) simply depicts a woman sitting alone at a small table, on which there is a cup of coffee. **6** However, the power of the picture comes from the viewer's gradual assimilation of details: the woman's clothing suggests a certain smartness, and an empty plate sits beside the coffee cup. On the shelf behind the woman—perhaps significantly—is a small bowl of colorful fruit. **7** They're presence contrasts with that of the precisely depicted brown radiator standing against the wall nearby. The more one explores the picture, the more **8** they unearth new questions and considerations. Is the painting a comment on urban isolation or **9** does, it simply record a moment of solitude and reflection within the busy levels of a city? These ambiguities of recognition are what hold the attention and, eventually, the involvement of the onlooker.

6

A) NO CHANGE
B) Unfortunately,
C) Fortunately,
D) Because

7

A) NO CHANGE
B) Its
C) Their
D) It's

8

A) NO CHANGE
B) they are unearthing
C) one unearths
D) one, unearthing

9

A) NO CHANGE
B) does
C) does;
D) does—

CONTINUE

Above all else, in every one of Hopper's paintings, the contrast between darkness and illumination [10] force us to consider the truth of his pictures. Sometimes—as in his most popular picture, *Nighthawks* (1942)—the darkness is all-encompassing and makes us aware of the gulf between our personal life voyages and those of others. At other times—as in one of his last pictures, *Office in a Small City* (1953)—Hopper reverses this motif. [11] Though he was less prolific during his advanced years, he was still creating new art into the 1960s. The picture blazes with the stark light of office windows and a cerulean sky: through one office window we see a man sitting at a bare desk, gazing through a second window just across the way. Is this a room with a view, or a view with hidden insights? Remember Henri's words: "What you feel" is what counts.

10

A) NO CHANGE
B) is forcing
C) forces
D) forced

11

The writer is considering deleting the underlined sentence. Should the sentence be kept or deleted?

A) Kept, because it provides important information about the main topic of the passage.
B) Kept, because it is the main point of the paragraph.
C) Deleted, because it does not discuss the artist central to the paragraph.
D) Deleted, because it is unimportant to the main topic of the paragraph.

CONTINUE

Test 10

Questions 12-22 are based on the following passage.

Smells Like Teen Rebellion

[1] If someone drills you in this or that order, it's natural to have the inexplicable urge to defy that order. [2] This, **12** <u>in short</u>, is the central mechanism of teenage rebellion. [3] It isn't that adults or young children like to listen to others any more than teenagers do, but rather that adolescents are more disposed to seek out their own choices. [4] Scientists have discovered one possible **13** <u>explanation, even</u> through adolescence, a teenager's mind continues to grow, but not uniformly. [5] It turns out that the emotion-oriented of the brain matures faster than the region that controls rational thought. [6] Unfortunately, this volatile mentality often leads to alcohol, drugs, sexual activity, bullying, and the general breaking of rules. **14**

12

A) NO CHANGE
B) instead
C) with regard
D) however

13

A) NO CHANGE
B) explanation: even
C) explanation, since even
D) explanation even

14

The writer plans to add the following sentence to this paragraph.

> Consequently, teenagers possess well-developed feelings but lack a fully-formed capacity for control.

To make this paragraph most logical, the sentence should be placed

A) before sentence 1.
B) before sentence 2.
C) after sentence 3.
D) after sentence 5.

In response to this, many schools have increased their efforts to spread awareness of such **15** elicit activities by enlisting speakers and organizing assemblies. Such efforts, however, often prove to **16** exacerbate these things. **17** Most adults do not take such programs seriously. In other words, you can tell teenagers over and over again that breaking the rules will only hurt them, but the more you speak, the more they will see your words as a challenge and want to "overcome" that challenge.

15

A) NO CHANGE
B) illicitly activities
C) eliciting activities
D) illicit activities

16

A) NO CHANGE
B) resemble a losing uphill battle.
C) be counterproductive.
D) work against the usual grain.

17

Which choice provides a specific example that supports the previous sentence?

A) NO CHANGE
B) The best students take such programs with a grain of salt and the worst ones actively work to disobey their messages.
C) Who can tell exactly how teenagers will react to such programs?
D) For myriad reasons, this is clearly not the best way to inspire good behavior in teenagers, especially the more difficult ones.

Test 10

18 Granted, some teenagers are very well-behaved. When a given rule has even a slim chance of being evaded, "that's just going to strengthen teenage desire and teenage feeling; that's going to make teenagers think, 'I need to fight to win,'" explains Kristin Laurin, a scientist 19 has conducted research on teen psychology. This amounts to saying that teens will probably end up on the wrong path if they 20 break these rules. This also amounts to saying that anyone who is special enough can still prevail.

21 At what age does this self-sabotaging phase of life conclude? It doesn't take science to prove that experiencing something firsthand leaves a stronger impression than hearing an account from someone else. In recent efforts to combat bullying, awareness organizations have brought innovative ideas to schools: these organizations simulate a bullying environment and twist the situation until each student in the participating groups 22 have had a taste of what it feels like to be bullied. Within the groups, more select groups form and naturally dominate the rest of the kids. When the simulation finally ends, each student is left with a vivid impression of what being bullied feels like, producing a higher likelihood that the students will not exhibit bullying behaviors in the future.

18

Which choice most smoothly and effectively introduces the writer's discussion of teenage behavior in this paragraph?

A) NO CHANGE
B) I cannot deny the simple fact that I was once a teenager, too.
C) If you think teenagers are bad, try dealing with toddlers.
D) DELETE the underlined sentence.

19

A) NO CHANGE
B) who has conducted
C) that did conduct
D) of them conducting

20

Which choice best combines the two sentences at the underlined portion?

A) break these rules, that
B) break these rules, but that
C) break these rules, and that
D) break these rules because

21

The writer wants to introduce the paragraph with a question. Which choice best accomplishes this goal?

A) NO CHANGE
B) Which of the aforementioned teenage transgressions is the most dangerous?
C) What then can schools do to help their students?
D) What percentage of adults never grow out of this phase?

22

A) NO CHANGE
B) are having
C) is having
D) has had

CONTINUE

Test 10

Questions 23-33 are based on the following passage.

The Freelancer's Dilemma

Working at home can be a difficult task for the unprepared. With the luxuries and comforts that we afford ourselves, [23] we can be hard to differentiate [24] among what is the "spare room" and what is the "home office." Discipline is in short supply when your copier is next to your television, your new business suits are pajamas, and your only office mate is your cat.

These are but the least of the challenges that face the typical "freelancer"—a term applied to any individual who works gig-to-gig, contract-to-contract, rather than settling into a single-contract, single-office job. Today, freelancers are common in fields as different as publication design, video production, and college teaching. [25] In addition, some fields that were once largely reliant on career employees with full-time contracts have been transformed into freelancer-based industries; without its freelancers, contemporary journalism might be in jeopardy.

It is undeniable that freelancers are fixtures in today's [26] economy. It is just as undeniable that freelance work can be immensely attractive. But the benefits of a freelance economy or a freelance lifestyle should not obscure the drawbacks, which are often substantial, and which [27] has received ever-increasing media attention.

23

A) NO CHANGE
B) they
C) you
D) it

24

A) NO CHANGE
B) between
C) throughout
D) both

25

A) NO CHANGE
B) On the contrary,
C) Unfortunately,
D) Evidently,

26

Which choice best combines the two sentences at the underlined portion?

A) economy, but also just as
B) economy and equally
C) economy, but it is also
D) economy, just as

27

A) NO CHANGE
B) have received
C) had received
D) is receiving

28 Many people who claim that the proverbial "9:00 to 5:00" work schedule is not for them turn to freelancing. A promising month-to-month contract can be terminated at a 29 moment's notice, and severance pay is nonexistent. Many freelancers are also active in industries that, as a matter of economic 30 sense—favor younger and less established workers: asked to choose between a web site designer with seven years of experience and a $40 hourly rate and a recent college grad with only a $14 per hour rate, most small- to medium-sized businesses would choose the latter.

Despite these harsh realities, freelancer horror stories are actually few and far between. (In fact, the rapid proliferation of freelancing web sites has made it nearly impossible for competent, disciplined freelancers to go without income sources for long.) The more persistent problems faced by freelancers involve individual working methods. 31 Some freelancers have a lot of trouble. This is a danger even for freelancers who have spent time in traditional workplaces, since a freelance lifestyle can seem like an invitation to relax and set your own schedule—even if the stated job expectations are rigorous.

28

Which choice best introduces the paragraph?

A) NO CHANGE
B) It is common knowledge that young people tend to command lower salaries than do seasoned veterans.
C) The entire workforce is currently experiencing a concerning dip in productivity.
D) With the considerable flexibility of freelancing comes only a small measure of job security.

29

A) NO CHANGE
B) moments
C) moment
D) moments'

30

A) NO CHANGE
B) sense; favor
C) sense, favor
D) sense favor

31

Which choice presents the most specific example of the difficulties freelancers experience?

A) NO CHANGE
B) Many freelancers report having such issues.
C) Working from home presents its own unique set of challenges.
D) Without extremely hard deadlines, freelancers easily begin to procrastinate.

CONTINUE

Some freelancers have consequently **32** <u>began</u> to band together and "co-work" by renting office spaces, a move that effectively removes professionals from their home environments while maintaining their occupational independence. **33** <u>Good work habits, as it turns out, can be contagious.</u> At times, entering an environment of diligent workers is all it takes to motivate a formerly undisciplined freelancer.

32

A) NO CHANGE
B) begun
C) begin
D) begins

33

The writer is considering deleting the underlined sentence. Should the writer make this deletion?

A) Yes, because the underlined sentence presents information unrelated to the paragraph.
B) Yes, because the underlined sentence presents a consideration that contradicts the main point of the paragraph.
C) No, because the underlined sentence presents information in support of the paragraph's main point.
D) No, because the underlined sentence presents an important counterargument to the paragraph's main point.

Questions 34-44 are based on the following passage and supplementary material.

Canine Minds: The Evolution of Man's Best Friend

— 1 —

Dogs have been domesticated 9,000 years longer **[34]** then cats have, yet this fact is not necessarily a guarantee that our affinity for dogs is stronger. Oxytocin, the hormone responsible for the initiation of maternal instincts in humans, is found in high levels in postpartum women and contributes to be the emotional bond between mother and child. The same hormone is found **[35]** in comparable amounts in both cats and dogs, and in their respective owners, indicating that the emotional connection between man and pet stems from a deep biological foundation.

— 2 —

[36] Cats and dogs possess different, but equally unique, evolutionary traits that connect them to humans. Dogs use left-side bias facial recognition, an advanced interpretation and communication tool, to detect human emotions. Imagine splitting your face in half, mirroring the left side and the right side individually, and **[37]** to merge together the two resulting left sides and the two resulting right sides; because no face is perfectly symmetrical, you will find that the left-side merger is quite unlike the right-side merger. Dogs are profoundly aware of this discrepancy and use only the left halves of human visages to determine the subtle changes that directly relate to human feelings.

34

A) NO CHANGE
B) more than
C) more then
D) than

35

A) NO CHANGE
B) around
C) about
D) within

36

Which choice most smoothly and effectively introduces the writer's discussion of dog abilities in this paragraph?

A) NO CHANGE
B) Some people strongly prefer dogs to cats.
C) Over time, humans have developed a subtle, unique way of communicating their emotions to dogs.
D) Over time, the dog has developed unique capabilities that have enhanced its symbiotic relationship with humanity.

37

A) NO CHANGE
B) merge
C) having merged
D) merging

CONTINUE

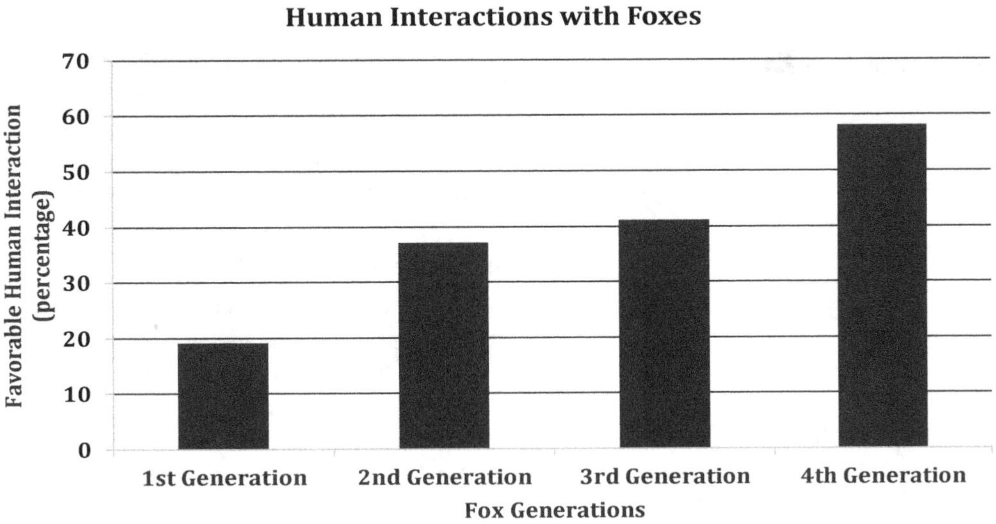

— 3 —

In an experiment that pinpointed the developmental aspects of domestication, Russian geneticist Dmitry Bleyaev set out to do with a few generations of silver foxes what it had taken other dog domesticators thousands of years to accomplish. Bleyaev's endeavor consisted of housing 3,000 wild silver foxes to observe their range of emotions. Only those animals that exhibited neutral to positive interactions (inquisitiveness, friendliness, playfulness) were allowed to reproduce. The next generation of foxes exhibited **38** fewer instances of these particular traits; repeating this procedure over and over produced **39** a majority of silver foxes suited to harmonious and productive interactions with humans.

— 4 —

Through extensive testing, researchers have proven that dogs are the only non-humanoid species capable **40** to respond consistently and accurately to pointing. One can only presume that these traits have their origins in the hunter-retriever alliance. In this relationship, the submissive beast locates the rewards of

38

Which choice offers the most accurate interpretation of the data in the chart?

A) NO CHANGE
B) the same amount of
C) no
D) more

39

Which choice offers an accurate interpretation of the data in the chart?

A) NO CHANGE
B) a few
C) an entire generation of
D) approximately fifteen

40

A) NO CHANGE
B) of responding consistent and accurate to pointing.
C) of responding accurate to consistent pointing.
D) of responding accurately and consistently to pointing.

CONTINUE

the hunt in exchange for food and shelter, with body language serving as the sole means of communication. [41]

— 5 —

To see if these personality traits could be a matter of learned behavior as well as genetic makeup, Bleyaev and his fellow researchers placed aggressive kits and fearful young foxes with den mothers who sought out human interaction. The younger animals [42] did not become more susceptible to domestication, and thus never learned to trust humans. Some argue that the results of Bleyaev's study are questionable. These skeptics believe that taming is solely a conditioned response. [43] Though the controversy continues, perhaps an even greater fraction accepts the findings.

Question [44] asks about the previous passage as a whole.

41

At this point, the writer is considering adding the following sentence.

> This finding, however, fails to explain why many humans report feeling instinctively afraid of canines.

Should the writer make this addition here?

A) Yes, because it restates the main point of the paragraph.
B) Yes, because it provides an important consideration crucial to the main point of the paragraph.
C) No, because it presents a consideration that is unimportant to the main point of the paragraph.
D) No, because it neglects to mention how humans relate to cats.

42

A) NO CHANGE
B) have not become
C) had not became
D) were not becoming

43

The writer wants to conclude by reinforcing the soundness of the experiment described in the paragraph. Which choice best accomplishes this goal?

A) NO CHANGE
B) However, it is difficult to find fault with Bleyaev's methods.
C) Yet, everyone is entitled to his or her own opinion.
D) Regardless, the conclusions of Bleyaev and his colleagues are based on too small a sample size to be reliable.

Think about the previous passage as a whole as you answer question 44.

44

To make the passage most logical, paragraph 3 should be placed

A) where it is now.
B) after paragraph 1.
C) after paragraph 4.
D) after paragraph 5.

STOP

If you finish before time is called, you may check your work on this section only.
Do not turn to any other section.

No Test Material On This Page

Answer Key

TEST 10

PASSAGE 1

Edward Hopper Paints America

1. C
2. C
3. B
4. C
5. D
6. A
7. B
8. C
9. B
10. C
11. D

PASSAGE 2

Smells Like Teen Rebellion

12. A
13. B
14. D
15. D
16. C
17. B
18. D
19. B
20. B
21. C
22. D

PASSAGE 3

The Freelancer's Dilemma

23. D
24. B
25. A
26. B
27. B
28. D
29. A
30. C
31. D
32. B
33. C

PASSAGE 4

Canine Minds: The Evolution of Man's Best Friend

34. D
35. A
36. D
37. D
38. D
39. A
40. D
41. C
42. A
43. B
44. C

Post-Test Analysis

This post-test analysis is essential if you want to see an improvement on your next test. Possible reasons for errors on the four passages in this section are listed here. Place check marks next to the types of errors that pertain to you, or write your own types of errors in the blank spaces.

TIMING AND ACCURACY

◇ Spent too long reading individual passages
◇ Spent too long answering each question
◇ Spent too long on a few difficult questions
◇ Felt rushed and made silly mistakes or random errors
◇ Unable to work quickly using error types and POE
Other: ______________________________

APPROACHING THE PASSAGES AND QUESTIONS

◇ Unable to effectively grasp the passage's tone or style
◇ Unable to effectively grasp the passage's topic or stance
◇ Did not understand the context of underlined portions
◇ Did not eliminate false answers using error types
◇ Answered questions using first impressions instead of POE
◇ Answered questions without slotting in and checking final answer
◇ Eliminated NO CHANGE and chose a trap answer
◇ Eliminated correct answer during POE
Other: ______________________________

Use this form to better analyze your performance. If you don't understand why you made errors, there is no way that you can correct them!

GRAMMAR AND SENTENCE STRUCTURE

◇ Did not test sentence for subject-verb agreement
◇ Did not identify proper verb form and verb tense
◇ Did not test sentence for pronoun agreement
◇ Did not identify proper pronoun form (subject/object, who/which/when/where/why)
◇ Did not test for proper comparison phrasing (amount/number, between/among) and number agreement
◇ Did not test phrase for correct adverb/adjective usage
◇ Did not see broader sentence structure (parallelism, misplaced modifier)
◇ Did not see flaws in punctuation (colon, semicolon, comma splice, misplaced commas)
◇ Did not see tricky possessives or contractions (its/it's, your/you're)
◇ Did not identify flaws in standard phrases (either . . . or, not only . . . but also, etc.)
◇ Did not use proper phrasing in sentences requiring the subjunctive
Other: ______________________________

STYLE, ORGANIZATION, AND WORKING WITH EVIDENCE

◇ Did not notice cases of redundancy and wordiness
◇ Misidentified an expression as redundant or wordy
◇ Did not notice flaws in essay style or excessively informal expressions
◇ Misidentified an expression as stylistically inconsistent or informal
◇ Created the wrong relationship between two sentences
◇ Created the wrong relationship between two paragraphs
◇ Created the wrong placement for an out-of-order paragraph
◇ Did not eliminate faulty or improper English idioms
◇ Did not properly read or analyze an insertion/deletion question
◇ Did not properly read or analyze the information in a graphic
◇ Understood a graphic, but could not identify the correct passage content
Other: ______________________________

CPSIA information can be obtained
at www.ICGtesting.com
Printed in the USA
BVHW010953270620
582466BV00009B/162

9 780996 406413